# Teaching world studies

JKUS (Hic)*

# Teaching world studies

An introduction to global perspectives in the curriculum

Edited by David Hicks and Charles Townley

## Longman
London and New York

0582497116

Longman Group Limited
Longman House
Burnt Mill, Harlow, Essex, England
and Associated Companies throughout the world.

*Published in the United States of America
by Longman Inc., New York*

*First published 1982*

**British Library Cataloguing in Publication Data**

Teaching world studies.
  1. International education
  I. Hicks, David II. Townley, Charles
  370.11'5   LB2365.I/

  ISBN 0-582-49711-6

**Library of Congress Cataloging in Publication Data**

Main entry under title:

Teaching world studies.

  Bibliography: P.
  Includes index.
  1. Curriculum planning. 2. History, Modern –
20th century – Study and teaching. I. Hicks,
David, 1942–    . II. Townley, Charles.
III. Title.
LB1570.T34   1982       375'.001      81-20750
ISBN 0-582-49711-6                    AACR2

Printed in Hong Kong by
Hing Yip Printing Co.

# Contents

# Notes on contributors

**David Bridges** is a lecturer in philosophy of education and curriculum theory at Homerton College, Cambridge. He co-ordinates in-service education at the college and is a member of the SSRC Cambridge Accountability Project. His publications include *Education, Democracy and Discussion* and several papers on world perspectives and international understanding. A former editor of *New Era*, he is currently editor of the *Cambridge Journal of Education*.

**Barry Dufour** is a lecturer in the University of Leicester School of Education, a post which he combines with that of tutor in Social Studies at Countesthorpe College. He is joint author of *The New Social Studies* and had recently completed *New Movements in the Social Sciences and Humanities* published by Maurice Temple Smith. He has also written several books for school pupils, including *The Eskimos: Tradition and Change*.

**Jim Dunlop** lectures at Jordanhill College of Education, Glasgow, where he is Director of the Jordanhill Project in International Understanding. He acts as a consultant to UNESCO and to BBC (Scotland) for the radio series, *International Understanding*. A founder member of the Modern Studies Association, he is also editor of *Modern Studies: Origins, Aims and Development*.

**Brian Gates** is Head of Religious Studies and Social Ethics at St Martin's College, Bowerham, Lancaster. He has written several journal articles on religious education and helped to produce the DES discussion film *Inside Talk*. His doctoral research was on religion in the developing world of children and young people, and he has recently edited a book for teachers on Afro-Caribbean religions published by Ward Lock.

**Tony Ghaye** is a lecturer in Geography and Teaching Studies at Worcester College of Higher Education. He has taught in Australia, Leicestershire and Sussex where he was Head of Geography in a secondary school. He is currently researching in geographical education.

**David Hicks** is Director of the Centre for Peace Studies, at St Martin's College, Lancaster. He was Education Officer for the Minority Rights Group for three years and wrote *Minorities: A Teacher's Resource Book for the Multi-ethnic Curriculum*, published by Heinemann. He has written several journal articles on global perspectives and is currently Co-Director of the Schools Council Project *World Studies: 8–13* (1980–83).

**Bill Kelly** lectures in Geography at Worcester College of Higher Education, having previously taught in secondary schools in Manchester and in Uganda. In 1980 he was the SOAS Teacher Fellow, in Development Studies, and has gained overseas study experience in India and in Ghana.

**Roger Morgan** is Co-ordinator, International Studies, Rolle College of Higher Education, Exmouth. He has responsibility both for British students abroad and for overseas students at Rolle College, and is also active in the UK Centre for European Studies and the National Association of Development Education Centres. He is currently researching in Development Education and is co-author of the SOAS publication *Development Studies: A Teacher's Handbook.*

**Robin Richardson** is Adviser for Multicultural Education with Berkshire Education Authority, Reading. From 1973–79 he was Director of the World Studies Project and has written many articles on World Studies. His books include the *Frontiers of Enquiry* series (Hart Davis), the *World Studies* series (Nelson), *Images of Life* (SCM Press), the World Studies Project publications and *Change and Choice: Britain in an Interdependent World* (CWDE).

**David Selby** is Director of the World Studies Teacher Training Centre at York University and was Head of the Humanities Faculty at Groby Community College, Leicestershire. He has taught in secondary schools and at University College, Cork. Author of *Toward a Common System of National Education*, he has written journal articles and edits the *World Studies Journal.*

**Hugh Starkey** lectures in French at Westminster College, Oxford. He was previously Head of Languages at the City of Ely College and warden of a teachers' centre in Cambridge.

**Charles Townley** is a tutor in the Division of In-Service Studies at Edge Hill College, and runs the Social Studies Curriculum Centre at Chorley, Lancashire. He is a past chairman of ATSS and was editor of the *Social Science Teacher* in its early years. He has published several articles in that journal and is joint editor of *Fundamentals of Sociology.*

# List of figures

# List of tables

# Foreword

On 19 November 1974, at its eighteenth session, the General Conference of the United Nations Educational, Scientific and Cultural Organisation drew up a recommendation to member states reminding them of their responsibility to ensure the education of all for the advancement of justice, freedom, human rights and peace.

The Recommendation suggested the following objectives as 'major guiding principles of educational policy':

(a) an international dimension and a global perspective in education at all levels and in all its forms;

(b) understanding and respect for all people, their cultures, civilisations, values and ways of life, including domestic ethnic cultures of other nations;

(c) awareness of the increasing global interdependence between peoples and nations;

(d) abilities to communicate with others;

(e) awareness not only of the rights but also of the duties incumbent upon individuals, social groups and nations towards each other;

(f) understanding of the necessity for international solidarity and co-operation;

(g) readiness on the part of the individual to participate in solving the problems of his community, his country and the world at large.

The Recommendation further stressed that:

Education should be directed both towards the eradication of conditions which perpetuate and aggravate major problems affecting human survival and well-being – inequality, injustice, international relations based on the use of force – and towards measures of international co-operation likely to help solve them. Education, which in this respect must necessarily be of an interdisciplinary nature, should relate to such problems as:

(a) equality of rights of peoples, and the right of peoples to self-determination;

(b) the maintenance of peace; different types of war and their causes and effects; disarmament; the inadmissibility of using science and technology for warlike purposes and their use for the purposes of peace and progress; the nature and effect of economic, cultural and political relations between countries and the importance of international law for these relations, particularly for the maintenance of peace;

(c) action to ensure the exercise and observance of human rights, including those of refugees; racialism and its eradication; the fight against discrimination in its various forms;

(d) economic growth and social development and their relation to social justice; colonialism and decolonisation; ways and means of assisting developing countries; the struggle against illiteracy; the campaign against disease and famine; the fight for a better quality of life and the highest attainable standard of health; population growth and related questions;

(e) the use, management and conservation of natural resources; pollution of the environment;

(f) preservation of the cultural heritage of mankind;

(g) the role and methods of action of the United Nations system in efforts to solve such problems and possibilities for strengthening and furthering its action.

# Preface

Professor Godfrey Brown of Keele University recently pointed out that, 'A global dimension for curriculum development is neither a luxury nor merely do-goodism. It is an element in survival.' This need has been recognised for some time but the continuing question is how we should implement such a dimension in the curriculum.

This book stems from the initiatives which have emerged over the past decade. Part 1 aims to clarify the underlying rationale and to highlight the central concerns and the critical issues in the field. Part 2 provides illustrations of approaches which have been implemented successfully. Part 3 explores the implications for those concerned with both the initial and in-service education of teachers, whilst Part 4 identifies curriculum materials which are currently available and brings together the various sources from which information and classroom support are available.

David Hicks
Charles Townley
May 1981

# Acknowledgements

We are grateful to the following for permission to reproduce copyright material:

Development Studies, SOAS, 1977 for our Figs. 15 and 16 (*Network of Course and Institutional Links/Constraints on Course Planning*); Ely Resource and Technology Centre for our Fig. 4 (*Ely Material on World Studies: The Rich and the Poor*); Jordanhill College of Education, Glasgow for our Figs. 5, 6 and 7 (*JPIU: Project Organisation/Appropriate Technology/Multilateral Aid*); Learning for Change in World Society, World Studies Project, London, 2nd edition 1979 for our Fig. 3 (*World Society: A Topic Web*).

# Part I
Issues and concerns

# Chapter 1 David Hicks and Charles Townley
# The need for global literacy

Children who are in school now will in the twenty-first century have to
cope with a future very different from today. The ability to cope with that
future will depend, in part, on being able to take a global, as well as a
national and local, perspective on current issues of conflict, change, development, peace and justice.

The 1970's, in particular, saw the emergence of new perceptions of the
world as a single system which, in turn, gave rise to the concept of the
global village. Over the course of that decade the quest for social justice
and economic welfare as global concerns resulted in a series of international
conferences. Whilst our attention, at the start of the 1980s, has been focused
on nuclear war, economic recession and unemployment, it is important
to recall the other crucial issues. Whereas the particular conferences may
now be forgotten, they served to focus attention on issues of global significance that still remain with us. Amongst them are: the environment,
world population, world food, the law of the sea-bed, the role of women,
world trade, world employment, arms limitation, human settlement and
climatic change. All highlighted the urgent need for radically new patterns
of global development.

Major issues such as these have been variously interpreted as mere hic-
cups on an historical time-scale and as a turning-point in evolutionary history. If the latter analysis is the correct one, and research evidence
increasingly points this way, current and future global crises should be seen
as error-detectors and as catalysts for encouraging desirable change (Mesarovic and Pestel 1975). Whether we are facing a series of temporary global
crises or a longer-term climacteric, it is a matter of some urgency that
education should take cognisance of such changes. These issues should thus
not only be reflected in what goes on in schools but also in teacher education.

## Awareness of global issues

What events and trends over the last two decades have led to this awareness
of the global nature of many contemporary issues? During the 1950s, as the
effects of the destruction of the Second World War receded, it seemed that
new developments in technology might lead to a higher level of material
prosperity. Anything seemed possible and the euphoria grew yet further
with the advent of the 1960s. It seemed then, to some, that a new age of
liberation might be dawning and certainly a distinct shift in consciousness

seemed to occur during this period. A series of far-reaching revolutions appeared to be under way, ranging from colonial wars of liberation, technological breakthroughs and rapidly rising material expectations to the birth of the women's movement, concern over minority rights, the development of a youthful counter-culture and release from rigid sexual mores.

Toffler (1970) argued that many of these trends could be related to a speeding-up of social change itself. He suggested that possibly the *rate* of change had even more implications than its actual direction and coined the term 'future shock' to describe the stress and disorientation caused in individuals and whole societies by such rapid change. He noted that during the 1960s levels of mental stress, drug-taking, alcoholism, mental breakdown and suicide had all increased, symptoms, he suggested, of increased human inability to cope with rapid change.

Others too began to sense that all was not well. A sense of crisis was becoming apparent by the late 1960s but it was interpreted in different ways. Some saw it as (Reich 1970):

a collection of problems not necessarily related to each other, and, although profoundly troubling, nevertheless within the reach of reason and reform. But if we list these problems, not according to topic but as elements of larger issues concerning the structure of society itself, we can see that the present crisis is an organic one, that it arises out of the basic premises by which we live and that no mere reform can touch it.

Reich went on to list these interrelated problems as: (a) disorder, corruption, hypocrisy, war; (b) poverty, distorted priorities, and lawmaking by private power; (c) uncontrolled technology and the destruction of the environment; (d) decline of democracy and liberty; powerlessness; (e) the artificiality of work and culture; (f) absence of community, and (g) loss of self. Within the United States, and other countries as well, it was the Vietnam war in particular which focused dissent. The spectacle of the most powerful military country in the world taking on a Third World peasant army thus eventually led to the greatest anti-war movement of modern times (Halstead 1978).

It was out of the dissonance of, on the one hand, expectations of new levels of liberation in all facets of life and, on the other, the growing sense of crisis that a highly vocal counter-culture emerged. Such movements seem to arise historically when a section of society sees traditional life becoming increasingly impossible during a period of rapid socio-economic change. Thus when everyday experience continually contradicts the dominant ideology of society, such that the discrepancies do not seem resolvable in the normal way, then a radical response may arise which totally rejects the conventional norms and bases itself on different goals and alternative life-styles.

Roszak (1970) wrote of this trend:

From my own point of view, the counter culture, far more than merely 'meriting' attention, desperately requires it, since I am at a loss to know where, besides among these dissenting young people and their heirs of the next few generations, the radical discontent and innovation can be found that might transform this disoriented civilization of ours into something a human being can identify as home. They are the matrix in which an alternative, but still excessively fragile future is taking shape ... all we have to hold against the final consolidation of a technocratic totalitarianism in which we shall find ourselves ingeniously adapted to an existence wholly estranged from everything that has ever made the life of man an interesting adventure.

Now whilst this may sound like the heady message of the 1960s heard remotely across an intervening decade, the fact remains that (a) the same problems are still with us but in even more accentuated form, and (b) although the alternative movement no longer occupies the headlines, the radical principles that blossomed from it more than a decade ago are now more easily available for recall.

In considering long-term socio-cultural change in the twentieth century the alternative/counter-cultural movement must warrant serious study, not only because of the depths of its alienation but also because of its creative vision in offering not only alternative ways of viewing the world but also more meaningful ways of living. One of the best chroniclers of its growth was Leech (1973), who discerned through the exploration of drugs, Eastern religions, occultism, liberation movements and political radicalism a pro-foundly spiritual quest. Similarly Musgrove (1974) was able to identify an interconnected set of values (related to power, boundaries, communication, work and co-operation) which were not merely confined to the young but part of a wider stratum threading through contemporary society.

Parallel with this growth of radical concern, indeed inextricably inter-twined with it, was a growing realisation that the problems to be faced were no longer local, or even national, but of global concern. Thus in the late 1960s increasing concern was expressed particularly over the so-called population explosion and what rapidly became known as the environmental crisis. Whilst such concerns may seem less urgent when faced with visions of nuclear war, it is important to remember that it was the environment and the many threats to the earth's delicate ecosystems that first gave rise to the image of the global village. It was concern about pollution, industrial growth, resource depletion, food production and population growth that lead to the whole 'limits to growth' debate and a challenging of the dom-inant theories about economic growth and highly technological futures (Meadows *et al.* 1972). Whilst in retrospect some of these early analyses may have oversimplified the issues, they nevertheless graphically high-lighted the global nature of problems.

Awareness of the global condition brought many positive responses, amongst the most notable of which was Schumacher's suggestion that 'small is beautiful' (1974). His suggestion that the pursuit of profit and 'progress' was at the root of many ills became, and still is, a major rallying-point for the disenchanted. As the nations of the world worked their way through a series of international crises, some of which have been mentioned above, the Organisation of Petroleum Exporting Countries (OPEC) irrev-ocably changed the global balance of power and the complexity of the issues

5

only seemed to increase. Thus the second report to the Club of Rome opened with these words (Mesarovic and Pestel 1975):

Suddenly – virtually overnight when measured on a historical scale – mankind finds itself confronted by a multitude of unprecedented crises: the population crisis, the environmental crisis, the raw material crisis, to name just a few. New crises appear while the old ones linger on with the effects spreading to every corner of the Earth until they appear in point of fact as global, worldwide, crises. Attempts at solving any one of these in isolation has proven to be temporary and at the expense of others; to ease the shortage of energy or raw materials by measures which worsen the condition of the environment means, actually, to solve nothing at all. Real solutions are apparently interdependent; collectively, the whole multitude of crises appears to constitute a single global crisis-syndrome of world development.

It was recognised that not only was the scale of such crises vastly different from previous historical events, but that the *causes* in fact were related to the best of intentions: conquering disease, controlling nature, exploiting natural resources. It was suggested that a major shift in priorities would be needed to make a transition possible to a viable world. One could choose either to see this as doom-watching or as a new beginning the report suggested, current and future crises could best be seen as 'error-detectors, catalysts for change, and as such blessings in disguise'. A similar theme was taken up by Stavrianos (1976), who argued close parallels between the 1970s and the Dark Age following the collapse of Rome: 'The Roman Empire, like our contemporary global civilization, was outwardly impressive and seemingly unassailable.' Both periods he suggests, being characterised by (a) economic imperialism, (b) ecological degradation, (c) bureaucratic ossification and (d) a flight from reason. Interesting food for thought.

Our awareness of particular global issues is often very dependent on the media: at one time oil supplies may be the focus of concern, at another trading arrangements between North and South, or the threat of global war. We have in fact been living with all of these, and more, for the last two decades, with first one issue held before us and then another. None actually go away, they are merely seen as less newsworthy at one particular time or highlighted at another by global politics. Amongst the most recent studies to highlight the global nature of our dilemmas was, of course, the Brandt Report (1980).

It certainly seems as if the 1970s may in retrospect be the decade that marked the 'end of the twentieth century dream' (Booker 1980) or even a 'failed experiment in urban-industrial living' (Clarke 1975). However future historians may judge this latter quarter of the twentieth century, it is clear that global issues demand our closest attention. How, for example, should such matters be dealt with in the classroom? What scope, if any, is there for the study of contemporary global issues in initial and in-service teacher education? And also, but certainly not least, *how* should such issues be taught?

## Educational responses to global issues

The different educational responses to global issues began to make themselves clear during the course of the 1970s. Amongst the more common phrases relating to this broad field are education for international understanding, global education or global studies, World Studies, development education and peace education. A global perspective may also be present in multicultural education, environmental studies and political education. The first group of phrases certainly have what might be called a 'family likeness' and Derek Heater has comprehensively reviewed many of the developments in his *World Studies: Education for International Understanding in Britain* (1980).

It is important, however, to clarify the differences and similarities between some of these responses, for they have generally come from outside the formal curriculum. The oldest, most classical, response is that of education for international understanding which goes back several decades and has been popularised by the United Nations Educational, Scientific and Cultural Organisation (UNESCO) and other UN agencies. Its focus is on *understanding* other countries and cultures. At the beginning of the 1970s, however, other responses began to arise and it is to four of these in particular that we now turn.

## World Studies

Awareness of the need to understand the world as a single system rather than as a series of separate parts led to the growth of what is known in the United States as global education or global studies. The keynote here is interdependence in the global village, and American developments, in turn, helped to stimulate the growth of World Studies in the UK. The American work is exemplified by bodies such as the Center for Global Perspectives in New York and the Mid-America Program for Global Perspectives in Education in Indiana.[1] The stress is on the need for a perspective that embraces the *whole* world rather than merely parts of it. It has been suggested (Hanvey 1976), for example, that a global perspective could be made up of the following five dimensions:

1. *Perspective consciousness* – the recognition or awareness on the part of the individual that he or she has a view of the world that is not universally shared, that this view of the world has been and continues to be shaped by influences that often escape conscious detection, and that others have views of the world that are profoundly different from one's own.
2. *'State of the Planet' awareness* – awareness of prevailing world conditions and developments, including emergent conditions and trends, e.g. population growth, migrations, economic conditions, resources and physical environment, political developments, science and technology, law, health, inter-nation and intra-nation conflicts, etc.
3. *Cross-cultural awareness* – awareness of the diversity of ideas and practices to be found in human societies around the world, of how such ideas and

practices compare, and including some limited recognition of how the ideas and ways of one's own society might be viewed from other vantage-points.

4. *Knowledge of global dynamics* – some modest comprehension of key traits and mechanisms of the world system, with emphasis on theories and concepts that may increase intelligent consciousness of global change.

5. *Awareness of human choices* – some awareness of the problems of choice confronting individuals, nations, and the human species as consciousness and knowledge of the global system expand.

In a similar way Anderson has suggested that an individual's involvement in the world requires certain cognitive, perceptual, emotional and social capacities. According to Anderson (1979), the ability to perceive one's involvement in global society thus requires the capacity to:

(a) perceive oneself and all other individuals as members of a single species of life – a species whose members share: a common biological status; a common way of adapting to the natural environment; a common set of biological and psychological needs; common existential concerns; and common social problems...

(b) perceive self and all humans as part of the earth's biosphere...

(c) see how each person, and the groups to which that person belongs, are participants in the world's socio-cultural system . . .

(d) perceive that people at all levels of social organization – from the individual to the whole society – are both 'cultural borrowers' and 'cultural depositors'; they both draw from and contribute to a 'global bank of human culture' that has been and continues to be fed by contributions from all peoples, in all geographical regions, and in all periods of history...

(e) perceive that people have differing perceptions, beliefs and attitudes about the world systems and its components...

Within the UK acceptance of the term 'World Studies' has been largely due to the pioneering work of the World Studies Project set up by the One World Trust in 1973.[2] Under the directorship of Robin Richardson the project early on developed a distinctive style of working, arising from a student-centred and school-based model of in-service curriculum development. The project has defined World Studies as a field of knowledge, being a generic term for (a) studies of countries and cultures other than one's own, and (b) studies of contemporary global issues and interaction between countries. It acknowledges that, by and large, World Studies is not a discrete subject on the timetable but that it refers to a general concern or dimension in the curriculum, e.g. in existing courses in geography, history, social studies or religious education for example. Having said this, much of the pioneering work in the UK has in fact been carried out as a separate subject on the timetable, as described in chapter 4.

The stress in World Studies is thus categorically on the need for a *global* perspective, on world-mindedness and allegiance to humanity as a whole. We are reminded that the global village is a single system, with all its various parts interdependent.

## Development Education

Development education had its origins in the late 1960s with the concern of the aid agencies, the churches and the United Nations over Third World development. The term is, of course, little used in formal education but is based on the belief that world development as an issue requires education to prepare people for it. The very term development raises a variety of questions. Does it mean simply economic growth? Basic human welfare? Development programmes designed by outside 'experts' or self-reliant development? If development, by any definition, involves change then it should surely be change from a worse to a better state. It has been argued that this should not be narrowly defined in economic terms of Third World poverty but should also be applied to the 'poverty of spirit' in the so-called developed countries.

It is, in fact, useful to visualise a spectrum of opinion in relation to development education. Thus, at one end it is seen to be *about* Third World problems and the way in which the rich countries can help. Further along the spectrum the concern is more on understanding global interdependence and changing attitudes to cope with such needs. At the other end of the spectrum is recognition that only structural changes both within our own society and in the global village will ever lead to any sort of meaningful development. At this end of the spectrum development has both local, national and global dimensions as this UN definition of development education makes clear: (JUNIC AD/FAO, 1975)

The objective of development education is to enable people to participate in the development of their community, their nation and the world as a whole. Such participation implies a critical awareness of local, national and international situations based on an understanding of the social, economic and political processes.

Development education is concerned with issues of human rights, dignity, self-reliance and social justice in both developed and developing countries. It is concerned with the causes of under-development and the promotion of an understanding of what is involved in development, of how different countries go about undertaking development, and of the reasons for and ways of achieving a new international economic and social order.

Such a definition of development education is certainly a challenging one and one which many of the proponents of this field would increasingly support. It is probably fair to say, however, that those not directly concerned with the field, and some of those who are, would take a much more conservative view of development education as properly being just teaching about the Third World on its own.

One of the main dilemmas within development education is often between its sponsors and its practitioners. This is particularly the case with aid agencies whose charitable status may conflict with their educational programme (Hutchinson 1980). If the latter involves letting oppressed groups speak for themselves and it also suggests strategies for change it may offend the agency's charitable status. That is, development education in wishing to promote a more just world may involve what are technically 'non-charitable' activities.

Hutchinson also suggests that the practitioners of development education may already be 'opening up new areas' which the sponsoring agencies themselves are ignoring. The question then arises as to where development education may actually lead its practitioners? Four areas for the agencies to break new ground in are seen to be: a closer look at the real complexities of development; listening more carefully to the voices of the oppressed; identifying a new generation of heroes; looking more carefully at often neglected socialist models of development.

One interpretation of the tension between sponsors and practitioners, and probably the most relevant, is that development education has in particular worked on its practitioners. Thus in educating themselves they have necessarily moved away from their sponsors' often narrow vision of Third World aid. They have come to see, as many of the churches have done, that development education is first and foremost about human development. The Third World is thus not just a geographical area but also the aged, homeless, unemployed, handicapped and oppressed minorities in Britain. On this basis development education is about personal change, politicisation and action here at home as much as about Third World development. Whatever the definition it is important, as both Storm and Richardson have reminded us, that the practical realities of the classroom are always kept in mind (ULIE 1980).

### Peace education

Peace education is an international field of concern arising out of the development of peace research during the 1960s. Whilst peace research initially concentrated on direct violence and war, the focus has gradually shifted to other forms of, less obvious, indirect violence or structural violence. Examples of the latter would include apartheid, economic oppression, discrimination against minorities and denial of human rights, i.e. violence that is built into social, political and economic structures. The focus has thus also shifted from what has been called *negative* peace (absence of war) to *positive* peace, i.e. ways of creating more equitable and just structures in society through non-violent social change.

The four problems of peace have been aptly summarised as: violence, injustice, poverty and environmental damage. 'Turn these four problems round and they read *absence of violence, economic welfare* (including satisfaction of fundamental needs), *social justice* (including satisfaction of human rights) and *ecological balance*. These four values are not a bad formulation of what one might mean by "peace"' (Galtung 1976).

The term peace education can be applied to both formal and informal education and, whilst the concerns of peace research may suggest its possible content, the most important stress is on its *form*, i.e. the form or process of education must itself be compatible with peace. It cannot, in other words, be merely education *about* peace but must also be education *for* peace. The method is thus as, if not more, important than the content. It has to exclude not only direct violence but also indirect or structural violence. In education this takes the form of one-way communication, not allowing the learners to communicate with each other or to turn the information flow the other way, not allowing them to share in identifying their own goals. Peace education is thus particularly about creating learning situations which involve participation, co-operation and dialogue, leading to increased self-reliance. It is particularly interested in exposing the hidden curriculum and analysing the quality of the relationships in any educational situation. It must also be future, rather than past or present, orientated because it is concerned about creating more just alternatives. It must, therefore, also be action-orientated and will draw much of its inspiration from the peace movement itself.

Like both development education and World Studies, peace education is a term rarely used in British schools. One innovative exception is the two-year course in Peace Studies for sixth formers pioneered at an international college in Wales.[3] Increasingly in the present climate of international affairs issues of peace and conflict are in the news. What *do* you answer when asked: 'Sir, would you tell us if the bomb was going to drop?'[4] The need to focus on peace is increasingly being recognised as a necessity for the 1980s. None of the other fields discussed here take the issue of peace as a focal concern. Certainly World Studies is likely to look, at some point, at issues relating to the arms race or the arms trade. However because its focusing idea is interdependence, these are only part of its overall concerns. The strength of Peace Studies here is that it *must* be centrally concerned with questions such as: Should we teach children about war? If so, *what* should we teach and *how*? It can also raise fundamental questions about institutionalised militarism, the nature of aggression, non-violent change and other such issues.

Whilst peace education may be the last of the four initiatives considered here to reach the margins of the educational consciousness, it may also in some respects be the most important. Its arrival is not only marked by the course referred to above but also by a special issue of the *World Studies Journal* on peace education,[5] and the creation of a new Centre for Peace Studies offering support for teachers.[6]

## Multicultural education

Whilst none of the chapters in this book have been directly inspired by multicultural education, this field is of critical importance to all those concerned about global perspectives in the curriculum. Multiracial education, as it was first known, was a reluctant response to the presence of colonial immigrants in the UK, encouraged by the government to come to the metropolitan country to help solve its labour problems. Multiracial education was thus originally seen as 'English for immigrants' or 'English as a second language'. Its key concern was, and still is, culture: a concern arising directly out of the colonial experience and subsequent decolonisation.

11

Multicultural education is beset with far more tension than any of the other fields that concern us here, simply because 'race relations' in Britain is an immediate, political issue, here and now. The tensions are compounded by the institutionalised nature of racism in the UK which permits both racial prejudice and discrimination to be present without it really being noticed. Needless to say this arises, in part, out of Britain's colonial and imperialist past. This means that multicultural education cannot be seen, or treated, in isolation. Changes in the curriculum or in educational policy will only be meaningful if matched by structural changes in society as a whole. Multicultural education is also, unlike World Studies, development education and Peace Studies, an *official* concern at the Department of Education and Science (DES), even if it lacks direction at policy level.

The key issues in multicultural education are several and have been well summarised by Street-Porter (1978). Underlying these issues is the whole area of the acquisition of racial attitudes during childhood socialisation. Attitudes towards minority peoples and other countries are thus picked up at an early age and are often both stereotyped and prejudiced. Minority groups are all too easily seen as problems in themselves, by teachers as well as pupils. This climate of prejudice will often result in the underachievement of minority-group children which may be coupled with problems of self-image, identity and cultural worth. Classroom difficulties may only enhance existing white prejudices rather than being seen as a response to the minority experience.

Cultural pluralism must eventually prevail in which minority rights (over say language or culture in the curriculum) become a natural, rather than a concessional, part of educational planning. James (1980) has suggested that teachers may already have been forced to the limits of what is possible within the structure of the school system, but nevertheless they are of vital importance in assisting or hindering the creation of a racially just society.

The curriculum needs have been succinctly summed up (Jeffcoate 1976):
1. An insular curriculum, preoccupied with Britain and British values, is unjustifiable in the final quarter of the twentieth century. The curriculum needs to be both international in its choice of content and global in its perspective.
2. Contemporary British society contains a variety of social and ethnic groups; this variety should be made evident in the visuals, stories and information offered to children.
3. Pupils should have access to accurate information about racial and cultural differences and similarities.
4. People from British minority groups and from other cultures overseas should be presented as individuals with every variety of human quality and attribute. Stereotypes of minority groups in Britain and of cultures overseas, whether expressed in terms of human characteristics, lifestyles, social roles or occupational status, are unacceptable and likely to be damaging.
5. Other nations and cultures have their own validity and should be described in their own terms. Wherever possible they should be allowed

to speak for themselves and not be judged exclusively against British or European norms.

The multicultural curriculum, however, is all too often thought of as something that is only needed in the multicultural classroom. Since children in the UK are all growing up in a plural society, and since racist attitudes occur in all schools, a multicultural – as against an ethnocentric – curriculum is needed in all schools. Part of this should be an understanding of the black experience in Britain. Finally, it is the black community itself which should define its own needs and in this case, as the Institute of Race Relations' statement to the Rampton Committee made clear, we should perhaps be talking about 'anti-racist not multicultural education' (1980).

## Some comparisons between the educational responses to global issues

Having outlined some of the main identifying features of World Studies, development education, peace education and multicultural education, what similarities and differences in fact emerge? Clearly each field has its particular strengths and weaknesses.

Development education focuses on the vital concepts of development and underdevelopment. If we take the UN definition quoted above it embraces development at all levels and in all countries of the world. On that basis World Studies could almost be said to be a form of development education. However, more commonly, due to its origins and sponsorship, development education focuses its attention on Third World countries. This is not necessarily a bad thing, although the danger lies in dwelling exclusively on poverty. Indeed development education has been generally slow to concern itself about ethnocentric and racist bias in its own teaching materials, compared with the level of concern in, say, multicultural education. Practitioners of the latter have rightly been concerned that development education materials may hinder their own work. It is up to the practitioners of development education to prove them wrong.

The strength of World Studies lies in the fact that it takes a much broader perspective than development education traditionally does. It is concerned about issues equally in North and South and tends to focus on interdependence rather than development as a theme. Its wide ranging concerns probably make this a better vehicle in the classroom for studying contemporary issues than development education with its more limited Third World image. It is freer also from constraints, having no sponsors with vested interests. The danger lies, perhaps, in the constant stress on *global* values and common attitudes, for in the search for these overriding concerns attention to cultural pluralism may be overlooked. Since World Studies would almost certainly agree with the 'small is beautiful' maxim, this is an interesting paradox. In multicultural education, in particular, there is concern about cultural autonomy, minority rights and ethnic identity. The stress is on the need to accept and value diversity. Similarly, while we urgently need a world view, there is at the same time a trend towards fragmentation into smaller, more humane units. Demands for autonomy and grass-roots participation, for control at the local level, may in the long term be more important than the globalisation of world society. If World Studies overlooks this it will certainly alienate itself from multicultural education.

Multicultural education is different from the three other fields of interest discussed here, not only for the reasons already mentioned, but also because it is the only label of the four which has any measure of widespread parlance. Because it arises out of critical issues in everyday life it may seem at times a more legitimate concern than the others. It has much it can learn, however, from development education, and Hicks (1979) has suggested that they are best seen as 'two sides of the same coin'. A multicultural curriculum is also necessary not just in multicultural areas but throughout the UK to replace the 'normal' ethnocentric curriculum. It is equally important that it concerns itself with more than just the background of minority groups in the UK. Whilst this may indeed be at its core, issues of race and minority rights are of global importance and this has been well illustrated in a recent teachers' resource book (Hicks 1981).

Peace education is the odd one out here for a variety of reasons, partly because it is the newest (in the UK) of these concerns and also because of its stress on pedagogy before content. It is about *how* we teach, how we view knowledge and education, it is about radical alternatives. Its own dilemma, or rather the dilemma of its practitioners, is whether peace education can ever really take place in institutions like schools and colleges which may be both hierarchical and bureaucratic. The approaches of peace education are, however, a vital part of everyday politicisation and consciousness-raising. It is teaching *for*, not merely teaching *about*, racial justice, global development and peace. The approaches of peace education also underlie the format of all conferences and workshops run by the World Studies Project, i.e. they try to create equity, antonomy, solidarity and participation. They are essentially part of what Wren called 'education for justice' (1977).

Now it is clear that whilst there is much in common amongst these responses, that there are in fact 'family likenesses', there are also important differences. In part these arise from the main focusing ideas of each field:

| | |
|---|---|
| World Studies | interdependence |
| Development Education | development |
| Peace Education | peace |
| Multicultural Education | culture |

and these differences have been briefly explored above. They also, however, arise from the ideological standpoints of practitioners as outlined in Table 1. Most of the responses discussed above thus contain their own conservative – liberal– radical spectrum and it is this spectrum which explains many of the tensions *within* each field. It also helps to explain, in part, the tensions *between* each field, for whilst radicals can see how much they share, conservatives may feel they have little in common.

The error, perhaps, is to take any of these concerns as *discrete* fields, for

Table 1 A map of some of the tensions (From: Richardson R., 'Tensions in World and School', *Bulletin of Peace Proposals*, Oslo, summer 1974)

| | Focus | 'Conservative' | 'Liberal' | 'Radical' |
|---|---|---|---|---|
| Aims | The political task | To defend the national self-interest with force if necessary | To create a system of world order – viz. laws to prohibit armed force | To create justice, both within and between countries |
| | The educational task | To evoke loyalty to the nation | To evoke loyalty to the world community as a whole | To develop the skills and attitudes of 'freedom fighters' |
| Classroom | Curriculum content | Own national history, culture, achievements, victories, great men | World history, other cultures, East–West conflict, United Nations | Relevant concepts – 'structural violence', North–South conflict, systems bias |
| | Resources for learning | Textbooks, 'chalk-and-talk' | Worksheets, hand-outs, 'evidence', newscuttings | Experiential – games, simulations, and involvement in real issues |
| | Teaching style | Class as basic unit, and teacher as instructor | Individuals or small groups as basic unit – teacher as guide | Variety of groupings and roles according to varying tasks |
| | Basic skills | 'Factual recall – dates, formulae, terminology, spelling | Skills of enquiry – assessing evidence, forming hypotheses | Skills of expression – language, other media, action in real issues |
| Background | School organisation | Clear boundaries – e.g. in hierarchy, distinct subjects, seclusion, segregation | Blurring of boundaries – participation, integrated studies, interaction | Variety of boundaries, according to varying tasks |
| | Schools in society | 'Academic' education for children of present élite | 'Equality of opportunity' – viz. emphasis on future élite | Variety of provision within and towards real social equality |
| | Theory of knowledge | Platonic – reality as wholly external to the human mind | 'Forms of knowledge' – ideas of distinctive intellectual disciplines | Existentialist – emphasis on subject – object dialectic, 'social construction' of reality |

if we do so we may then miss out on the perspectives that the others have to offer. Too often one can become caught between the *roots* (i.e. distinctive characteristics) of one's field and the need to justify it in the *classroom* (where its title may be meaningless). It is probably best therefore not to consider development education, World Studies, multicultural education and peace education as distinct fields, but rather as offering organising concepts for curriculum planning: development, interdependence, culture and peace. They are complementary, not mutually exclusive. What is clear is that they should be used to develop what might be called 'global literacy',[7] 'that is, basic understanding of the contemporary world, its problems and its evolving systems of international relationships' (UNESCO 1976a). What it now remains to do is to indicate the legitimation and support that grew up during the 1970s for such concerns.

## Legitimation and support for global perspectives in the curriculum

What official recognition has there been of the need for global perspectives in the curriculum? What support from the UN, from the government, the DES or teachers' unions? These are important questions, because the answers to them will indicate both the legitimation and support that is available for such claims.

The key document must be the Recommendation adopted by the General Conference of UNESCO at its eighteenth session in 1974, called in full the *Recommendation Concerning Education for International Understanding, Co-operation and Peace and Education relating to Human Rights and Fundamental Freedoms*. This clearly set out the international concern for a global perspective in the curriculum and amongst the objectives to be 'regarded as major guiding principles of educational policy' were (UNESCO 1974):

(a) an international dimension and a global perspective in education at all levels and in all forms;
(b) understanding and respect for all peoples, their cultures, civilisations, values and ways of life, including domestic ethnic cultures and cultures of other nations;
(c) awareness of the increasing global interdependence between people and nations;
(d) abilities to communicate with others;
(e) awareness not only of the rights but also of the duties incumbent upon individuals, social groups and nations towards each other;
(f) understanding of the necessity for international solidarity and co-operation;
(g) readiness on the part of the invidual to participate in solving the problems of his community, his country and the world at large.

The document also outlines 'the major problems of mankind' which, it was argued, needed to be studied in an interdisciplinary way. These included: human rights, peace and war, the eradication of racialism, world development, pollution and the conservation of natural resources.

The UK government was, of course, a signatory to the Recommendation which offered considerable moral support for those already working in World Studies and development education. Two years later the DES issued Circular 9/76 which drew the attention of all local education authorities (LEAs)and voluntary colleges of education to the Recommendation (DES 1976):

The Secretaries of State attach importance to the message of the recommendation having the widest possible dissemination and impact and look to all those to whom this circular is addressed to consider the best ways in which, in their local circumstances, the recommendation can be used. In due course the United Kingdom will be required to report to UNESCO on the measures which it has taken to implement the recommendation . . .

In the same year teachers' unions at the World Confederation of Organisations of the Teaching Profession (WCOTP) agreed on a series of recommendations for 'Education for a global community'. These were reported on in the journal of the National Association of Teachers in Further and Higher Education and included (NATFHE Journal 1976):

1. Encourage open discussion which allows students to develop a respect for all human beings.
2. Champion the cause of social justice for all students in their classes, schools and communities.
3. Promote the concept of a global community by including in all curriculum development where possible appreciation of diverse cultures.
4. Make appropriate use of the mass media and seize all other opportunities to publicise the concept of a global community.
5. Ensure that one's own training and professional education includes a realisation of the objectives of 'Education for a global community'.
6. Eliminate prejudice and bias from their teaching, be selective, and show the individual how to assume his or her role in a global society.
7. Assist young people towards comprehending their responsibilities with regard to the interdependence of individuals and groups of all nations.

Gradually therefore official recognition was given to issues of global concern. Indeed the Green Paper published by the DES in 1977 referred to the fact that 'we live in a complex, interdependent world and many of our problems in Britain require international solutions. The curriculum should therefore reflect our need to know more about and understand other countries'.

The Ministry of Overseas Development at this time also set up a Development Education Fund which, as in other European countries, was to ensure that part of the overseas aid budget should be spent on development education in the UK. The need for this had been made clear by a survey of public opinion on overseas aid which described the country as suffering from a state of 'national introversion' (Bowles 1978) and in which both ethnocentric and extremely racist views had often been expressed. The setting up of the fund, which was later axed by the Conservatives, allowed many innovative ventures to get off the ground and the success of these has recently been set out in the World Studies Journal.[8] Another milestone was

17

the setting up of the Standing Conference on Education for International Understanding in 1978 backed by the then Secretary of State for Education, Shirley Williams.[9]

It was against this background that a host of smaller ventures were 'filling in the detail'. Amongst these were the education departments of aid agencies such as Christian Aid and Oxfam, the Centre for World Development Education with its resources for teachers, the growth of development education centres and the setting up of the World Studies Teacher Education Network. The two influential publications in these fields were, and are, *The New Era* and the *World Studies Journal*, the former having a venerable pedigree of several decades and the latter being originally the brainchild of a Leicestershire Community College with the help of a grant from the Development Education Fund.[10]

The most influential work in this field has come from the World Studies Project which, under the direction of Robin Richardson from 1973 to 1979, pioneered many developments in exploring 'global literacy'. It has considerable expertise in running workshops and conferences for teachers, a countrywide network of schools and colleges and several impressive, and extremely useful, publications to its credit. Today the project continues to exert its influence by being jointly responsible for the curriculum project *World Studies 8–13*.

It was only relatively recently that Professor Godfrey Brown noted that curriculum innovation in these fields depends on 'a very small minority of individuals who are doing their best against all odds . . .' (Brown 1978). It is fair to say, however, that these odds are now changing as the case studies in this book illustrate. They have been chosen to illustrate both the breadth of what is going on and also some of the most innovative work in schools and initial and in-service education. Even Wright's (1979) criticism of the missing global dimension in Schools Council activities has now been met by the curriculum project *World Studies 8–13* (1980–83) jointly sponsored by the Schools Council and the Rowntree Charitable Trust. It is based in Bristol with the World Studies Project, and Lancaster with the Centre for Peace Studies and will be producing an attractive teacher's resource/handbook on teaching World Studies to the 8–13 age range.[11]

It is appropriate, we think, to end this first chapter with some reminders and questions for the proponents of a global perspective in the curriculum. Whilst the case studies that follow illustrate some of the most interesting work that is going on at the start of the 1980s, it would be wrong to imply that it is sufficient. Not only do more schools, more colleges and more schools of education need to give global perspectives in their curricula, they also need to consider both the quality and the focus of concern. Do we pay enough attention to ethnocentric and racist bias in our teaching materials?[12] Do we attempt to combat myths and stereotypes, for example, concerning world food?[13] Are we equally concerned about militarism, the arms race and disarmament?[14] What thought do we really give to alternative, safer and more peaceful, futures?[15]

# Notes

1. The Center for Global Perspectives, Inc. is at 218 East 18th Street, New York NY 10003, USA. The Mid-America Program for Global Perspectives in Education is at Indiana University, Bloomington, Indiana, USA.
2. The World Studies Project may be contacted at 24, Palace Chambers, Bridge Street, London SW1V lJA. Its considerable expertise is exemplified by its publications: *Learning for Change in World Society* is an excellent resource book for teachers; *Ideas Into Action* describes case studies of global perspectives in the secondary curriculum; *Debate and Decision* is a handbook for courses and meetings.
3. Atlantic College Peace Studies Project, United World College of the Atlantic, St Donat's Castle, Llantwit Major, Cardiff, S. Glamorgan CF6 9WF.
4. See for example Michael Reidy's 'What should we tell our pupils?' Talkback, *Times Educational Supplement*, 31 Oct. 1980.
5. The Summer 1980 issue of the *World Studies Journal*, 1 (4), was on peace education. Back copies are available from: Groby Community College, Ratby Road, Groby, Leicester LE6 0FP.
6. The Centre for Peace Studies is at St Martin's College, Lancester LA1 3JD. It offers support and advice on all issues related to teaching about peace and conflict. It is currently involved in running the curriculum project *World Studies 8–13* (see below).
7. Parallels might well be drawn here between the term 'global literacy' and 'political literacy'. Whilst they obviously differ in meaning, although with some overlap, the stress on literacy suggests the vital need to acquire particular skills. For an interesting introduction to 'political literacy' see Crick, B. and Porter, A. (eds) (1978) *Political Education and Political Literacy*, Longman.
8. 'Development education — the story of a fund', *World Studies Journal*, 2 (4), 3–4, 1981 (see 5 above).
9. Standing Conference on Education for International Understanding, Extramural Division, School of Oriental and African Studies, Malet Street, London WC1E 7HP.
10. See Chapter 12 for addresses and details.
11. *World Studies 8–13* (1980–83) is being run by Simon Fisher, World Studies Project, 12 Fairfield Road, Bristol BS3 ILG and David Hicks, Centre for Peace Studies, St Martin's College, Lancaster LAI 3JD. The project will be carrying out its dissemination programme in 1982–83 and will be producing a handbook/resource book for teachers.
12. The whole area of ethnocentric and racist bias in teaching materials is an important one. Zimet, S. (1976) *Print and Prejudice*, Hodder and Stoughton, provides an excellent review of the research. A more detailed study of British racial attitudes and 'images' of the Third World is made in Hicks, D. W., *Textbook imperialism: a study of ethnocentric bias in textbooks with particular reference to geography*, unpublished Ph.D. Thesis, University of Lancaster, 1980.
13. Essential reading on world food issues in George, S. (1977) *How The Other Half Dies: The Real Reasons For World Hunger*, Pelican, and Lappé, F. M. and Collins, J., *Food First: Beyond the myth of scarcity* (1980 ), Souvenir Press, Ltd, London; (1979) Ballantine, New York.
14. See Thompson, E. P. and Smith, D. (eds) (1980) *Protest and Survive*, Penguin Special. For classroom context see Betty Reardon, 'Obstacles to disarmament education' in *Bulletin of Peace Proposals*, 10 (4), pp. 356–7, 1979, International Peace Research Institute, Oslo. On teaching resources Graham Pike's 'Resources and agencies for disarmament education', *World Studies Journal*, 1 (4), 34–6, 1980, is most useful.
15. See for example Robertson, J. (1978) *The Sane Alternative: Signposts To A Self-Fulfilling Future*, from Spring Cottage, 9 New Road, Ironbridge, Shropshire TF8 7AU.

# Chapter 2    Robin Richardson
## Culture and justice: key concepts in World Studies and multicultural education

In summer 1977 the British government issued a document entitled *Education in Schools*. It was circulated widely by the DES and became known colloquially as the Green Paper. It included amongst other things a brief statement which was seized on eagerly and gratefully by supporters of World Studies, multicultural education, development education, education for international understanding, and so on. We quoted the statement in our various publicity leaflets and applications for funds, and in the prefaces of our various publications, as a succinct and weighty summary of what we were up to.[1] We did not notice – or if we did ourselves notice we trusted that no one else would – that the statement was seriously illogical and inadequate. The statement had two halves, and much the same *non sequitur* was present in each. It went as follows:

Our society is a multi-cultural, multi-racial one and the curriculum should reflect a sympathetic understanding of the different cultures and races that now make up our society. We also live in a complex, interdependent world and many of our problems in Britain require international solutions. The curriculum should, therefore, reflect our need to know more about and understand other countries.

One objection to this dual statement – the one half about multicultural Britain, the other about global interdependence – is that it commits a form of the naturalistic fallacy: it derives an 'ought' about the curriculum from an 'is' about society. The relationship between schools and society, however, is very problematic. Changes in society do not necessarily have to be accepted or welcomed by schools, and neither in schools nor in society should changes be considered independently of the distribution of power and, therefore, of questions about whose material interests are being promoted, and whose are being challenged. '*Our* society...' says the Green Paper. '*We* live...' The tone is that of 'we're all in the same boat' – a rallying call which typically comes from the captain rather than from the crew and whose function, if it is successful, is to mobilise deferential respect for the authority structure in which the captain has certain distinctive rewards. 'We're all in a multicultural boat' may similarly be (but need not be) part of a collusion with, rather than a challenge and resistance towards, the structures and institutions which result in racial discrimination, and which breed racist beliefs.[2]

A further objection to the statement in the Green Paper is to do with what is actually being proposed. Even if you accept its basic propositions about multicultural Britain and global interdependence as unproblematic, and even if (it is not at all difficult) you accept that certain new realities in national and world society have implications for the curriculum of schools, still it is by no means clear that 'sympathetic understanding of different cultures' and 'knowledge of other countries' are required as priorities. Surely what primarily follows from the proposition that 'we live in a complex, interdependent world', for example, is that we should study the nature of dependence, therefore of dominance, therefore of power. Who is dependent on whom for what, and what are the goods and bads which actors in international society possess and use? And who, any way, are the main actors in international society? Are they adequately conceptualised as 'countries' rather than as, say, élites within countries and as all sorts of non-governmental organisations, including trans-national corporations? These are the main questions.[3] Knowledge of other countries is no doubt required to answer or handle them, but surely such knowledge is neither a logical nor a strategic priority.

Similarly one may object to the proposition that 'sympathetic understanding of different cultures and races' is a priority derived from the observation that 'our society is multicultural'. The priority, surely, is to understand how and why society became multicultural, who benefits and who suffers from the present arrangements, how racism in both individuals and institutions can be resisted and removed, and how both harmony and justice, not just the one or the other, can be promoted. White teachers and educational administrators no doubt need, as part of this understanding, to have a sympathetic knowledge of different cultures and races − or more accurately, of how particular ethnic groups, and individuals within particular minority groups, experience and articulate the world around them. But such knowledge is neither sufficient nor an immediate priority. For minority-group pupils, as distinct from white teachers and administrators, the priorities include confidence in their own culture and identity, competence in resisting assaults on themselves, and skill in creating change.[4]

It is interesting, in order to highlight and summarise the main criticisms which can be made of the Green Paper statement, to speculate about what a completely different kind of statement would have looked like. Such speculation is also useful for drawing attention to the Green Paper's strengths. One can consider, for example, something such as this:

Our society contains conflicts of interest between social classes, between the sexes, between generations, between the dominant, mainly racist white majority on the one hand and ethnic minorities of Asian or Caribbean background on the other. Within world society as a whole, Britain's ruling élite is part of the North: it is in economic conflict with the South, and actively colludes with and benefits from patterns of repression and exploitation in Third World countries. As part of the West it is in conflict also with the East, and wastes vast sums of money on armaments. The curriculum of our schools should help pupils and teachers and the local communities to which they belong, to understand the power structures in which they participate as victims or as beneficiaries, and should help them develop commitment to, and practical skill in working from their various positions

21

towards, greater equality, peace and justice, locally, nationally and internationally.

This alternative statement clarifies, explicitly or implicitly, a series of separate but interrelated tensions. Its key concept, for example, is power, whereas the key concept in the Green Paper is culture; its key value is justice, not harmony; its political ideology is socialist, not liberal; it has a radical, not reformist, approach to change ; it reflects the outlook of ethnic minorities in Western countries, not the white majority; in world terms it reflects the standpoint of the South rather than the North.

It may be that one day a government will come to power in Britain, and in other Western countries, which will issue or endorse a statement on multicultural education and World Studies similar to this alternative to the Green Paper. In 1977, however, it would not have been politically possible for the British government to say much more, or much differently, than it did. For this reason if for no other it is useful to examine the Green Paper statement with regard to its strengths and uses, not only its weaknesses. There are five main points worth emphasising. First, the statement makes much better sense than does its alternative to the vast majority of primary school teachers. Rightly or wrongly, teachers of younger children feel that 'controversial' questions about social justice and the distribution of wealth and power should be left until the secondary school. With younger children, they feel, it is more important to emphasise the needs and qualities which all human beings have in common than to draw attention to dissent, dispute, conflict. Certainly it may be that primary schools are far more protective and paternalist than they should be, and that harmony is too highly valued, in comparison with values such as fairness, individuality, reality, in their ethos. The fact remains that the Green Paper statement is supportive for valuable curriculum development of certain kinds in primary schools, and therefore not to be dismissed lightly.

A second important point about the Green Paper statement, closely related to the first point about the age-group of pupils, is that it usefully emphasises where many courses in World Studies and multicultural education can most appropriately start in actual practice: with culture rather than with power as the key concept, and with a liberal, reformist approach to the issues rather than a socialist, radical one. To say that this is where courses may usefully start is not, of course, to say where they should finish. A third point is that the Green Paper is implicitly commending humanities, particularly history, literature and the arts, rather than the social sciences: the statement is in consequence ill-balanced, certainly, but nevertheless it is worth recalling that equally a statement which referred only to the social sciences, ignoring humanities, would be ill-balanced. Fourth, the implicit emphasis is on individual attitudes and understanding rather than on structural and political change – the Green Paper is descended in this respect from the famous UNESCO declaration that wars begin in the 'hearts and minds' of human beings. The emphasis is false in so far as it implies that changes in attitude and understanding amongst individuals are sufficient for the creation of a more just social order, within and between countries. It is valuable, however, in so far as it emphasises that programmes of social change need to be based on a dialectic between political action and personal change, and that it is often with the latter, personal change, that they begin. The emphasis on personal change – and also, incidentally, on the humanities as distinct from the social sciences – was eloquently expressed by Camus, in his great lecture 'Create Dangerously'[5]:

Great ideas...come into the world as gently as doves. Perhaps then, if we listen attentively, we shall hear, amidst the uproar of empires and nations, a faint flutter of wings, the gentle stirring of life and hope. Some will say that this hope lies in a nation ; others, in a man. I believe rather that it is awakened, revived, nourished by millions of solitary individuals whose deeds and works every day negate frontiers and the crudest implications of history. As a result there shines forth fleetingly the ever-threatened truth that each and every man, on the foundation of his own sufferings and joys, builds for all.

When organisations and projects quote the Green Paper statement, in order to give themselves greater weight and legitimacy, they may seem in effect to be adopting a top-downwards, or trickle-down, approach to educational change : they seem in effect to be saying 'multicultural education is important because the government says so'. Certainly important objections can be and must be made of top-downwards approaches to change, and it is always as well to be sceptical about the usefulness of official policy statements and recommendations as actual initiators of change. The fact remains that the Green Paper has been useful as a support and protection, and as a lever or counter in various negotiations. One of the lessons of the 1970s, so far as World Studies and multicultural education are concerned, is that legitimation is important, not a luxury, and that therefore a top-downwards approach to change has its value. To say this is by no means, of course, to underemphasise the importance of bottom-upwards change as well. Rather, it is to acknowledge that educational change takes place inside very complex organisations, and that the proponents of change need to know well the structures of formal and informal influence within those organisations. A conceptual scheme used in this connection in the 1970s by the Mid-America Program for Global Perspectives, Indiana University, distinguished between 'legitimisers', 'influence leaders' and 'inside advocates'. These are distinct roles in a school or college rather than, necessarily, distinct individuals. The legitimiser is the person or committee who can provide or withhold financial support for a new development in the curriculum. The influence leader provides moral support, or alternatively can mobilise demoralising opposition. The inside advocate both argues a case in principle and works out detailed proposals for practical application. Proponents of World Studies and multicultural education need to identify and influence all three of these roles inside each separate school or college.[6] The Green Paper statement does not give new ideas to inside advocates: but certainly it strengthens their hand as they negotiate with legitimisers, and it is useful as a preliminary summary as they approach influence leaders. This is a fifth point in its favour. There are very few schools

23

and colleges in Britain, or in any other Western country, in which the alternative statement suggested here earlier would be more effective from these two points of view.

To summarise, the Green Paper statement can be criticised, but also it can be defended. Table 2 tabulates the various tensions which exist between the Green Paper on the one hand and the alternative on the other. In effect it is also a summary of the main debates and dilemmas in which proponents of World Studies and multicultural education have been involved during the last ten to fifteen years, and which are likely to be increasingly important in the years ahead. Every new project or publication can be examined with these tensions in mind as a checklist. Where does it stand with regard to each dimension or tension? Is it attracted to the one pole much more than to the other, and if so which? Or is it equally attracted to both poles, and therefore in a state of tension? To what extent is it consciously and explicitly aware of its own position?

Table 2   Tensions in World Studies and multicultural education

|  | Green Paper | Alternative |
| --- | --- | --- |
| Key concept | Culture | Power |
| Key value | Harmony | Justice |
| Ideology | Liberalism | Socialism |
| Attitude to change | Reformist | Radical |
| Style of change | Top-downwards | Grassroots-upwards |
| Focus of change | Individuals | Structures |
| Work location | Practitioners | Theorists |
| Educational location | School | Community |
| National location | White majority | Ethnic minorities |
| World location | North | South |
| Academic discipline | Humanities | Social sciences |
| Age-group | Younger pupils | Older pupils |
| Classroom strategy | Starting-point | Final objectives |

In order to be able to ask and answer such questions with greater precision, it is useful to take the key concept of culture and to consider how we should teach about other countries and cultures if, at the same time, we wish to remain in close contact with the key concept of power. What does the Green Paper phrase 'sympathetic understanding' actually mean, or begin to mean, if a teacher wishes to, or is ready to, live with the tensions recalled in Table 2? In the next few paragraphs seven separate principles will be proposed. Several of them can be appropriately introduced with a brief passage from a novel by Thomas Hardy. Hardy describes how Angel Clare, a middle-class intellectual, goes to live and work amongst people in the Dorset countryside, people whom he has until now dismissed with the negative stereotype of Hodge. Other words developed by town dwellers over the years to express the same stereotype include country bumpkin, provincial, yokel, clodhopper, rustic, peasant. This is how Hardy (1891, Ch. XVIII) describes Clare's encounter:

The conventional farm-folk of his imagination, personified by the pitiable dummy known as Hodge, were obliterated after a few days residence. At close quarters no Hodge was to be seen. His host and his host's household, his men and his maids, as they became intimately known to Clare, began to differentiate themselves as in a chemical process. ...The typical and unvarying Hodge ceased to exist. He had been disintegrated into a number of varied fellow-creatures – beings of many minds, being infinite in difference; some happy, many serene, a few depressed, one here and there bright even to genius, some stupid, others wanton, others austere...into men who had private views of each other as he had of his friends...men every one of whom walked in his own individual way the road to dusty death.

It is a beautiful and remarkable description of the goals which a teacher may have in mind when studying other cultures and countries with her or his pupils. Hardy in effect provides three main guidelines. First, he emphasises that Clare sees the country people as different from each other – they are not a monolithic, homogeneous mass. E. P. Thompson has argued that 'the deformed human mind is the ultimate doomsday weapon – it is out of the human mind that the missiles and the neutrons come'.[7] A major aspect of the deformation, he claims, is the propensity to make no distinctions amongst those who are defined as the enemy : they are all merely Other, outside ourselves, non-people. Whether or not wars and other ills do arise primarily from hearts and minds of men and women, as UNESCO said, as distinct from the institutions and processes which men and women have created, is for the moment beside the point. Thompson and Hardy (and many others) are surely right to insist that one minimal condition of peace and justice is that we should break down generalisations, strenuously permit our enemies 'to differentiate themselves as in a chemical process'. In autumn 1979, when most of the Western media were frantic with indignation against Iran, one journalist wrote bravely and simply as follows, emphasising this first preliminary guideline in all our dealings with other countries and cultures (Tweedie 1979):

Iranians are not all students, mullahs or heroin smugglers. There are Iranian plumbers, birdwatchers, piano-tuners, potters, horticulturalists, weavers, and hairdressers. There are lazy, timid, depressed Iranians, Iranians who hate crowds, agrophobic and claustrophobic Iranians, and Iranians who bite their nails. Some Iranians dislike the East as much as others dislike the West. Some believe in women's equality and abhor violence of any kind. Some are even atheist.... The whole pattern of the build-up towards violent or unjust action taken by one group or country against another is grounded in an effort to reduce that group or country's individuals from an infinity of characteristics to one harshly outlined caricature....

A second guideline for approaching other cultures, closely connected with the first, is that people should be seen as directing their own lives, and moved by anxieties and hopes, and intentions and will-power. They are not merely cogs in a machine, pawns on the board of history, roles in an impersonal system. All too often, the Swedish psychologist Stig Lindholm (1975, pp. 10–11) has commented, we have what he calls external relationships with people in other countries, cultures, classes and groupings: 'one regards the other person as an object, which in turn implies that the person is regarded as a pawn, or one whose behaviour is guided or determined by external causes, rather than his or her own desires and objectives;...one views the other more as the occupant of a given role than as an individual;...the external relationship implies a dehumanisation, a depersonification, of the other person.' The advertising campaigns of Western aid agencies, and all too many development education materials, implicitly reflect and commend external relationships. With internal relationships, however, of the kind into which Angel Clare enters with the farmer and his family and friends, 'the other person is conceived of as an individual, a living person with goals and intentions; the person is not static, like the occupant of a role, but rather he is in the process of developing, or possesses an innate potential to develop.' One aspect of internal relationships is that one readily conceives the people in another culture as having opinions about each other: '(they) had private views of each other,' writes Hardy, 'as he had of his friends; (they) could applaud or condemn each other, amuse or sadden each other by the contemplation of each other's foibles or vices.' Books such as *Endless Pressure* by Ken Pryce (1979) or *Petals of Blood* by Ngugi wa Thiong'o (1977) similarly show a great variety of perspectives, hopes and intentions, and also great powers of self-direction, and great courage and capacity to resist oppression, amongst people all too often seen by white Westerners as homogeneous and impersonal.

It follows, if people in another culture are seen as 'varied fellow-creatures', that they cannot be seen as wholly evil or as, in that infamous phrase of Kipling's about the white man's burden, 'half-devil and half-child'. Strenuous resistance to enemy images – what the German peace researcher Dieter Senghaas calls the 'endevilment' (*Verteuflung*) of enemies (quoted in Nicklas and Ostermann 1979) – is built by, amongst other things, the open-minded study of other cultures. This is the third guideline which Thomas Hardy implicitly proposes in his account of Angel Clare: the 'other' is not evil. It is a challenge to all kinds of racist – for example, to the anti-Semite, described by Sartre (1946, pp. 279–80) as follows:

(For the anti-Semite) the Jew is assimilable to the spirit of evil. His will...is one which desires to be purely, gratuitously and universally evil, it is the will to evil. Evil comes to the world through him; all that is bad in society (crises, wars, famines, upheavals and revolts) is directly or indirectly imputable to the Jew. The anti-Semite is afraid of discovering that the world is badly made: for then things would have to be invented, modified, and man would find himself once more master of his fate, filled with agonising and infinite responsibility. He localises all the evil of the universe in the Jew. If nations wage war, it is not due to the fact that the idea of nationalism in its present form involves imperialism and conflict of interests... If there is class struggle, it is not caused by economic organisation...but because Jewish ringleaders, hook-nosed agitators have seduced the workers. Thus anti-Semitism is primarily Manichaeanism; it explains the course of the world by the struggle between the principles of Good and Evil.

Sartre's account of the anti-Semite is an accurate description of the white racist in Western societies, and also of the anti-Soviet and anti-Communist stance which is reflected in the Western mass media. Substitute the term stupid instead of evil, and Sartre's account is in addition applicable to the anti-Irish attitudes which are expressed daily in countless so-called jokes in English pubs, offices, factories, clubs, theatres, TV studios: it is perhaps even more sick and reprehensible to conceive of human beings as bright/thick than as good/evil. Sartre emphasises in passing that the anti-Semite and the anti-racist are wholly different from each other in the structure of their minds, or any way ought to be. The former is merely opposed to evil, and assumes that good will automatically follow if evil (the Jew, the foreigner, the minority group) is eliminated or repatriated. The latter, however, has to seek good 'in anguish, to invent it, to debate it in action, to verify its consequences and finally to saddle oneself with the responsibilities of the moral choice thus made' (Sartre 1946, p. 282). This kind of distinction between the racist and the anti-racist is of immense importance: for there is an underlying danger that the latter as well as the former may be Manichaean, committed merely to the destruction of evil rather than to the creation of good. The danger has been well pin-pointed by a publication from the Peace News Collective:[8]

The British Left is thriving on the threat posed by the National Front and other fascist organisations. More of us are marching than at any time for ten years . . . . Rock against Racism and Whatever-you-fancy Against the Nazis badges abound: it looks like we're on a winner here . . . . Concentrated in the NF, we find most of the worst attitudes popular in Britain. This makes them just the sort of enemy the Left seems to need for it to come together with some common purpose – fascism represents an extreme form of almost everything we oppose.

It is from the study of culture, more than from the study of power, and from actual personal encounter with people in other cultures, that one derives the power to combat not only racism but also Manichaeanism. Here again is the Peace News Collective:

Everything in our society conspires to make us feel bad about ourselves, hence to project our badness onto scapegoats. Making racists feel still worse about themselves fuels racism in the long run. Hardened racists know in their heart of hearts that they've lost their way. Being anti-Black is often a testing out, a cry for help, for resisting with love. If we anti-racists need racists as our scapegoat niggers, we aren't 'combating racism', we're adding to it...I am pleading for a sensitive style of dialogue with racists. We need to learn creative listening. We need to acknowledge with them our own racism, give examples of our own hang-ups, say what enabled us to change and what we've learned from Black people and encourage our opponent to see encounter with Black people as an opportunity to learn too.

References to creative listening, dialogue and encounter emphasise a fourth important principle for teaching and learning about other cultures and countries : it is important to see people in these other countries as beings with whom one can interact. That is, one can learn from them, one can be changed. In true dialogue, as distinct from point-scoring or self-serving conversation, one is examining another's mind and perceptions in order the better to understand oneself. Angel Clare learns about, amongst other things, his own identity and mortality as he encounters people who 'walked each in his own individual way the road to dusty death'. It is broadly similar learning – about oneself, and about human nature and society more generally – that is always attained, at best, in the study of other cultures. We turn to Pryce's West Indians, or Ngugi's Kenyans, or Tolstoy's Russians, or whoever, in order to learn not only or even primarily about them, but about ourselves. Such learning is, certainly, painful, even shocking. It involves accepting Auden's suggestion that education should induce 'the maximum amount of neurosis that an individual can take without breaking'.[9] For it involves culture shock: 'only a thoroughly engaging and profoundly shaking personal experience', it has been suggested, 'can break through the barrier of ethnocentrism...; every opportunity must be taken by members of staff and students to expose themselves to foreign cultures' (Medellin 1976). This exposure involves becoming a stranger, a foreigner, an immigrant; the stranger knows 'that a man may lose his status, his rules of guidance, and even his history, and that the normal way of life is always far less guaranteed than it seems,' (Schutz 1964). Learning from a foreigner involves becoming in some measure a foreigner oneself; and surviving with the other's help: and being, therefore, grateful. Commitment to democracy and social justice – that is, to principles of fairness in relationships between 'us' and 'them', myself and others – remains brittle and fragile if it is not accompanied by, and indeed if it is not grounded in, such gratitude.

'Encounter', 'dialogue', 'culture shock', 'shaking personal experience', 'stranger', 'gratitude': these are dramatic words, and certainly it is important to emphasise that the Green Paper's 'sympathetic understanding' of other cultures is neither easy nor cosy. At the same time it is important to acknowledge that many interactions and interdependencies in the modern world are reasonably matter-of-fact and unthreatening. This point leads to a fifth principle for teaching and learning about other countries and cultures: what we think of as 'us' is in fact affected by 'them', often very deeply affected. The 'British way of life', or whatever, is a seductive and dangerous myth: it has been affected and enriched over many centuries through its contacts with other ways of life, and is economically dependent in the present on materials, labour, expertise, capital, markets, elsewhere. *Here* is the world – not over there somewhere. This crucial point for World Studies and multicultural education has been developed in detail by Chadwick Alger and his associates in the United States, in their study known as 'Columbus in the world, the world in Columbus'. It is explicated also at length in the most important single book of the 1970s on World Studies, by the American scholar Lee Anderson:[10]

Each of us is caught up in a network of international links and relationships that encircle the planet like a giant cobweb and make the 'globalness' of the contemporary world a pervasive and ubiquitous element in the routines of everyday life. Indeed, the global character of our lives is like the air we breathe. It has become so commonplace that we often take it for granted, and unconsciously assume that it is a natural and unchanging feature of the human condition.

A major part of World Studies, according to Anderson and Alger, is conscious examination of the globalness which we tend to take unconsciously for granted. It is accomplished by such apparently mundane activities as looking at the origins of the goods in a local supermarket, the news in one's local newspaper, the names in one's local street directory. It is important for the sake of intellectual honesty: globalness is a fact. Also it is important for moral and political reasons. 'As people perceive more clearly the ways in which international relations impinge on their everyday lives,' writes Alger (1977), 'involved interest in the foreign policies of governments should increase.... The capacity of citizens to remove the perceptual screens that prevent them from seeing the present international dimensions of their own communities is a prerequisite for the development of capability for participation in alternative global futures.'

Sixth, it is important not only to uncover the globalness of the modern world, and to make thus explicit the many reasons which 'we' have to be grateful to 'them', but also to uncover the reasons why negative stereotypes of others so frequently arise and are maintained. Why did Angel Clare previously think of country people as mere Hodge? Did the fault lie in just his own self – the way his own mind constructed the world, jumped to conclusions and typifications? Or in the middle-class, urban culture into which he had been socialised? Or in the exploitative economic relations which existed at that time between town and country? Was it the dual function of 'Hodge' to obscure and to justify an economic system in which the rewards and the power were unjustly distributed?

Broadly similar questions can be, and must be, asked about race relations in Western countries: is racism caused by, or is it itself the cause of slavery and colonialism in the past, and neo-colonialism and internal colonialism (through migrant workers) in the present? Either way, what are the mechanisms of racism, both in individuals and in institutions, and in the interaction between them? How are both individual racism and institutional racism most effectively resisted? What are the objective conflicts of interest between Whites and Blacks? The Green Paper's 'sympathetic understanding' involves such questions about the origins of negative stereotypes and about conflicts of interest. The questions of course have to be not only about race relations but also about the East – West and the North – South conflicts, and all other conflict formations between 'us' and 'them'.

Seventh, the study of other countries and cultures should not be divorced from the study of peace and justice, that is, from the study of management and resolution of conflict. The central question of political education, as identified by members of Her Majesty's Inspectorate (HMI) in a paper widely distributed and discussed in the late 1970s, is also a central question in World Studies and multicultural education: 'What happens when people disagree?' (HMI 1977, p. 57.) One answer is that they fight a zero-sum battle, and the stronger wins, establishing a *Pax Romana, Americana, Britannica*. Another answer is that there is a stalemate because of 'reciprocal vulnerability', therefore peaceful coexistence.[11] This second alternative produces a system of laws, contracts and obligations which people observe through the fear of unpleasant consequences if they do not. A third approach is that for reasons of morality rather than of *realpolitik* disagreement is managed such that all people's and parties' interests and perceptions are treated as in principle equal, regardless of their power base.

In so far as the first and second of these two approaches are studied in World Studies and multicultural education, teachers and students are engaged in political education. In so far as they focus on the third alternative, they are engaged in moral education. The tension between *realpolitik* and morality is inescapable in any study of justice: it is a tension also, incidentally, between pessimistic and optimistic views of human nature. The fact that the language of morality and democracy is frequently used for reasons of politics – that is, to protect or promote a group's own control over scarce resources – is not a reason for ignoring the tension. On the contrary, the rhetoric of justice, not only the reality, is an important topic for attention and study.[12]

A close critical examination of the Green Paper, to summarise, enables us to draw up seven general guidelines for teaching and learning about other countries and, more generally still, for the whole field of World Studies and multicultural education. The guidelines can be stated as a series of questions, as follows :

1. Are we helping students to differentiate, so that they do not speak of all Russians, all Muslims, all Europeans, all Blacks ?
2. Are we helping students to perceive foreigners as human beings similar to themselves, with hopes, anxieties, intentions, will-power ?
3. Are we helping students to perceive foreigners therefore as morally various, not wholly evil? Do they avoid the equation us/them = good/bad?
4. Are we helping students to interact with and learn from other cultures? Are we helping them therefore to cope with culture shock?
5. Are we helping students to understand the concept of interdependence – the notion that there are close cultural and economic connections between their own country and other countries?
6. Are we helping students to understand that us/them stereotypes have their roots in economic and political structures, not in individual personality alone?
7. Are we helping students to understand the concept of justice in its two main aspects, politics and morality?

This chapter draws to a close with a further brief summary of World Studies and multicultural education. This additional summary similarly seeks to unpack the Green Paper statement from a more critical perspective, and to emphasise the key concept of justice as well as that of culture. It is cast in the form of a statement of general educational aims and objectives, and is considerably more detailed than the list of seven questions. It could readily be used – or a statement along broadly similar lines could readily be used – as a focus for discussion and evaluation in individual schools and colleges, in negotiations with bodies such as examination boards, and in approaches to the providers of in-services courses. To draw up a statement such as this, it is important to note, is to engage in some of the first steps of rational curriculum planning:[13]

To plan a curriculum rationally, I suggest, does demand an awareness of the ends of the business, and the characterisation of such ends is logically prior to the determination of appropriate means. This is a *logical* priority of ends over means I am asserting. It means that rational consideration of a curriculum demands clarification of the ends prior to determination of the appropriate means, for without a grasp of the ends, the significance of the means *as* means cannot be grasped.

The statement which follows, of the proposed ends of World Studies and multicultural education, is summarised visually in Fig. 1.[14] The principal emphasis in this visualisation is that there is a two-way relationship between each pair of general objectives. Knowledge affects attitudes, attitudes in their turn affect knowledge, both affect skills, and so on. Knowledge, attitudes and skills are not appropriately thought of as occupying separate domains, each distinct from the other. Figure 1 also proposes distinctions between three separate levels of knowledge, and between four main themes. The three levels of knowledge – description, analysis, evaluation – merge with each other and affect each other, but can be kept apart for the sake of preliminary clarity. The four main themes – culture, interdependence, conflict, justice – are inevitably arbitrary, but at least they have a common-sense appeal, and could be used as a basis for syllabus planning.

## The aims and general objectives of World Studies and multicultural education

### Aims

Students should be developing the knowledge, attitudes and skills which they need in order to participate effectively and responsibly in a multicultural society and an interdependent world.

*Notes on the aims*
1. 'Effective' participation is that which protects or promotes the student's own interests, and the interests of the ethnic group and national society to which he or she belongs.
2. 'Responsible' participation is that which recognises and respects the rights of others, both in one's own national society and in world society as a whole.
3. The balance between effective and responsible participation is always difficult to secure and maintain. In practice it involves different practices and decisions, therefore different emphases within the list of general objectives which follows, in different locations and situations.

31

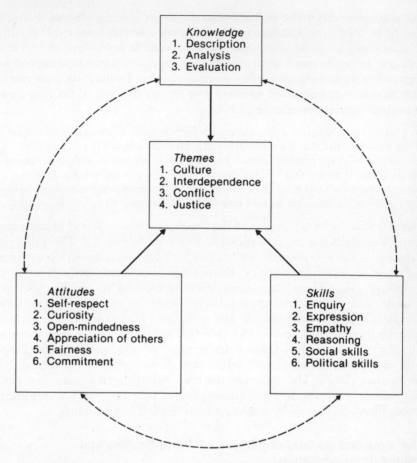

Fig. 1 The general objectives of World Studies and multicultural education: a visual summary

4. The objectives have implications for all subjects in the school or college curriculum, but are relevant in particular to history, geography, social studies, religious education, language and literature. Some of them are also very relevant to art and music.

5. It is axiomatic in this list of objectives, but unstated, that effective participation in society involves for most people remunerative employment, and that formal qualifications in mathematics, science and language are therefore of fundamental importance.

## General objectives – knowledge, attitudes and skills

*1. Knowledge*

*1.1. Knowledge of culture and cultures*

*1.1.1. Description.* Students should be able to perceive and describe the main ways in which the culture of their own ethnic group and national society is similiar to, and different from, the culture of others.

*1.1.2. Analysis.* In order to make these comparisons and contrasts students need concepts such as human biology (growth, nutrition, health, perception, cognition, emotion) and non-material human needs (e.g. for love and affection, meaning, self-realisation); life cycle (including family life and sex roles); religion (in its various dimensions – beliefs, custom, myth); technology (energy, fossil fuels, electronics, appropriate technology); politics, the management of conflict, processes of decision-making, distribution of power, sanctions and rewards.

*1.1.3. Evaluation.* Students should respond with personal views and judgements on both their own culture and other cultures.

## 1.2. Knowledge of interdependence

*1.2.1. Description.* Students should be able to perceive and describe the main ways in which events and trends in one part of the world can affect, and be affected by, events and trends elsewhere.

*1.2.2. Analysis.* In order to analyse interdependence students need the concept of economic cycle, with its component concepts of investment, extraction, processing, distribution, marketing, consumption, reinvestment; and the main concepts of ecology, environment, conservation, pollution; and concepts of historical causality with regard to politics (particularly the distribution of power), technology (particularly communications), and culture.

*1.2.3. Evaluation.* Students should respond with personal views and judgements on controversial issues and theories related to interdependence.

## 1.3. Knowledge of conflict

*1.3.1. Description.* Students should be able to describe some of the main international and intercultural conflicts of the twentieth century, and to identify examples of intercultural conflict in their personal experience or from personal observation.

*1.3.2. Analysis.* In order to understand these issues, students need the concept of objective conflict of interest; concepts of misperception, misunderstanding, stereotype, prejudice, racism, sexism; oppression, exploitation, discrimination, structural violence; revolutionary, reactive violence; escalation, vicious circle.

*1.3.3. Evaluation.* Students should respond with personal views and judgements with regard to the causes and mechanisms of conflict.

## 1.4. Knowledge of peace, law, justice

*1.4.1. Description.* Students should be able to describe the main features of a peaceful and just settlement, both within societies and between societies, and with regard to both the creation and maintenance of peace and justice.

*1.4.2. Analysis.* In order to describe and discuss peace and justice, students need concepts such as rights, equality, fairness, due process of law,

rule of law, representation, legitimacy; grass roots, governmental, consti-
tutional, civil disobedience, non-violence, armed struggle; security, diplomacy. They should be able to illustrate these concepts with regard to their
own society, both in the present and in the past, and also with regard to
other societies.

*1.4.3. Evaluation.* Students should respond with personal views and
judgements with regard to the good life and the good society, and with
regard to how values should be secured and maintained.

## 2. Attitudes

### 2.1. Self-respect

Students should have a sense of their own worth as individuals, confidence
in their own ability to understand complex issues and solve problems, and
pride in their own particular social, cultural and family background.

### 2.2. Curiosity

Students should be interested to find out more about issues related to living
in a multicultural society and interdependent world, particularly in the first
instance those issues which directly affect themselves.

### 2.3. Open-mindedness

Students should approach issues with a critical but open mind, and should
be ready to change their ideas and commitments as they learn more.

### 2.4. Appreciation of other cultures

Students should be ready to find aspects of other cultures of value to themselves, for example to learn from them and to be grateful for them.

### 2.5. Justice and fairness

Students should value democratic principles and processes at local, national
and international levels.

### 2.6. Commitment

Students should be ready to commit themselves to the creation and maintenance of more just social order – for example, through active membership
of particular organisations or campaigns.

## 3. Skills

### 3.1. Enquiry

Students should be able to find and record information about international
and multicultural issues from books, maps, statistical tables, diagrams, photographs, newspapers, audio-visual materials, and should be able to inter-
view people with specialist personal experience.

## 3.2. Expression

Students should be able to explore and express their ideas and feelings in a variety of ways – written prose, conversation, discussion (including committee discussion), speeches, drama and music, pictorial expression of various kinds.

## 3.3. Empathy

Students should be able to imagine the feelings and perspectives of other people, particularly people in cultures and situations different from their own.

## 3.4. Reasoning

Students should be able to compare and contrast, categorise, generalise, hypothesise, form conclusions; and to marshal arguments, and explain and justify their views with sound reasons and evidence.

## 3.5. Social skills

Students should be able to express their views, wishes and feelings clearly and considerately in various situations – for example, in their relationships with each other, in group discussions, in meetings with members of other societies or ethnic groups – and to understand accurately the words and behaviour of others.

## 3.6. Political skills

Students should be able to join with others to influence and to pressurise decision-making at various levels – within their local community and the education they are currently receiving, and in national and international affairs.

## Notes

1. For example, the statement was quoted by the Centre for World Development Education at the start of each booklet in a series entitled *The Changing World*; by the Council for Education in World Citizenship, the Standing Conference on Education for International Understanding, and the World Studies Teacher Education Network in their publicity papers; by the World Studies Project at the start of its book *Debate and Decision*; and by the World Studies course at Groby Community College, Leicestershire.
2. Critiques of multicultural education elaborating this point include those of Dhondy, (1978), Hall (1980) Carby (1980) Mullard (1981) and Stone (1981). The political framework of the critique has been well stated by Sivanandan (1976).
3. Burton (1972) and Anderson (1979) argue that the focus of study should be world society, not other countries or international relations. Authors who have emphasised a dominance/dependence model of world society include Caldwell (1977) and Galtung (1973, 1975).
4. These priorities are vividly emphasised in the writings of Chris Searle (1973, 1975, 1977). Banks (1974), argues in detail that less powerful groups in society, for example ethnic minorities, should have a distinctive curriculum, to equip them to struggle more effectively for their rights.
5. Lecture at the University of Uppsala, December 1957, reprinted in Camus (1961), pp. 176–91.

6. *Debate and Decision* (Richardson, Flood and Fisher 1979) is in effect a resource for facilitating discussion amongst legitimisers, influence leaders and inside advocates.
7. Thompson and Smith (1980) p. 52. Yergin(1977) provides an excellent historical survey of the growth of anti-Soviet images in the 1930s and 1940s.
8. Paton (1979). There is further elaboration of the concept of White awareness in Katz (1978) and of Manichaeanism in Hodge, Struckmann and Trost (1975).
9. Quoted in Coggin (1980). Hampden-Turner (1970) argues at length that true radicalism includes the capacity to risk and survive culture shock.
10. Anderson(1979) p. 33. British educational materials illustrating this emphasis include Taylor and Richardson(1980) and Braun and Pearson(1981).
11. The phrase 'reciprocal vulnerability' is from Mazrui (1975). Mazrui argues that this is an essential feature of what he calls mature interdependence. The other essential feature, he says, is an egalitarian ethic.
12. Brian Wren (1977) has provided an excellent discussion of education for justice, itself based on the philosophical work of John Rawls and the pedagogical theory and practice of Paulo Freire. See also Hicks (1981).
13. Hirst (1973) p. 13. Jeffcoate (1976). Heater (1980) concludes his important book on World Studies with the view that 'a sound and generally acceptable theoretical framework is vitally necessary. To provide this the common ground between the liberal and radical schools of thought must be identified and strengthened.'
14. This statement of general objectives is developed from one contributed to the handbook by Fisher, Magee and Wetz(1980).

# Chapter 3 David Bridges
## 'So truth be in the field . . .?' Approaches to controversy in World Studies teaching

### Introduction: the controversiality of World Studies

The first point I need to establish concerns the essentially controversial nature of the central and characteristic subject-matter of 'global education', 'education for international understanding', 'peace education' and other related subject-matter, all of which I shall refer to under the generic term of 'World Studies'. This controversiality is indicated by the way the literature about World Studies in schools[1] speaks constantly of World Studies teachers' attempts to *change* the attitudes and beliefs of their pupils, of other teachers and, where they have any contact with them, of parents. World Studies teachers indeed often report on their sense of professional isolation and their need for moral support from like-minded people at conferences and through professional corresponding networks – not least because, as one participant explained at the end of a particularly supportive weekend conference: 'Teachers involved in teaching World Studies are often on the fringe of the teaching world ideologically and socially.' (Bridges 1975.) The simple point to observe is that, whether they are dealing with national and global loyalties, international patterns of trade, the equitable distribution of the world's wealth, conflict resolution, the exploitation of natural resources or racial discrimination, World Studies teachers are handling issues which divide popular and indeed expert opinion, divide the teaching profession at large and indeed divide World Studies teachers themselves as soon as they get beyond banal generalities to judgements about particular issues.

The precise nature of the controversiality of World Studies teaching matter deserves closer analysis, for it is not all of a kind. It may be useful to distinguish three types of controversiality which arise respectively out of the ignorance of one party; out of the incompleteness of available factual knowledge; and out of irreconcilable values.

There are plainly some actual social controversies which are in a sense unnecessary because there are facts available which would readily indicate that one side of the argument was mistaken. Factual questions about the scale of immigration into the British Isles need not be the subject of controversy – though they often are – provided we are clear about what would count as an immigrant. There is enough information around to establish whether or not as a matter of fact the wearing of seat belts saves lives – *this* question need not be a matter of controversy – even if the further question as to whether or not the wearing of seat belts should be made a legal obligation remains controversial. Such questions remain the subject of social controversy simply because some people remain ignorant of or stubbornly impervious to the available evidence.

There are, however, other issues which still essentially rest upon questions of fact but which remain controversial because no one can really claim to have the full information which would resolve the difference(s) of view. This may be especially the case where the information needed to resolve them lies in the future, i.e. where they rest upon some prediction of what *will* happen...if we continue to use up natural resources at our present rate; if the South African government does not change its racial policy; if we find no alternative to the nuclear deterrent as a means of preserving 'peace', etc., etc. Even more limited predictions about the effects on a country's economy of financial or technological aid programmes can turn out to be confounded by the variety of forces bearing upon a particular circumstance and by the uncertain way in which human beings respond to events (including predictions about how they will respond to events!). Thus, even where we are dealing with questions which are logically questions of fact, we can find ourselves in the middle of controversy arising out of the incompleteness or complexity of the factual data.

Apart from this, however, there is a third source of controversy which underlies every aspect of World Studies, and this is the controversy which is rooted in competing personal and social values. Values enter into World Studies teaching in a variety of ways, but they are always central. The fundamental motives for the development of education for international understanding, global education, education for a world society and World Studies were rooted in a concern to replace a narrow chauvinist loyalty to one's own country, tribe or race with a broader loyalty to humanity as a whole (or at least to extend the narrower loyalty to include the larger one). The US Institute for World Order expressed its educational goals in terms of four values which indicate the main categories of concern embraced by the World Studies movement: peace (and the avoidance of violence); welfare (and the end of poverty); ecological balance (and the avoidance of the pollution and depletion of the natural world); social justice (and the end of oppression).[2] The University of Oslo World Indicators Program produced a more complex list of these values which included: personal growth; diversity; socio-economic production; equality; social justice; equity; autonomy; solidarity; participation and ecological balance (quoted in Hepworth 1979).

Now there is one sense in which these values are non-controversial. Presumably no one (well, hardly anyone?) would prefer violence, injustice, poverty and pollution to peace, justice and freedom from poverty and pollution. But this level of agreement is bland and naive. People can agree that a just society is desirable and have radically different views (cf. Plato and Marx) of what would characterise a just society. The principles of peace, poverty and ecological balance are, similarly, ones which allow fundamentally competing interpretation and application. Not only this but, as Hepworth points out, many of these values are potentially and in our experience conflicting ones, and we have to make evaluative choices between them (Hepworth 1979). Indeed many of the key issues in World Studies rest on different views as to what priority should be given to two valued principles which conflict: to what extent is a group of people justified in using violence as a means to securing social justice or to oppose political oppression? What sacrifice of individual autonomy is justified in the interests of the prevention of pollution or the establishment of an equitable economic order? etc., etc.

Perhaps we can discern in the English language literature on World Studies which has emerged in the last ten years or so (and I think particularly of those sources so usefully brought together under Robin Richardson's aegis in the World Studies Project and in the issues of *The New Era* which he has edited) a rough kind of values consensus in the area of liberal socialism with occasional radical overtones (!). But I suggest (a) that even such a consensus papers over highly significant areas of disagreement; (b) that this kind of values stance is one which clearly stands apart from major values systems to be found amongst, for example, Muslim or Jewish theocrats or the plentiful dictatorships of the right or the left; and (c) that this values position could certainly not command universal agreement amongst teachers or parents even in, for example, the British Isles. This last observation is particularly pertinent, since it is precisely the purpose of many World Studies programmes to replace what are regarded as unworthy, outmoded or inappropriate values and attitudes popularly held, by the new global values embodied in their teaching. The emphasis is on 'learning for *change*' (see Richardson 1976) and change largely against rather than in support of the direction of popular opinion. As Robert Hanvey (1979) observed rather dismally in relation to opinion in the United States, 'parent demand for international/global education is almost non-existent'. But this observation did not discourage him from recommending 'hands on' experiential participatory learning in global education as one of the best ways 'to hook the kids'.

So, the teacher of World Studies is inevitably involved in handling in the classroom ideas, beliefs, attitudes and social and political values of a deeply controversial nature. What of it? Well, this observation leads me, as it has led others inside and outside teaching, to ask how the teacher ought to handle subject-matter of this kind in the classroom. What pedagogic or ethical principles ought to govern the teacher's classroom style and strategy?

In what follows, I want to discuss four responses to this question embodied in teacher stances which I shall discuss under the following headings: (a) proselytisation and indoctrination; (b) neutrality; (c) reason and impartiality; and (d) 'oppressive tolerance' and counter-indoctrination.

## Proselytisation and indoctrination

World Studies teachers, and more especially those outside the classroom who advocate World Studies, are I believe characteristically enthusiasts (some even fanatics) for a moral, social or political cause. They want to save the world from one form or another of self-destruction and create a world in which people can live fruitfully and happily together. They are commonly attached to pressure groups concerned with aid for the Third World, opposition to nuclear weapons or the pollution of the environment, or support for oppressed sections of the world community. They are people with deeply held opinions, which they believe to be of critical importance to mankind. Their natural and perfectly altruistic inclination is to promote that opinion for all they are worth. As teachers they have a precious opportunity (responsibility?) to shape the opinions of the young, of the new generation who (and this has been the aspiration of successive generations) may grow up to create a better world than our own generation has so far succeeded in doing. Why should teachers not advocate, proselytise, argue, persuade with all the skill at their command on behalf of those convictions which they themselves believe to be so important? If some want to call such an approach indoctrinatory, let us not be put off by its overtones of disapproval but seek plainly and expertly to secure firmly in children's consciousness principles which we believe to be for the ultimate good of themselves and of the world community.

I do not want to get too entangled here between different styles of advocacy and indoctrination or to examine whether all advocacy is indoctrinatory. What I want to characterise is an energetic teaching approach which sacrifices or subordinates most ethical and educational considerations to do with *how* beliefs or attitudes may be inculcated in children to a determined effort at their successful inculcation. What are we to make of this approach in the World Studies context? More particularly what objections if any can be presented against it?

I think there are at least four closely related objections which might well dissuade a World Studies teacher from this stance.

First, we would have to recognise that, whatever it achieves, this approach would fail to respect the diversity of belief and opinion which (given as I have argued the controversial nature of the subject-matter) is likely to be found amongst the children concerned and their parents. The principle of respect for persons and hence respect for their beliefs is so central to the ethics of the value systems supposed to characterise World Studies that it would be contradictory to offend it so blatantly in the name of defending it.

Secondly, such a stance and the procedures associated with it offend against another value which often appears in the World Studies catalogues (see e.g. The World Indicators Program to which I have already referred), and that is personal autonomy. Robin Richardson spelled out a version of this principle in an early (1973) lecture introducing the World Studies Project, (acknowledging his debt to J. P. White (1973) and others):

Education aims to provide frameworks in which people may learn freely to choose the values by which they live. Such freedom involves: first, knowledge of various possible values; second, knowledge of what is chosen; third, awareness of the future as well as the present; fourth awareness of psychological and political obstacles to the realisation of one's chosen values, and of what, psychologically and politically, helps and nourishes them; fifth, respect for other people's right similarly to choose freely the values by which they live. This involves (of course) an awareness that involved in other people's freedom are the very same kinds of knowledge that are involved in the exercise of one's own.

Perhaps not all World Studies teachers would accept this view of education or of personal autonomy, but anyone who did would clearly have difficulty in accepting the style of teaching described in this section which at the same time restricts the range of alternative opinion set before pupils, abandons the concern to develop their own critical capacities and exemplifies precisely that kind of oppressive relationship (albeit benevolent and paternalistic) to which, again, another part of the World Studies value system is opposed.

There is a third set of reasons for rejecting the indoctrinatory stance which I illustrated. These are related to the observation that it is simply dishonest to present as true what cannot in any ordinary way (of reference to evidence or argument) be established as true. The passion of one's own conviction is no substitute for 'publicly' demonstrable reasons, evidence and argument. Equally, it is dishonest to present as the only belief deserving serious attention what is not in fact the only belief which receives attention from those whose judgement in other respects one might acknowledge to be deserving of respect.

Fourthly, it seems to me that it does and should matter to World Studies teachers not only *what* children come to believe but *how* they hold those beliefs. More explicitly, we achieve relatively little if we simply replace one dogma, one prejudice, one unintelligent and irrational belief, one closed mind... for another. We have little enough entitlement to the assumption that we, our generation, have not only at last got all the right answers to the ancient problems of human life, but can foresee how they can be applied in the rapidly changing decades ahead. Whatever wisdom we imagine we have acquired must include the realisation that new generations of people will need to re-examine our values (including those we hold most dear), test and criticise our beliefs and adapt our wisdom to the changing circumstances of their own age. If our pupils are to be able to handle our ideas in this way they have to receive them not as categorical truth or dogma but with a full appreciation of the strength and weakness of the evidence and thinking which underlie them and of the ideas which contend with them for credence. Apart from anything else, if beliefs are, as World Studies teachers generally hope, to be a springboard to action, then they need to be held as something more than received wisdom. As John Stuart Mill (1971 edn) warned: 'However unwillingly a person who has a strong opinion may admit the possibility that his opinion may be false, he ought to be moved by the consideration that, however true it may be, if it is not fully, frequently and fearlessly discussed, it will be held as a dead dogma, not a living truth.'

## Neutrality

The rejection of proselytising and indoctrination or the fear of either typically leads people to urge on the teacher of World Studies (or, equally, teachers working in other obviously controversial areas like political, moral or religious education) a concern for 'balance' in their presentation, a concern that the teacher should either put both sides of an argument with equal enthusiasm or perhaps refrain from presenting either.

These kinds of concern are rather nicely illustrated in the responses which the group of teachers from Groby Community College in Leicestershire received when they circulated for comment a new World Studies syllabus which they were proposing to introduce. The first comment comes from a local MP (Aucott *et al*. 1979):

While I am sure that this course is well intentioned, there seems to me a very real risk that it might turn out to resemble indoctrination rather than education, to present matters of opinion and controversy as if they were matters of fact, and to contain an excessively political content. I trust, therefore, that you will do everything you can to guard against these risks and in particular to enable those taking the course to develop their critical faculties by presenting them, in the fairest way possible, with a critique of the arguments and views set out in the syllabus. If this should prove impossible, I think it would be better not to offer this type of course at all.

A slightly more sophisticated comment came from the Geography department in the school, but the notion of balance expressed is I think very much the same (Aucott *et al*. 1979):

The syllabus seems to have a distinct bias towards the view that the 'First' World (however defined) exploits the 'Third' World (however defined). This is not an established fact overall and it is important in schools to give a full range of facts and opinions. Again to present ourselves and the rest of the 'First' World as heartless exploiters is unhelpful; the real world situation is far more complicated than that. Clearly a balance has to be struck between saying nothing and giving too simplistic a picture to immature pupils. The exploitation of the so-called Socialist countries of Eastern Europe by the Soviet Union (and of Cuba) should be mentioned alongside criticisms of say the Western oil companies. Always, a full, balanced view should surely be our aim. It will always be hard to achieve.

What seems to be called for in these statements, as I think in a long tradition of scholarly teaching, is a style of pedagogy in which the teacher presents to her[3] pupils as many sides of a controversy as possible without, at least initially, indicating by the manner of presentation which she personally supports. I shall refer to this style as 'affirmative neutrality'.

There are a number of drawbacks associated with this approach. It pushes the teacher into a role which involves the transmission of a rather large amount of information in a form which may mitigate against reflective criticism by pupils. It is particularly difficult for the teacher to be at one and the same time the source of so much opinion and the chairman of a discussion. In addition of course, it is extraordinarily difficult in practice thus to present a range of opinions without this presentation being coloured or at least limited by the teacher's own views.

These were among the considerations which led those responsible for the Schools Council/Nuffield Humanities Curriculum Project to define and explore a somewhat different teaching strategy which they referred to as 'procedural neutrality'. I believe that this strategy and the research associated with it has particular relevance to the World Studies teacher so I propose to comment on it in a little more detail.

The Humanities Curriculum Project (HCP) (The Schools Council/Nuffield Humanities Project, 1970) was faced with a very similar problem to that which I have presented in this paper: what role should the teacher adopt in the classroom in relation to subject-matter which (in this case by definition) is controversial? The role that the HCP invited teachers to explore was that of the neutral chairman of a classroom discussion. It was not imagined for one moment that the teacher was in fact neutral in relation to the issues under discussion or that she would pretend to be. The teacher would simply enter into an explicit role clearly explicated to her pupils in which she would refrain from supporting one or other position in the controversy under discussion. To support her in this role and assist her in maintaining a position as procedural chairman, information about the controversy and different points of view relating to it would be available in the form of packs of material – newspaper cuttings, poems, letters, photos, cartoons, etc. – in HCP terminology the 'evidence' for the discussion.

To understand better the rationale for the kind of 'negative' or 'procedural' neutrality proposed by the HCP it may be useful to rehearse the five 'major premises' upon which the work of the HCP was based. These were (The Schools Council/Nuffield Humanities Project 1970):

 (i) that controversial issues should be handled in the classroom with adolescents;
 (ii) that the teacher accepts the need to submit his teaching in controversial areas to the criterion of neutrality at this stage of education, i.e. that he regards it as part of his responsibility not to promote his own view;
 (iii) that the mode of enquiry in controversial issues should have discussion rather than instruction as its core;
 (iv) that the discussion should protect divergence of view among participants, rather than attempt to achieve consensus;
 (v) that the teacher as chairman of the discussion should have responsibility for quality and standards in learning.

Associated with these five premises was the overall aim of the HCP which was 'to develop an understanding of social situations and human acts and of the controversial value issues which they raise' (The Schools Council/Nuffield Humanities Project 1970).

Now there has developed quite a body of literature about HCP in general and the notion of procedural neutrality in particular. At the risk of oversimplification, I want to pluck out of this three arguments which I have come to regard as the most significant ones in support of the stance of neutrality and then comment on two arguments of particular interest which have been offered against the strategy.[4]

The main argument in support of procedural neutrality starts from the HCP's decision to have as its teaching aim the *understanding* of certain controversies. As Lawrence Stenhouse (1975), the Project Director, has suggested, 'given a dispute in society about the truth of a matter, the teacher might wish to teach the dispute rather than the truth as he knows it'. What HCP chose to do was to teach the dispute and to try to get young people to appreciate the range of different perspectives available socially and indeed amongst themselves on the issues under discussion. This implied valuing and protecting a divergence of opinion (see premiss 4) rather than seeking consensus. It also implied restricting the teacher from intentionally, or quite contrarily to her intentions, giving her authoritative legitimation to one particular view.

This brings us to the second major consideration underlying HCP's support for procedural neutrality, what one might refer to as its empirical base. Time and time again in the research team's observation of classroom discussion and interviews with 'students' the HCP was faced with the power and pervasiveness of pupils' expectations that in any school setting there was a right answer to a question, and that right answer was the one which the teacher indicated was her answer to the question. The pupils' task was to discern, learn and return that right answer. Other answers were of little or no relevance in the school context. I paraphrase but I think I represent fairly the gist of the experience of the HCP. Expressed in these terms the problem of authority is not just that of the teacher's intention but also of her pupils' expectations. She may not intend to use the authority of her position to support a particular opinion but this is not sufficient to prevent this from being precisely what happens in practice. According to Elliott (1975): 'Years of educational conditioning may make it extremely difficult for students to understand and accept the teacher's renunciation of the role of 'expert' so ingrained is the notion by their past educational experiences...(The teacher) can so easily deceive himself into believing that students are not ascribing authority to his views, when in fact they are.' The only way out at least perhaps 'at this stage of education' (see premiss 2), is for the teacher to refrain altogether from supporting any side in the controversy.

The third argument underlying the advocacy of procedural neutrality is one which takes us into the logical or epistemological status of the value judgements which underlie the kind of controversial issues handled by HCP and indeed, as I have already argued, the kind of issues which regularly feature as part of World Studies teaching. This argument rests on the observation or premiss that although reason, argument and evidence marshalled according to 'publicly' recognised procedures can take you so far in ethical argument — for example ruling out certain empirical claims as contrary to observation and certain arguments as internally inconsistent — there comes a point in such argument where fundamental differences of view remain which cannot be resolved by reference to those same publicly recognised standards of reason, or at least, to be more precise, where the question as to whether reason can resolve these differences of view is itself controversial even at (or especially at) the most sophisticated level of ethical or meta-ethical argument.[5] This being the case it would be quite improper (dishonest) for a teacher to present as objectively correct an opinion which must essentially rest upon a foundation of what one might regard as arational or criterionless choice.

This notion of 'the neutral teacher' received a predictable bombardment of criticism in the educational press. The change of role proposed challenged fundamentally many assumptions about teaching. It was certainly not easy to implement in practice, and many teachers found the struggle out of proportion to the gain. Some simply realised that, when the chips were down, they cared more about promoting certain substantive opinions than encouraging the exploration of divergent opinion in group discussion. (The National Union of Teachers' representatives on the HCP's steering committee, for example, effectively prevented the HCP from extending its neutral teacher approach to the issue of race relations.) The Schools Council Moral Education Project directed by Peter McPhail objected to the neutral chairman role in terms of children's interest in and right to know the teacher's own opinions (McPhail *et al.* 1972).

These responses I shall leave without further comment. There are however two other lines of argument about this teaching strategy which I would like to explore a little more fully.

The first concerns the question 'what are the values of the neutral teacher?' Or more especially 'what values is the teacher promoting through her neutrality?' This sounds paradoxical but it is not. The HCP never imagined that the neutral teacher was in fact value free. She refrains from taking a stance on the substantive issues under discussion precisely in order to promote other qualities of learning and learning outcomes which she considers desirable – including, for example, the values associated with the activity of discussion itself, respect for the opinions of others, concern for evidence, a sense of the worth of one's own judgement and an increasing reliance on that judgement as a basis for one's opinion. The 'neutral' teacher is not without commitment. Rather, as the HCP introductory booklet put it: 'The teacher's commitment is to education, not to his own views' (The Schools Council/Nuffield Humanities Project, 1970.) However, if the social values that a teacher wanted to promote were in fact of a roughly liberal democratic order, she might well discover that her ends were better served through the so-to-speak 'hidden curriculum' of procedural neutrality than through any explicit attempt at their promotion. A particularly interesting case of this phenomenon occurred in connection with the HCP's trials with its (subsequently censored) Race materials. (The evaluation study suggested that marginally, but by a statistically significant degree, teachers who adopted the stance of procedural neutrality were more likely to encourage tolerant interracial attitudes than those who sought actively to promote such attitudes (see Verma and Macdonald 1971). The authors of the study have since had occasion to qualify the validity of the initial research and to extend their study into wider comparisons (see Verma and Bagley 1978), but its general force is still supported and offers intriguing possibilities to the World Studies teacher who shares the kind of values which I have indicated.

The second important question raised about the strategy of procedural neutrality concerns the attitude of the teacher towards rational argument and the place of rational argument in the discussion of value questions. I will discuss this question in the context of my comments on the next teaching stance – that of rational and impartial leadership.

## Reason and impartiality

I take neutrality to imply a strategy through which either one supports alternative points of view equally (affirmative neutrality) or one withholds support from any point of view (negative or procedural neutrality). Impartiality differs from neutrality in that it allows or even requires differential support to opinion, provided that the different level of support is related to their objective merits rather than any other consideration to do with, for example, one's personal interest, advantage or feeling.

That all is subject to argument, that no person counts for more than his argument counts, even the teacher, and that all statements are subject to rational criticism – all this is part of the rational commitment and is picked out in the conception of impartiality.... To be impartial is to consider views and interests in the light of all possible criticisms and counter-claim, and to ignore any kind of special pleading, whether from authority or whatever, from myself or whomsoever. (Bailey 1975)

Charles Bailey, who defined impartiality in these terms, argued that it should be this principle rather than that of neutrality which should guide the teacher in handling controversial value issues in the classroom. The classroom discussion in his view should have the objective not just of expressing an interesting range of opinion but of employing rational criticism to try to establish the truth of the matter.

In another attack on the idea of neutrality Mary Warnock (1975) offered a rather more didactic version of the teacher's role, but again one that emphasised her responsibility for teaching pupils 'how to draw rational conclusions rationally':

Unless the teacher comes out into the open, and says in what direction he believes that the evidence points he will have failed in his duty as a teacher. For what his pupils have to learn is not only, in an abstract way, what counts as evidence, but how people draw conclusions from evidence.... Thus the teacher must if he is to teach his pupils to assess evidence fairly, give them actual examples of how he does this himself. His pupils may disagree with him. The more adult they become, and the better their earlier experience of arguments, the more capable they will be of weighing the probabilities differently. But unless they see before them the spectacle of a rational man drawing conclusions rationally, they will never learn what rational probabilities are.

Now it would be odd to deny the general desirability of helping children to respect reasons and argument and to come to hold their opinions on the basis of reasons and argument. From this point of view impartiality would seem to be preferable to both indoctrination, which bypasses the activities of rational deliberation, and neutrality, which even if it does not offend against rationality on the face of it stops short in its support for it.

There are, however, two important reservations to this conclusion both of which arise out of arguments I have already indicated in support of the strategy of negative or procedural neutrality.

The first of these reservations concerns children's abilities to separate the authority of a teacher's social position in the classroom (and the examination hall) from the authority of reasons, evidence or argument she may adduce in support of an opinion she holds. The teacher may sincerely and earnestly urge her pupils to treat her opinion just like any other and to judge it by reference to the evidence which supports it, not the authority or otherwise of its source. But when pupils are so accustomed to accepting no better reason than 'because I say so' and when, institutionally, teacher's opinion coincides so universally with right opinion, the transition to the impartial assessment of evidence is psychologically not an easy one. As I have argued elsewhere (Bridges 1979), for the teacher to adopt the stance of negative neutrality and withhold her opinion from discussion altogether for a time may be a useful transitionary stage in weaning pupils from dependence on her authority.

The second reservation takes us into more profound problems of moral philosophy or meta-ethics. The critical question here is to what extent ethical questions or questions of moral value are amenable to rational argument as against arational preference. I have already indicated that members of the HCP took the view either that such questions were not ultimately resolvable by reference to reason or that whether or not they were was itself a controversial question. This view underlay at least one form of the argument in favour of neutrality. By contrast, Charles Bailey suggests that there are indeed good reasons for preferring some moral positions to others and that more specifically a commitment to rationality itself entails a commitment to a range of substantive and important values. This view underlies his argument in favour of impartiality.

The significant point for World Studies teachers here is that they need perhaps to be a little clearer and more consistent as to where they stand on this meta-ethical question about values and about the implications of their stance. Are values essentially and logically controversial – or are they so simply because some people have not followed the argument correctly? The confident assertion of values as a central motive for, and component of, World Studies programmes suggests that their proponents regard these as having some objectively defensible and universal value independently of the subjective preferences of a particular proponent, independently even of her particular social or cultural affinities. People speak of the evil of apartheid, for example, in a manner which suggests a judgement rooted in considerations more fundamental and universal than one expressed in terms of what is right or wrong *for me* or for *our society*. At the same time, however, the allegiance of World Studies teachers to ideas of a multicultural society and their endorsement of cultural pluralism often lead them into a kind of social relativism. I am not sure that such a position can be consistently maintained. Certainly its implications would come uneasily from the lips of most World Studies teachers – 'racial apartheid is wrong unless you happen to live for example in South Africa where it's right'? And the morality of seeking change in society becomes difficult to explain in a context in which we are supposed to derive our moral precepts not just in fact but rightly from those which already pervade that society.

But let me not try to resolve 2,000 years of moral argument in a footnote. My central point here is that the rationale for one's teaching strategy in relation to the values that feature so centrally in World Studies syllabuses must be consistent with and rooted in a defensible view of the logical status of those values, and in particular in some judgement on the extent to which they can be rationally and objectively defended. In particular I suggest that the issue between those who defend neutrality and those who argue for impartiality is importantly related to a difference of perspective on this meta-ethical problem.

## 'Oppressive tolerance' and counter indoctrination

The longstanding liberal preference for openness of discussion, balanced presentation of all sides of an argument, the tolerance and even encouragement of dissent and the impartiality or neutrality of those with special authority is based centrally on a conviction that these are the conditions which are best conducive to the development of knowledge and understanding at the personal and at the social level. John Stuart Mill's essay *On Liberty* (1971 edn) is a classic source for this opinion:

In the case of any person whose judgment is really deserving of confidence, how has it become so?

Because he has kept his mind open to criticism of his opinions and conduct. Because it has been his practice to listen to all that could be said against him; to profit by as much of it as was just, and expound to himself, and upon occasion to others, the fallacy of what was fallacious. Because he felt that the only way in which a human being can make some approach to knowing the whole of a subject is by hearing what can be said about it by persons of every variety of opinion, and studying all modes in which it can be looked at by every character of mind. No wise man ever acquired wisdom in any mode but this; nor is it in the nature of human intellect to become wise in any other.

The same tradition of thought is expressed in Voltaire's *Philosophical Dictionary* (1971 edn): 'We should tolerate each other because we are all weak, inconsistent, subject to mutability and to error.'... and in John Milton's famous speech against the licensing of books, *Areopagitica* (1958 edn):

Where there is much desire to learn there of necessity will be much arguing, much writing, many opinions; for opinion in good men is but knowledge in the

making. Under these fantastic terrors of sect and schism, we wrong the earnest
and zealous thirst after knowledge and understanding which God hath stirred up
in this city.... So Truth be in the field, we do injuriously, by licensing and
prohibiting, to misdoubt her strength. Let her and falsehood grapple; whoever
knew Truth put to the worse, in a free and open encounter? Her confuting is the
best and surest suppressing.

What these extracts illustrate are three central ingredients of what I would
refer to as the liberal epistemological tradition.[6] First, the importance of the
ready availability of the full range of opinion on an issue (a free market in
ideas); secondly, an acknowledgement of the fallibility of opinion including
our own; and thirdly, a confidence in the free competition of ideas as a
condition for the emergence of true or, given our second consideration, the
best opinion available.

This kind of view enjoys considerable popularity in liberal/progressive
educational circles. It has not, however, passed unchallenged. One form of
challenge in particular has, I think, particular relevance to approaches to
teaching in the World Studies field. I refer to the radical critique of the
liberal theory of free discussion and more especially to Herbert Marcuse's
important and seminal essay *Repressive Tolerance* (1976 edn).

I am not sure that I can do anything like justice to Marcuse's argument
in a short space, but let me try to give enough indication of it to prompt
the interested reader to pursue it at source.

The first stage in the argument (as I shall present it) is to make the point
that the merits of tolerance, impartiality and free discussion presuppose the
existence of conditions, which however, do *not* exist even in so-called democratic societies, notably the equal availability and expression of alternative
opinions. The dice, claims Marcuse (1976 edn), are heavily loaded in favour
of those opinions which support the status quo:

The antagonistic structure of society rigs the rules of the game. Those who stand
against the established system are *a priori* at a disadvantage, which is not removed
by the toleration of their ideas, speeches and newspapers.

Similarly the liberal position presupposes the rationality, autonomy and
open-mindedness of those who attend the expression of alternative opinion.
Instead in reality we are faced with manipulated and indoctrinated individuals who parrot, as their own, the opinions of their masters (Marcuse 1976
edn).

From this Marcuse (1976 edn) concludes that the actual effect of the
indiscriminate toleration of opinion, oppressive and liberationist, regressive
and progressive, is simply to reinforce the forces of oppression and con-
servativism – all the more perhaps by allowing them the appearance of
being tolerant of dissent and open to criticism.

The active, official tolerance granted to the Right as well as to the Left, to
movements of aggression as well as to movements of peace, to the party of hate
as well as to that of humanity. I call this non-partisan tolerance 'abstract' or
'pure' inasmuch as it refrains from taking sides – but in doing so it actually
protects the already established machinery of discrimination.

Accordingly, says Marcuse (1976 edn), if people are to become truly autonomous and freed from the prevailing indoctrination we would need to take apparently undemocratic measures:

They would include the withdrawal of toleration of speech and assembly from groups and movements which promote aggressive policies, armament, chauvinism, discrimination on grounds of race and religion, or which oppose the extension of public services, social security, medical care etc. Moreover, the restoration of freedom of thought may necessitate new and rigid restrictions on teachings and practices in educational institutions which, by their very methods and concepts, serve to enclose the mind within the established universe of discourse and behaviour.

Indeed

the trend would have to be reversed; they would have to get information slanted in the opposite direction.

This policy of selective tolerance and the deliberate slanting of opinion of course requires some judgement by some person or persons as to what precisely are the progressive and liberating opinions as distinct from the regressive and oppressive ones. For someone who is so acute in his criticism of other people's presuppositions Marcuse seems to have a startlingly simplistic confidence in the self-evidence of these distinctions. He is also relatively unforthcoming on the identification of those who will somehow make those distinctions on behalf of the blinkered masses. It is, he suggests (1976 edn):

everyone 'in the maturity of his faculties' as a human being, everyone who has learned to think rationally and autonomously. The answer to Plato's educational dictatorship is *the democratic educational dictatorship of free men* (my italics).

At this point Marcuse's position gets particularly contorted. He appears to want to avoid the idea of a kind of Platonic educational élite sorting out the ignorant or misguided masses. But at the same time he has to concede that on his own analysis of society the mass of the people must be unable to make the kind of discrimination he is after. (If they can then his analysis of society breaks down.) So the educational revolution has to be imposed on the majority by a minority. Moreover let us be clear that the new enlightenment, the new way of perceiving the world, justice and injustice, oppression and liberation, will be one which, if anything, is the product of closer, more restrictive (and why not more oppressive?) intellectual management than that which it replaces. It is difficult to see why one should suppose the post-revolutionary thinker to be any less restricted intellectually than the thinker whose place he has taken.

On my reading, Marcuse's position founders on the problematic nature of judgements about social progress and regression and on the contradictions between his concern to combat totalitarianism and oppression and his need to re-establish it as his own instrument of change. I think too that he may simply exaggerate as a matter of fact the power and potency of the indoctrinatory processes at work in a democratic society (though others have no doubt underestimated them). It is after all immensely difficult to distinguish in any individual's thought the extent to which his ideas, beliefs or values are the result of indoctrination or autonomous reflection. It would be interesting to have Marcuse's own account or to explore for ourselves the educational or social conditions which enabled Marcuse and other like-minded critics of the 'oppressive' society to develop the intellectual equipment which they use so forcefully to analyse the structure and weaknesses of that society. Perhaps if we could extend to more people the advantages of *their* upbringing we might establish that democracy of free men to which Marcuse aspires without taking to expedients which would seem to fly in the face of its aspirations.

If I find it difficult to accept some of Marcuse's conclusions I believe nevertheless that World Studies teachers can study his criticism to advantage. In particular those who want their pupils to be able to give serious consideration to a full range of alternative opinions will have to be alert to the social and psychological barriers which will inhibit access or the giving of serious attention to ideas which challenge fundamentally the deep-seated orthodoxies of their own assumptions or of society. This is indeed a key practical question for the World Studies teacher, though not for her alone. I do not however believe that it is answered by attempts to replace one sort of indoctrination, one sort of oppression, one sort of one-sidedness, one sort of myopia... by another.

## Conclusion

Where does all this leave us? I do not ask this question rhetorically or purely for effect. It is a question which has nagged at me for nearly fifteen years, since I started teaching World Studies in school myself. However, let me try and pull out of my previous discussion the positive principles which have underlain my comments. They include, most importantly I think, the following:

1. A respect for persons, which I take to include respect for children's and parents' rights to hold opinions which differ from our own and a readiness to understand these opinions ourselves;
2. A concern to cultivate and develop the personal autonomy of young people – including in that the understanding and self-confidence which are conditions of free choice;
3. An honest acknowledgement of the true state and status of opinion – including in that an open recognition of the uncertainty, the provisionality, the controversiality of judgement and recognition of the albeit problematic distinction between fact and value;
4. A readiness on behalf of the teacher to detach from her opinion as far as is possible the authority which belongs to her social role or personal charisma and to rest it instead on the authority of reason alone;
5. A concern that one's pupils as far as possible grasp along with any opinion that we teach the reasons, evidence and argument underlying that opinion;

6. A concern to teach the controversy and not just one person's view of the proper conclusion of the controversy;
7. A concern to cultivate in our pupils and ourselves a constant alertness to, and ruthless criticism of, especially those beliefs which we take most for granted.

Those principles do not tell anyone how to teach World Studies, but they do indicate conditions which I would want to argue any World Studies teacher should strive to satisfy. They have of course much wider educational application. This I am relieved to observe, for I am reluctant to conceive of World Studies teaching as something which has objectives far apart from more broadly educational ones. Indeed, though this may be a little simple-minded, I dare say that if we had firmly established an educational system founded upon the seven moral and educational principles I have indicated we might have progressed a good way towards those 'global values' with or without 'World Studies' in the curriculum.

## Notes

1. See for example successive issues of the *World Studies Bulletin* (now incorporated in *The New Era*).
2. For an elaboration of these values see Reardon (1976).
3. I dislike the contortions of style I get into when I try to use pronouns which do not have the appearance of relating exclusively to the male or female gender. I have chosen therefore on this occasion to refer to the teacher as 'she' with the hope that male colleagues will not thereby suffer any greater crisis of identity than their female counterparts have endured for many years. I have eschewed the opportunity to replace 'chairman' by 'chairperson' on the pleading of woman colleagues who find this style of recognition of their competence trivial, patronising and superfluous.
4. For a fuller discussion of this topic see Bridges (1979).
5. For a version of this argument see Elliott (1973).
6. For a fuller commentary on this tradition see Bridges (1979).

# Part II
Projects and courses

# Chapter 4    David Selby
# World Studies and the core curriculum

## An integrated approach to an interdependent world

Ronald Higgins, in his brilliant and chilling book, *The Seventh Enemy* (1978), has identified six immense and impersonal threats which are converging to undermine the fabric of the world's political, social and economic life. These he lists as 'the population explosion; the maldistribution of food; the shortage of vital resources; the degradation of the environment; the misuse of nuclear power; and the growing tendency of science and technology to escape humane control'. 'These trends,' he writes elsewhere (1979), 'are not irreversible. But nor are they soluble by clever people in white coats. Appropriate technologies can help but there is no technological fix. It is political arrangements and therefore human values and priorities that will restrain (or accelerate) the present gallop towards multiple calamity.'

Higgin's conclusion is of profound significance for education in the 1980s. By implication, he is pointing an accusing finger at the 'parish pump' curriculum still obtaining in many educational institutions at all levels. Whereas it should be a key task of educationalists to alert their charges to the problems we face globally and to their obligations and personal accountability as emergent world citizens, most students remain insufficiently versed and practised in world citizenship and in global awareness and concern.

A perusal of single-subject humanities syllabuses available is indication enough that an underlying global perspective is by and large conspicuous by its absence in the British school curriculum. Students taking O-level or CSE Twentieth-century History, for instance, may well consider Third World topics but only as the final quarter of a Eurocentric two-year course, whilst students taking World Geography tend to work in concentric circles outwards from the UK, through Europe, and, finally, to the 'far reaches' of the globe. In such courses the processes and interactions which constitute the 'global village' will be but rarely etched in sharp relief and the personal, local and national obligations attendant upon membership of an interdependent world will be but little reflected upon. Likewise, treatment of global considerations in economics, religious education and sociology tends to be, at best, marginal (Turner 1978).

Failure to inject a thoroughly global perspective into the humanities single-subject disciplines arises in part out of the defence mechanisms operative amongst the practitioners of such disciplines, trained as they were in initial teacher education institutions which themselves often failed to convey a

55

world viewpoint. On top of that there is the inevitable time-lag between the emergence of a new perspective at the philosophical level and its realisation in practical terms. Perhaps more important, however, is the fact that each and every single-subject discipline is an inadequate vehicle for the comprehensive treatment and study of global issues. Topics of crucial importance for an understanding of the modern world such as population, trade and North–South relations cannot be satisfactorily treated from a purely economic, geographical, historical, moral, anthropological or sociological perspective, although the insights and skills offered by each specialism are invaluable. The interdependent world presupposes an integrated approach to curriculum development.

## CSE World Studies: aims and rationale

In late August 1978, 190 fourth-year students at Groby Community College began a two-year course leading to the college's new Mode 3 CSE in World Studies. The syllabus was drawn up to meet the need, as we saw it, for a course offering both a global perspective and overcoming the limitations of any single-subject treatment of the issues involved. The aims of the syllabus were set out as follows:
1. To encourage students to set their thinking about the modern world within a global framework.
2. To foster amongst students an allegiance to mankind in general as against an allegiance to national, local or sectional interests.
3. To help students become aware of the widening gap between the richer and poorer countries, and of the consequences likely to follow if global inequalities are not remedied.
4. To encourage respect for cultural diversity.
5. To help students identify and respect those values shared by mankind in general.
   The basic premises of the Groby World Studies CSE syllabus is that there are certain definable problems of human organisation on this planet which can only be fully understood from a global point of view and which can only be treated on a global basis. Central to the syllabus is the concept of the 'global village', the word 'village' underlining the fact that the contemporary world is a single system with all its various parts interdependent. Developments of a social, political, economic, environmental or technological nature in any quarter of the 'village' can have significant repercussions in many – possibly all – other quarters. Thus 'viewed against a backdrop of the whole of man's history, the continuing transformation of the world from a collection of many lands and peoples to a system of many lands and peoples is a profound change in the human condition. The emergence of the contemporary world system carries with it far-reaching implications for the task of socialising and formally educating young people' (Anderson and Becker 1968). In the first place, it becomes vitally important that students be introduced to a new framework within which to develop their thinking and loyalties. They should be shown that they

have a double allegiance – an allegiance to their own nation and people and an allegiance to mankind in general – and that where a conflict exists between the two, the larger loyalty subsumes the smaller.

At the same time the prospects for the future, should global loyalty not transcend national loyalty, need serious consideration. In the socio-economic sphere, it is becoming imperative that students be made aware of the fact that the world's wealth is not equitably distributed and that, unless a global strategy is evolved to remedy the inequalities existing, the 'global village' may well lurch from crisis to crisis in their lifetime and beyond.

Finally, whilst making every effort to foster respect for cultural diversity, students should be encourage to identify and respect those values shared by the whole species – the 'attitudinal glue', as it has been called, which can 'bind together the moral impulses necessary for human co-operation' (Henderson 1975).

The 'global village' approach to studying the modern world (as against the 'places' and 'events' approaches common to Geography and Modern World History courses) presents problems in terms of syllabus construction in that it is, by definition, non-linear. To accept that the world is a single system with interdependent parts is to reject the notion that any particular problem, set as it is in time and place, can be understood by exclusive investigation of that one problem. Does 'Poverty in the Third World' go under the heading of 'Natural Resources', 'Overpopulation' or 'Global Inequalities' as a study topic? Is the remedy for Third World poverty to be found in aid organisations and programmes, intermediate technology, population control, dismantling well-established trading systems or in a compound of these – and other – factors? Do we put southern Africa in the conflict, human rights or race section of a syllabus?

## CSE World Studies: a conceptual model

To extricate ourselves from the tangles and dilemmas raised by questions such as the above, we adopted the useful conceptual model suggested by Robin Richardson for contructing World Studies syllabuses (1977). The four concepts in the model (Fig. 2) are in themselves mutually dependent.

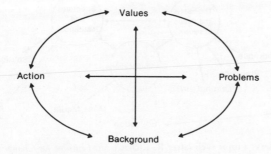

Fig. 2   A conceptual model for World Studies

Projects and courses

A global problem is only perceived as such given certain values on the part of the beholder. Values, likewise, determine one's analysis of the underlying causes of a problem and one's decisions as to a particular course of action. Action (i.e. an attempt at tackling a problem) may well lead to a shift of values in the light of experience and to fresh insights into the problem and its underlying causes. From this central conceptual hub, Richardson (1976) has developed a World Studies topic web (Fig. 3), a diagram

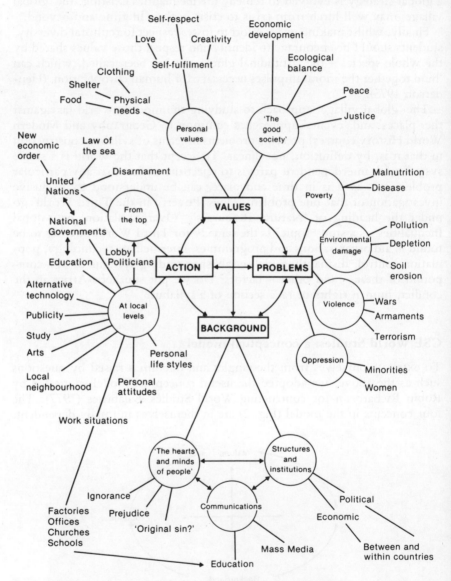

Fig. 3  World society: a topic web (after R. Richardson, *Learning for Change in World Society*, World Studies Project, London, 2nd edn 1979)

which maps out the field of World Studies as a subject or dimension in the curriculum and which illustrates how closely interwoven are the topics likely to appear in a World Studies syllabus.

In the syllabus, as written down, no attempt is made to draw attention to the many interconnections existing between the various topics listed. Nor is mention made of the ongoing interaction between background, problems, action and values which is central to our classroom strategy. The listing of topics is convenient but the reader ought not to be misled into thinking that the World Studies course religiously follows the order of the syllabus as set down below (Sections I–V).

When we look at poverty (Section II:2), for instance, we also give some consideration to North–South conflict (Section II:4), to the work of the UN and aid organisations in combatting poverty (Section III:2,3), to dismantling structural violence (Section III:7) and to population control (Section III:8), although all of these topics are given fuller consideration at other points in the course. The teaching and learning, in other words, involves an elaborate system of cross-referencing.

Nor is the locality of the school overlooked as a resource. Failure to identify events, trends and situations illustrative of the syllabus within the locality would tend to invalidate the very concept of a single world system upon which the syllabus is constructed.

Whilst Section I of the syllabus deals with background and Section II identifies the key problems, Sections III and IV are concerned with what has been described as 'action'. Broadly speaking, 'action' can be taken at two levels; it can be taken at the 'top' by those involved in national government or with international organisations or it can be taken at the grass roots by individuals or small groups. Section III deals with the former type of action and Section IV with the latter. Under Section IV students are given the opportunity to involve themselves in a project at grass-roots level. The experience they gain may be reported and analysed as their research project. Alternatively, they can choose a research project title from within the twelve study areas listed in Section V of the syllabus.

A word, too, on content. The syllabus is all-embracing and it may be thought too full. It should, however, be pointed out that a case-study approach is adopted to most of the topics listed. An exhaustive approach to each topic would be both unrealistic and counter-productive. Furthermore, it is worth mentioning – although it is a point mentioned later – that material for the final examination is only selected from Sections I, II and III of the syllabus.

*The syllabus*

*Section I: The global village*
1. The term 'global village' introduced and explained.
2. Origins and evolution (theories of the formation of the earth and of the structure of the earth's crust – plate tectonics).
3. Sizes and shapes (comparative study of differing size of land masses; the

sea area and land area compared; the annihilation of distance with modern technologies and transport developments).

4. Climatic zones.
5. Natural resources (including water) – their distribution and uses; the sea as a natural resource.
6. Human resources (population figures, racial groupings).
7. Developed and developing countries; the Third World; the Fourth World – the terms introduced and explained (including basic facts).

*Section II: The global village is a village at risk*

1. Population.
2. Poverty and affluence (including hunger and malnutrition; drought; the geography of world disease; the diseases of affluence and the diseases of poverty; incapacity in the face of natural disaster; illiteracy; the uneven distribution of wealth and income between the developed and under-developed worlds).
3. Conflict and violence (including ethnic, religious and ideological conflict; war; the arms race; the threat of nuclear war; torture; refugees; conflict over the ownership of the sea-bed).
4. Structural violence (oppression as perpetrated by organisations, governmental systems, trading systems and widely held opinion which, in its effect, achieves the same end-result as actual physical violence). Apartheid in South Africa; the role of women in certain societies; minority groups in Central and East Africa, Russia, India, Sri Lanka and Canada; migrant workers in Europe and, most importantly, the relationship between the 'rich world' and 'poor' world'.
5. Reactive violence (including anti-colonial movements; freedom-fighting; terrorism; student and youth protest and, most important of all, the Third-World response to structural violence as it has developed since the oil crisis of October 1973).
6. Destruction of the environment (spoliation of the natural environment – pollution, resource depletion and misuse, the energy crisis, desertification and urbanisation).

*Section III: Pointers towards a better world*

1. Towards world government and co-operation (an outline history of world government theories and movements including the UN Charter for a world-elected assembly; the emergence of political groupings transcending the nation state, the European Economic Community (EEC), the European Free Trade Association (EFTA), Comecon, the British Commonwealth, etc.; international co-operation in weather prediction, communications and outer space).
2. The United Nations Organisation; its aims, history, work, structure and achievements; the aims, work and achievements of its specialised agencies (including the Food and Agricultural Association (FAO), the international Labour Organisation (ILO), United Nations Educational,

Scientific and Cultural Organisations (UNESCO), United Nations Children's Fund (UNICEF), Office of the United Nations High Commissioner for Refugees (UNHCR), United Nations Relief and Rehabilitation Administration for Palestine Refugees (UNRRA), United Nations Relief and Works Agency (UNRWA), World Health Organisation (WHO), and specific case studies of same.

3. Some other international bodies and their work (including the Red Cross, Christian Aid, International Voluntary Service (IVS), Save the Children Fund, Voluntary Service Overseas (VSO) and the World Council of Churches).
4. International policing, law and security (including UN policing in Korea, Suez and Cyprus, Interpol, extradition agreements and the International Court of Justice).
5. Human Rights (including the Declaration of Human Rights, the Declaration of the Rights of the Child, the European Court of Human Rights, Amnesty International).
6. Peacebuilding. Peace movements, arms control and disarmament.
7. Dismantling structural violence on a global scale: United Nations Conference on Trade and Development (UNCTAD); its work and conferences; aid programmes, intermediate technology.
8. Population control – some national and global strategies.
9. Alternative life-styles and technologies.
10. Conservation.

*Section IV: Involvement*

'In a global age where worldwide interdependence makes itself felt in the daily lives of most human beings, it is critical that individuals learn how they might exercise some measure of control and influence over the public affairs of global society, as well as over the public affairs of their local communities and nations.' (Anderson and Becker 1977.)

'We must encourage and assist our students in identifying their own value and action priorities in light of their concern about particular global issues. We must help them discover their own strengths and learn how they can be most effective. We must help each person find his or her entry point for action.' (Shirman and Conrad 1977.)

This section involves an examination by students of how they, as individuals, can contribute meaningfully to the welfare of the global village. In attitudinal terms, it is of central importance. At a point sooner or later in the course, many a thoughtful student, oppressed by the burden of world problems to which he/she is introduced will challenge the usefulness of World Studies. 'Why tell me all this, if I can't do anything about it?' If an invitation to action is not then forthcoming, attitudes to the course – and more important, to the issues being considered – will be adversely affected. Included amongst the forms of involvement discussed in class are:

1. The UNESCO Associated Schools and Colleges Project and how it can help the individual foster international understanding.

2. Community relations work.
3. Participation at local, national and international level in the work of an international environmental organisation (e.g. Friends of the Earth).
4. Participation in the work of IVS, UN, Population Concern or a similar body at local or national level.
5. Money-raising to help fight world poverty, hunger and disease.
6. Projects connected with the school such as school recycling projects or monitoring the school's use of energy and other resources.
7. Running a 'globally-conscious' home (conservation, etc.) and 'globally conscious' shopping.
8. Local projects involving experimentation with or development of alternative technologies.
9. (a) A voice in local politics
   (b) A voice in national politics
   (c) A voice in European politics
   (d) A voice in world politics

   What channels are open to the individual so he/she can make known his/her views concerning global issues?

10. A global problems and solutions publicity campaign in the locality.

After brief consideration of the above in class, students working individually or in groups, are invited to involve themselves in a local project of their choosing and, later, to write up their experience and conclusions as their research project.

*Section V: Cohesive forces within the global village*

Those students choosing not to involve themselves in a project under Section IV are asked to choose a research project title falling within one of the following areas:

1. Common factors in world beliefs and ideologies.
2. The universal appeal of sports, games and athletics.
3. Developments in the use of space.
4. The universal appeal of art, science, films, fashion, music, cookery or literature.
5. The study of an art form or craft of a particular country, culture or continent with an examination of its wider influence and appeal.
6. Our concern to preserve the archaeological and architectural heritage of mankind.
7. Family, home life, education, work and community (including law and order) in particular parts of the world.
8. Travel, transport and tourism.
9. Communications systems and mass media.
10. World leaders (political, religious and cultural).

*Objectives and assessment*

By the end of the two-year course we expect CSE students to:
1. Be able to recognise and recall relevant information.
2. Have a knowledge of the key concepts in the syllabus.

3. Have given evidence that he/she can plan, organise and pursue independent enquiry.
4. Have shown that he/she can present the results of that enquiry, and other course work, clearly and accurately.
5. Have given evidence that he/she can explain in his/her own words the arguments surrounding current global issues and developments and can form his/her own judgement.
6. Be able to express his/her point of view clearly and accurately in speech.

These six testable objectives – as against the broader syllabus aims listed earlier – are assessed through: (a) course work; (b) a research project; (c) an oral examination; (d) two written examinations. The course work constitutes 20 per cent of the overall assessment, the research project 30 per cent, the oral examination 10 per cent and the written examinations 40 per cent.

Assessment of Objective 1 (recognition and recall of relevant information) constitutes 20 per cent of the overall assessment; of Objective 2 (knowledge of key concepts) also 20 per cent; of Objective 3 (ability to plan and organise independent enquiry) 15 per cent; of Objective 4 (presentation of results) 10 per cent; of Objective 5 (ability to explain and form judgements) 25 per cent; and of Objective 6 (ability to express views in speech) 10 per cent.

Assessment of CSE course work is based on the standard of the student's ten best pieces of work, two arising out of Section I of the syllabus, and eight out of Sections II and III. One 'piece of work' is defined as being a relevant written response or written and graphic response to any part of the course or syllabus. It might be an essay on a particular topic, a critical review of a film seen, a piece reflecting on ideas put forward by a visiting speaker, a story intended to highlight some aspect of a global issue, or it may take some other form.

The course work is assessed with regard to Objectives 2 (7 marks), 4 (5 marks) and 5 (8 marks).

The major research project has a limit of 5,000 words. Alternatively, the student may choose to present four shorter projects of no more than 1,250 words each. The major project or each shorter project may be an account and analysis of practical work undertaken by the student following consideration of Section IV of the syllabus. On the other hand, a title may be chosen from within one of the areas listed in Section V of the syllabus.

Where students opt to write one major research project, they are asked to prepare and present a 'plan of campaign' prior to commencing work on the project. The 'plan of campaign' contains a project title, a statement of the aims of the project, a description of how the project is to be tackled and an initial list of resources to be consulted. It is incorporated into the project together with any subsequent amendments made by the student in the light of ongoing research. In addition, a student preparing a major research project is asked to keep an involvement/research diary which: (a) describes the student's experiences; and (b) serves the purpose of demonstrating her/his ability to plan, organise and pursue independent enquiry. An edited version of the diary – up to 2,500 words – constitutes the first half of the major project. That, together with the 'plan of campaign', is assessed under Objective 3 of the syllabus (i.e. out of a total of 15 marks). The second 2,500 words of the major project is in the nature of an evaluation of the student's research/involvement experience, containing personal opinions/ reflections and demonstrating knowledge of issues and arguments. This latter half of the project is assessed under Objectives 2, 4 and 5 (total: 15 marks). Afterwards students are given an oral examination of not less than ten minutes on the project (the plan of campaign, difficulties encountered whilst collecting information, the project itself and the views expressed therein). Each oral examination is recorded on cassette tape for purposes of moderation.

Where students opt to write four shorter projects, they are likewise required to prepare a 'plan of campaign' and keep a diary for each project attempted. The four projects are marked out of 30 and an average taken. The oral examination is in this case based upon two of the projects presented.

The research project/four short projects are assessed with regard to Objectives 2 (3 marks), 3 (15 marks ), 4 (5 marks) and 5 (7 marks). The oral examination assesses Objective 6 (10 marks).

A written examination on Sections I, II and III of the syllabus is taken by students at the end of the course, and consists of two papers.

Paper I, lasting 1½ hours, contains 50 questions requiring one- or two-sentence answers and testing the candidate's ability to recall information (Objective 1). There are 2 marks for each question, thus a possible total of 100 marks, to be scaled down to 20.

Paper II, lasting 1¾ hours plus 15 minutes reading time, contains three sections. The first section requires short paragraph answers and tests knowledge of key concepts (Objective 2); the second consists of 10 questions requiring short answers based on stimulus documentary and/or visual material (Objective 5); the third is a major essay question testing knowledge of key concepts (Objective 2), and the ability to explain the arguments surrounding current global issues and developments and the ability to form an independent judgement (Objective 5).

## The quest for an O-level

Soon after the 190 students began World Studies in August 1978, it became clear to the teaching team that certification at O-level was a priority we could no longer ignore. Some fifty fourth-year students regarded by humanities teachers in our (11–14) feeder High Schools as having sound O-level prospects had been given the opportunity of taking O-level Geography instead of CSE World Studies. Most had opted for Geography. As we saw it, World Studies would remain at a disadvantage, a poor cousin subject eschewed by the most able, unless it was also offered at O-level. Only when World Studies became a joint O/CSE course could we get to grips with another key task we had set ourselves; the elevation of World

Studies to a place in the college's compulsory fourth- and fifth-year curriculum alongside subjects such as maths, PE and English.

Where were we to find a compatible O-level syllabus which would allow us to teach in mixed-ability classes (streaming would hardly be compatible with a course bent upon de-streaming globally!) and which would enable the final decision over O or CSE examination entry to be made as late as possible in the course? Why not write our own Mode 3 O-level syllabus? A visit to the offices of an O-level examination board seemed to confirm all we had heard from colleagues in other Leicestershire schools about the current attitude to Mode 3 O-levels. The boards, we had been forewarned, alarmed at the onward march of proposals for a 16+ examination, were in no mood to countenance new Mode 3 proposals, especially in 'strange new subjects like World Studies'. Indeed, sensitive to widespread articulation of concern over 'falling standards', the boards were becoming increasingly prickly in their relationship with schools already operating their own Mode 3 syllabuses. 'Put your ideas on paper,' advised one board official, 'but I can't promise anything.' We came away from our meeting realising that to prepare a Mode 3 O-level in World Studies would involve a mountain of work, negotiations and renegotiations with the odds heavily stacked against our proposals ever being accepted. News from a neighbouring school that two years of negotiation with one board had come to nothing confirmed our worst fears.

What options remained open? Firstly, we could approach one of the handful of Leicestershire colleges operating their own Mode 3 O-level and request permission to follow their syllabus and take their examination. Secondly, we could scour the handbooks of the examination boards in search of an existing syllabus which would lock in with our CSE in World Studies.

A perusal of local Mode 3 O-levels quickly ruled out the first option. The concept of interdependence, the underpinning feature of the CSE World Studies syllabus, was accorded at best secondary importance, and the global issues central to the syllabus tended to be incorporated in the final third or quarter of a Humanities course placing greatest emphasis upon the locality and upon British life and society.

We thus turned our attention to syllabuses being offered by the examination boards and it was at this point that we came upon the Joint Matriculation Board's (JMB) O-level syllabus in Integrated Humanities. The syllabus is extremely flexible in terms of both method of assessment and subject-matter. The teacher is

free to adopt whatever method of assessment he or she feels appropriate in relation to the teaching course and educational strategy being followed in the centre. For assessment purposes teachers may wish to make use of project work, work done as classroom or homework exercises, discussion situations, 'examinations' designed and conducted by the centre on the course of study or the particular topic, or a combination of any of these techniques.

No final examination is set by the Board but an elaborate inter-school moderation system is laid down as are detailed criteria for assessment. A student must present work on five topics, each topic being assessed on a scale of marks from 0 to 30. The overall maximum of 150 marks has to be made up of marks awarded for four 'qualities', using the following mark ranges:

1.  Knowledge                                                      55–75 marks
2a. Ability to locate and select evidence                         20–30 marks
2b. Interpretation of evidence and evaluation of argument         25–45 marks
2c. Presentation of explanations, ideas and/or arguments          20–30 marks

There is nothing to prevent a school varying the marks available under each 'quality' from topic to topic, although it is a lot easier for both student and teacher if the five topics are assessed to a fixed mark scheme.

The mode and method of assessment we found very attractive both in its own right and for our purposes. By judicious use of the mark ranges offered by JMB, we could create an O-level mark scheme which was more or less compatible with the CSE scheme. In addition, there was sufficient content overlap. The Integrated Humanities syllabus offers ten topics for study of which either four or five must be chosen: 'The Community', 'Law and Order', 'People and Work', 'Mass Media', 'Consumer Affairs', 'Education', 'The Family', 'Persecution and Prejudice', 'Poverty' and 'War'. The latter three topics form a major part of the World Studies syllabus and, in addition, we decided to take advantage of the Board's readiness to consider for approval one school-designed topic by submitting our own on 'The Environment'. Covering environmental spoliation, resource depletion, conservation and alternative life-styles and technologies (Aucott *et al.* 1979), this topic effectively covered areas of the CSE syllabus not covered by the JMB syllabus. What about a fifth topic? We pondered on this one until the self-evident dawned upon us. Students of O-level potential could be advised to devise a strategy for their involvement or research project so that the end-product could be entered for O-level under one of the seven topic headings we would not otherwise be covering. Hence, a student working on a UNESCO Associated Schools Project information exchange as his/her 'involvement' project could concentrate upon collecting information on, say, schooling in one or more countries and thus meet the requirements of the Integrated Humanities syllabus. Alternatively, a borderline O-level candidate could begin a major research project under Section V of the CSE syllabus (e.g. 'Family Life in Other Countries') and have no difficulty in entering his/her work as the fifth O-level topic (in this case as a 'Family' topic).

By organising the two-year course around the CSE syllabus, can we cover all the aspects of each topic as listed in the Integrated Humanities syllabus? The short answer is that we cannot. That, however, presents no real stumbling-block, as the JMB makes it quite clear that it does not expect the syllabus to be followed to the letter. The syllabus states[1]

The specification of the detail of the sections of each of the topics is not intended to establish a uniformity of content; it is intended as advice and guidance to the teacher designing a course and as providing a framework within which the study of each topic will form an internally consistent field of study and the combination of any five of the topics forms a coherent Integrated Humanities course.

*Strategies for a consultation*

Having hit upon an O-level syllabus flexible enough in content and mode of assessment to lock in with our CSE, we immediately made known our intention of offering World Studies at both levels. The announcement not only had a galvanising effect upon many of the students already taking the course but it also brought into sharp relief the question of whether World Studies should become part of the college's compulsory curriculum as from August 1979. As planning for the academic year 1979/80 was well under way, a decision on the latter point had to be made as swiftly as possible. The principal, supportive of World Studies but keen to ensure that parents were fully consulted, asked us to put our case at a public meeting so that parental reaction could be assessed.

Accordingly, we decided from the outset to seek the support of influential figures within the catchment area; figures who would tend to reassure parents doubting the wisdom of our proposal by the very fact that they were seen to favour compulsory World Studies. We were thinking of college governors, local councillors, local clergymen, and well-known and well-respected teachers working in local primary and high schools. Allies with particular expertise were also required: representatives from the worlds of business, industry and further and higher education, for example, who could speak with authority about the relevance of O/CSE World Studies for the school leaver entering a career or taking his studies further. Under this same category of allies with particular expertise came influential representatives from World Studies circles capable of setting developments at Groby within the context of developments nationwide. Further, we hoped to have as allies our consumers – a selection of fourth-year students from across the ability range prepared to discuss their experiences within the World Studies classroom.

Out of these initial ruminations emerged a format for the World Studies consultation. The idea of a traditional-style parents' meeting, chaired from the dais, was discarded from the outset. Instead, we opted for a format which would more accurately reflect the ethos, as it was developing, of the World Studies classroom and which would also facilitate in-depth consultation. The evening, we decided, should begin with a multi-media presentation outlining the aims and content of the World Studies course, explaining the qualifications to which it would lead and seeking to anticipate likely queries about and objections to our proposal. The presentation, we felt, should be planned and executed by the entire teaching team. After the presentation, parents would be invited to repair to the Humanities area to put their questions to and hear the points of view of people invited to sit on six panels or 'stalls'. The stalls would be manned by:
1. Students currently following the course.

2. Parents of students following the course and prospective parents.
3. Teachers from the two feeder High Schools and from a local primary school.
4. Local employers and trade unionists, to discuss the acceptability for employment purposes of a CSE or O-level qualification in World Studies.
5. Lecturers and tutors from further and higher education establishments, to discuss the acceptability for admission purposes of a qualification in World Studies.
6. Leading figures in the World Studies field in touch with developments throughout the country.

At each stall there would be a teacher from the Humanities Faculty and a parent-member of the School Association Committee, whose task it would be to note down the questions and opinions put forward so that these could be taken into consideration when a decision was made on compulsory World Studies. In addition, the Business/Industry panel, the Further and Higher Education panel, and the National Experts panel would each be in possession of a dossier of letters written in response to our request for opinions on the CSE syllabus. On display during the second part of the evening would be a selection from the range of teaching and learning resources available for World Studies. The students present would also have their work files available for parents to browse through.

The format seemed ideal for our purposes. It allowed for free-ranging and in-depth consultation. The use of stalls permitted a person-to-person exchange of views and reduced the likelihood of parents being too inhibited to speak as they so often are at a formal meeting chaired from the front. It was also an approach more likely to avoid the embattled positions so often evident at a formally run meeting where a participant, having made known his standpoint, is reluctant to lose face by shifting his position. A two-hour consultation also allowed for shifts of attitude as a result of a series of one-to-one conversations. The format was also a way of avoiding red herrings of an emotive nature. (How often have we seen a parents' meeting on the curriculum deflected from its original purpose by one or two dominant personalities ready to do battle about the credibility of CSE qualifications or about mixed-ability teaching!) Another consideration making the format an attractive proposition was that it permitted parents to put their questions to the person best able to answer them, which would not have been the case had all questions been fired at a World Studies team facing the serried ranks of parents. The eventual success of this format has been described by Aucott et al. (1979), members of the team concerned.

## The core curriculum in operation

Approximately 320 fourth-year students now take the two-year World Studies course at Groby each September. Three fifty-minute periods per week are allotted to the course which is taught to half a year group at a time by a team of six teachers. In addition, a compensatory teacher is on hand to give assistance as and when necessary. The course is taught on a mixed-ability basis throughout, but different work is set to meet O and CSE requirements in the fifth year. CSE students continue to present projects, essays and thoughtsheets to the pattern established in the fourth year, whilst potential O-level students work to a pattern of extended essays, knowledge tests and data-handling units taken under test conditions. The extended essays are marked out of 14, 4 marks being awarded for knowledge (JMB 'quality' 1), 3 for location and selection of evidence ('quality' 2a), 2 for interpretation and evaluation ('quality' 2b) and 5 for presentation of arguments ('quality' 2c). The test is marked out of 10 solely on 'quality' 1; the data-handling unit out of 6 entirely on 'quality' 2b. Students failing to score sufficiently highly on O-level extended essays, tests and data-handling units are encouraged to review their position and opt for CSE, their essays then being remarked to the CSE scheme of assessment.

For each unit of the course, a 'mainstream' topic booklet has been devised alongside a simpler version written in conjunction with the Head of Compensatory Education and a 'Readings and Things' pamphlet containing a range of more advanced material. The booklets provide the backbone of the course but are complemented by the regular use of more active methods.

Films such as *The War Game, Eye of the Storm, The Survival Game, Spare a Thought* and *Five Minutes to Midnight* are shown regularly[2] following the techniques described by Whitaker (1980) and Taylor and Richardson (1979). A range of filmstrips and slides is also used as are debates, discussion exercises, visiting speakers, simulation games and the experiential units described in *An Experience-Centred Curriculum* by David Wolsk (1975). The texts which we find best convey the idea of an interdependent world are Stuart's *The Unequal Third*, (1977), Turner's *World Inequality* (1978) and the four titles by Richardson in the Nelson World Studies series (1978).

The involvement aspect of the course has, not unexpectedly, been the most problematic. In the first year there were some extremely imaginative initiatives, including the preparation of a 'Rock against Racism' opera, the designing and building of a windmill and a number of 'cultural evenings' in which students presented the food and culture of a particular part of the world. Most, however, fell upon stony ground partly because of lack of adequate monitoring by staff. Firstly, we allocated far too little time within the World Studies classroom and, secondly, the range of projects was so wide that teachers had neither the time nor expertise to provide adequate guidance. Since then, at least one fifty-minute period per week has been made available for consultation on major projects and for in-school project work during the fifth year. In addition, a pro forma for plans of campaign and for the monthly monitoring of project diaries has been brought into use and so we now experience far fewer casualty projects. A member of staff has been given a scale point partly for assisting with the planning and overall monitoring of projects, a practical reflection of the importance the college and faculty accords to involvement. It has to be said, however, that involvement, challenging students, as it does, to develop a high level of commitment and to flex their political muscles, will always be an uneasy bedfellow of the fifty-minute-period, thirty-period-a-week, timetable.

Mention should also be made of the fact that World Studies now appears as a sixth-form O-level course which, at the time of writing, is taken by upwards of thirty students. It is hoped that we will before long be able to prepare students for an AO examination in Development Studies during the same timetable slot. Student pressure is building, too, for an A-level in World Studies. There have already been a significant number of cases of successful O-level students wanting to take their studies to a higher level. At the moment the only way to meet this demand seems to be to use one of the more flexible and progressive A-level General Studies syllabuses on offer (Selby 1980).

Finally, a word on World Studies and the community college. Community consultation was vital in achieving widespread acceptance of and support for World Studies. Our consultation format had allowed for an in-depth dialogue with parents and with community interests of a kind envisaged in the Taylor Report (1977), *A New Partnership for our Schools*. The Taylor Committee says:

In our view a school is not an end in itself; it is an institution set up and financed by society to achieve certain objectives which society regards as desirable and it is subject to all the stresses to which society itself is subject. It is vital, therefore, that teachers have the support of people outside the school in the increasingly difficult task of attaining these objectives and dealing with these stresses.

Support we had certainly received from parents and other members of the community who as a body appeared far more receptive to change than the stereotype (defence mechanism?) common in many a staffroom would have us believe. One panellist wrote:

It is my belief that curriculum change is often approached from the wrong direction. Innovators attempt to introduce change by increasing the driving forces instead of attempting to release the pressure of restricting forces. The interesting feature of the World Studies evening was that it approached the problem from both ends at the same time! It is sobering that educational innovation, founded as it must be on an act of faith, depends upon the creation of relationships of mutual trust between teachers and pupils on the one hand, and teachers and parents on the other.

Partnership with the community has remained vital to the operation of the course. We rely heavily upon individuals, groups and interests in the community as resources for our work, whether as questionnaire respondents or as visiting speakers or for the expertise and insights they can bring to bear upon involvement projects. On the other side of the same coin, one of the aims of a number of involvement projects is to inform members of the community about global issues and to exhort them in turn to commitment and action. This adult education aspect is vital. Indeed, the success of the World Studies movement may stand or fall upon its commitment to adult education for it is, without doubt, a serious blind spot to concentrate exclusively upon the education of those less likely to be in a position to influence events for some time and to ignore those who can influence events *now* especially when the issues of concern have, in most cases, already reached crisis proportions. For this reason, the college has also begun 'We Agree' workshops to seek consensus between groups of adults on global issues. World Studies, in short, cannot thrive within a fenced garden. Seeking to bring down barriers globally, it cannot afford to raise the drawbridge on the local community without serious loss of credibility[3].

## Notes

1. Copies of the Integrated Humanities O-level syllabus can be obtained from the Joint Matriculation Board, Manchester M15 6EU.
2. These films, and others suitable for World Studies, are available from Concord Films Council, 201 Felixstowe Road, Ipswich, Suffolk IP3 9BJ.
3. For consideration of the relationships between World Studies and community education, see *World Studies Journal* (1980), **2** (1)3–17.

# Chapter 5    Hugh Starkey
## World Studies and the development of new resources

### Origins of the World Studies course

One of the options offered to pupils at City of Ely College prior to 1976 was a course called European Studies. The course was intended for those pupils who were not taking an examination in a foreign language. It contained some elementary language work and a larger element of background studies, mainly concentrating on aspects of daily life in Germany. The course was typical of such courses which sprang up in schools all over Britain in the early 1970s, coinciding with the development of the comprehensive school system. These courses were developed partly on pragmatic grounds and partly out of ideological conviction, the two elements being in tension.

Britain's entry into the EEC made schools receptive to the possibility of introducing European Studies courses as promoted by the Centre for Contemporary European Studies at Sussex University where the academic framework for such courses was being developed. Schools were reluctant, however, to devote prime curriculum time to the subject. On the other hand, comprehensive schools soon discovered that although a foreign language could be successfully taught to all pupils in the early years of secondary school, the less academic pupils made little further progress in language learning after the second or third year of study. These pupils, many of them thoroughly disaffected after their experience of failure in language learning and often having developed a positive antipathy to all things foreign, were offered a European Studies course instead. However, there was neither the appropriate course framework nor the appropriate pedagogy available, nor even the appropriate teaching materials for a course whose clients were primarily non-academically inclined. This was precisely the case in Ely, where teachers found great difficulty in motivating pupils taking European Studies and therefore derived very little satisfaction from the course themselves.

The World Studies Project in London, unlike the Centre for Contemporary European Studies, was not based at a university and it had been exploring teaching methods appropriate to all pupils. Its publications stressed the importance of the affective as well as the cognitive domain (Richardson 1976). Such developments paved the way for a course appropriate to pupils who would derive little benefit from a purely academic approach.

The new Head of Languages appointed to City of Ely College in 1976 had been involved with the World Studies Project and immediately proposed the replacement of the unpopular European Studies course with a course of World Studies. In a memorandum to the principal dated May 1976 the aims of a World Studies course were outlined as follows:

The World Studies course assumes that the citizen of tomorrow should be equipped to adapt to change and be able to work together with others in an increasingly international community. She or he will require to understand some fundamental facts about the world as a whole and its problems and will need to be able to evolve a system of values against which to test the various concepts of progress which will present themselves in a lifetime stretching into the twenty-first century. It will also be important to learn about some of the ways in which individuals and groups can take action to bring about desired changes.

The rationale for such a course replacing European Studies was presented thus:

One of the functions of a modern languages department within a school is to produce an understanding of what is meant by a culture and to encourage empathy with people of other national cultures. The importance for pupils of studying a foreign culture is in preparing them to be future citizens by giving them a new perspective on their own country's values and culture, whereby these are seen to be relative and not absolute. The initial approach to a foreign culture may be through the study of a foreign language. This initial approach may be constrained by the ability of pupils to comprehend and produce the foreign language and the foreign culture may be taught increasingly via the medium of the pupils' mother tongue. Once this has happened, the rationale for concentrating on our near neighbours France and Germany, whose cultures and values are in most respects similar to our own, disappears.

The arguments may have had a persuasive effect, but the fact that someone was volunteering to take over a difficult option group was probably even more eloquent. The change was approved. The syllabus was written during the summer and the course started in September 1976, preparing for its first CSE Mode 3 examination in May 1978.

## Teaching strategies

The World Studies course is allocated two seventy-minute lessons and a thirty-five-minute lesson per week for five terms. The four course units are covered at a rate of one unit per term, with the final term for revision and finishing project work. The time available is comparatively generous and the course takes up the same share of the pupils' week as other major subjects such as maths and English, namely $12\frac{1}{2}$ per cent.

There is no intrinsic reason why pupils should be *a priori* interested in the course and, indeed, for reasons mentioned above there is likely to be some overt hostility. Although in theory pupils have opted for the subject, they may well, in practice, have opted against all the other choices. Motivation of pupils is an essential prerequisite to the successful teaching of this course which will otherwise be nullified, not necessarily by hostility so much as by the complacent, unquestioning apathy of pupils from a quiet, relatively isolated, white, rural community.

Motivating pupils to wish to learn more about the world is, in any case, part of the course. As the initial memorandum, quoted above, suggested, the course is not just a question of learning about the world, but rather about developing positive attitudes towards constructive change. Although some learning of facts and figures is necessary, the mere studying of maps and statistics, however interestingly presented, neither motivates nor changes attitudes. Studying textbooks, even if appropriate ones are available, is not a popular activity. Lectures by the teacher and copying notes do little to improve motivation.

On the other hand, many activities are enjoyed by pupils and these are able to lead to real interest and questioning. Case-study material describing life for families in other countries and cultures is always well received, whether presented by magazine features, slides, photographs, films, television programmes or, best of all, by real people visiting the classroom.

Activities involving visits outside the classroom are also popular. These have included a survey of the countries of origin of the goods displayed in High Street windows, or the cars parked in the cathedral car park; a linguistic town trail with examples of writing in public places in a dozen languages; taking a foreign visitor on a guided tour; visiting a museum or a commune; interviewing local people, by appointment. Such activities also help to develop confidence and responsibility.

Games and simulations are also useful in promoting real understanding. In particular they can illustrate activities where chance may play a large role, such as farming, and they can also be most useful in learning about trade.

Discussion is also a most important method of exploring and clarifying ideas. The skill of questioning is also one that should be acquired during the course and is an important element of developing discussion skills. Both these can be developed through a close examination of visual material such as slides or photographs. The World Studies Project, in particular, has developed many interesting ways of structuring discussion activities and these have proved most successful in practice (Richardson 1976). Many of these ideas are incorporated in the teaching materials produced in Ely.

Another way of motivating pupils is to enable them to participate in structuring their own learning. Project work is a well-known example of this approach, but pupils can also discuss the structure of a unit of work and choose the kind of lessons they wish to participate in. As an example of this, pupils were presented with a worksheet at the beginning of the summer term 1977 which gave brief details of twenty possible lead lessons, including talks, simulations, visits and opportunities to meet people. The class was asked to discuss the list, choose twelve activities and put them in an appropriate sequence.

The pupils were surprised, as they had never been asked their opinions in this way before. However, the discussion and explanation was fruitful and not only served to introduce the term's work and to show pupils the

74

outline of their course, but also enabled them to identify with the course as a co-operative venture rather than something imposed on them.

A lead lesson is usually followed up with discussion and note-taking, revising and elaborating on the points introduced. An example of the overall teaching strategy is given in this extract from a diary kept by the teacher during the course. The period covers one month at the beginning of the autumn term in the fourth term of the course. The topic being introduced is the New International Economic Order. It illustrates the variety of lead lessons, and the teacher's concern with developing attitudes as well as imparting information.[1]

*September*

| | |
|---|---|
| Wednesday, 7th | Showed film *Indonesian Boomerang*,[2] a film distributed by Christian Aid in which an Australian teacher visits Indonesia and attempts, with difficulty, to communicate what he has learnt to his family and his pupils. Discussed pupils' impressions of Indonesia and provided some background. |
| Thursday, 8th | Single lesson. Follow-up discussion of points made in film. Class still showed hostile and inward-looking attitudes, especially fear of Communism, sense of intellectual superiority over Africans, Asians, etc. Film obviously hadn't had immediate impact on attitudes! |
| Monday, 12th | Showed *Indonesian Boomerang* again – Richard Bainbridge, local Christian Aid organiser, led discussion. Discussion off to a slow start – usual silliness, but developed very well, e.g. 'If you send them tractors you'll just put people out of work.' Also 'We should try to solve our own problems first' – ambiguous that statement! Our problems identified as: unemployment, inflation, race. |
| Wednesday, 14th | Writing on *Indonesian Boomerang*. Introduction of terms: colony, empire, primary product – examples of primary products. |
| Thursday , 15th | Continuation of talk on colonialism. Used Sri Lanka and tea as an example.[3] Seems to be a good grasp of facts and concepts. Group is still hardline on attitudes. At least there is interest in the subject-matter once the lesson gets going. |
| Monday, 19th | Showed *The Survival Game*, a film made for the Ministry of Overseas Development, in which James Burke attempts to explain the way in which the world trading system is loaded in favour of the developed countries. Pupils were involved – applauded, etc. with studio audience. Pupils wrote what they thought of the film – contributions were |

|  | read out anonymously. Pupils felt it was dull in parts – but explained trade issues clearly. |
|---|---|
| Wednesday, 21th | Made notes on *The Survival Game*, based on points in the teaching notes provided with the film. Recall of the film was excellent and in detail. At one point Alec – remembering TV item – raised the question of India's nuclear capability. 'Why does India spend so much money on a nuclear weapon when millions of people are starving?' Answer suggested by class: because she feels threatened. Also discussion on why the Indian family were made to look sad and dirty. 'That's the way people think of them.' Why? 'That's what they're shown on TV?' Pointed out circularity of argument. Does that image correspond to what e.g. Iain Guest's slides showed? 'Yes.....well, no! They were clean and happy.' |
| Thursday, 22nd | Single lesson – had asked them to write an outline of a project on a world-scale problem for homework – only 2 had! Some claimed they didn't understand the word 'outline'. Spent lesson compiling list of some world-scale problems based on war and violence, energy and pollution, poverty, unemployment, etc. |
| Monday, 26th | Simulation games   1. Making and improving – from Richardson (1976) a game in which 'goods' are 'manufactured' and sold. Raw materials, tools and components can be bought and profits reinvested. Groups set up their own production line. Groups made TVs and 'cars' from paper, templates, pencils and scissors. Very successful and enjoyable game. Pupils certainly learnt meaning of capital, investment, specialisation, reinvestment of profits, value-added, etc. Pupils worked hard at it, in spite of initial scepticism. |
|  | 2. New game with unequal resources and a trading element. Not quite so successful in outcome (or was it?) Third World won! They easily obtained technology (loaning templates) then used monopoly of raw materials to force price up tenfold. Certainly concept of supply and demand and price increases shown. |
| Wednesday, 28th | Notes and discussion following up Monday's game. Supply and demand introduced. |
|  | – Question: What might two groups without paper have done in a less restrained situation? |
|  | – Answer: Gone in and taken it. |
|  | – Response: Well, that's rather like colonialism. |

How did the Third World group win Monday's game? – (a) it cheated but (b) it got its technology easily and quickly. In real life Third World doesn't get the technology. If it does, it can't sell its goods to the market because of quotas and tariffs. (Thought: improve the game by putting quotas on Third World goods!)

Thursday, 29th    Selecting projects and asking questions: e.g. Nigel – racism; David, Kevan – food; Karl, Greg, Peter – arms race; Malcolm – unemployment.

*October*

Monday, 3rd    Visit of Scott Sinclair from Development Education Centre, Birmingham. Spoke of Ghana – the colonial legacy. Showed Ghana's dependence on cocoa, which is processed in Europe. Also the way communications are geared towards trade with Europe, not neighbouring countries. Stressed the initiative and resourcefulness of Ghanaians.

Keeping a diary of a course, as it is taught, can prove invaluable for subsequent analysis and evaluation. Even these brief extracts begin to bring the classroom situation alive again.

## Pupil perceptions of the course

Further evidence of pupils' perceptions of the course and their reactions to it comes from two interviews conducted in private with a group of three pupils by a Cypriot researcher, Andreas Panayides, who was studying at Cambridge Institute of Education at the time. The interviews took place during the fourth and fifth terms of the course. They were taped and transcribed and the following are short extracts.

A.P.: What do you think your teacher, Mr Starkey, is primarily concerned to teach you through this World Studies?

Nigel : To give us a bare outlook of the world's situation.

Stephen : A general idea on the world statistics. I, we've done a few projects on tea and world organisation and stuff like that.

Peter : I agree with the notion of giving us a better outlook of the world as it is today – trying to see how poor people are, and how lucky we are in having our clothes, and our food, because people in the world are starving.

A.P. : Well, do you think Mr Starkey is concerned to change your attitudes or your values towards all these world problems?

N : Yes, I think he is trying to change our attitudes, yes.

S : He's giving us quite a big outlook on everything really, I mean he is trying to get over to us....

N: (cutting S): He's giving us the facts for us to sort out what we think ourselves about the situations.

S : It's quite a big outlook on mainly poor countries really.

N : Yes, Third World countries.

A.P. : Well, what do you feel you yourself are getting out of this course?

N : We're learning things we never knew existed.

S : Yes, about the world, because at the start we never knew what conditions were like in Sri Lanka on the tea plantations. We thought it was quite a good life in the start. But after, we learned they only get something like 25p a week. We didn't know that.

N : If we see something on telly now, we may not have known before the situation, we now may understand it more – something that comes on telly.

S : What we just took for granted about all the poor people and stuff like that, we used to think they just wasted their money and stuff like that. But we see for ourselves what it's like.

N : We see they need more children to go out and work to bring more money into the house.

S : Yes, we always thought it was stupid having seven or eight children, but they do this so that when they get older they've got children to look after them.

A.P. : How important to you is the fact that you are preparing for a certain exam? I mean, does this help you or hinder you?

N : Well, it varies really. If you pass, you get a pass in it. It's a CSE pass.

P : It's not really important. It's just an interesting thing to do.

S : Because it's not really established yet. You may go to some employer and say you have this World Studies, grade 2, and they won't know what you're getting on about.

P : In a few years time it may be useful, but not at the moment.

N : We are learning things that other pupils in school may not get a chance to learn.

S : Yes, we're the first people to actually do this course.

A.P. : Well, would it make any difference if you were preparing for exams?

P : Not really. We wouldn't bother to do so much work then.

S : Yes, I think so, because we've now got exams.

N : We need to get some projects done because that goes towards the exam marks.

S : Yes, and it helps us, and makes us concentrate more on the project, right, and we get it finished properly rather than leave it half done. It's definitely to persuade us to work harder because of the exam.

N : I agree with Stephen, yes.

A fuller version of these interviews together with teacher comments can be found in Starkey and Panayides (1978). They vividly illustrate pupils' awareness of their own changing perceptions of the world.

## Revision of the course

The experience of the first two years of the CSE course suggested that the syllabus was in many ways too academic and the load of course work and project work was too great. The unit on Language was particularly difficult to cover satisfactorily, although its *raison d'être* was still valid. The syllabus was also too rigid. A World Studies course should be able to respond to and examine issues of the day, in 1979 a revolution in Iran and starvation in Kampuchea, for instance. And so a revised syllabus was submitted and accepted which gives scope for the teacher to take advantage of opportunities which arise and to study topics which are of current interest.[5] Below is the new syllabus in outline:

## Assessment

(*a*) *Coursework*

(i) A folder consisting of the fifteen best pieces of coursework from the two-year course. Each piece to be the pupil's own response to an element of the course: 20 per cent.

(ii) Two projects, each worth 15 per cent. Project 1 to be started in Year 1 and to be an exploration in greater depth of a topic from Units 1 or 2. Project 2 to be an exploration in greater depth of topic from Units 3 and 4. Total 30 per cent.

(*b*) *Examination*

Paper 1 – short, factual answers:   15%

Paper 2 – longer answers:   35%

## Syllabus

*Unit 1   The world today – some case studies*

*Objectives*

(i) To enable pupils to compare their own culture and society with those of a variety of other countries.

(ii) To illustrate the effect of such factors as political system, national wealth, historical and geographical factors on the lives of individuals in different countries.

*Syllabus*

At least six case studies illustrating the way of life, the problems, achievements and aspirations of people in a number of countries. A consideration of ways in which their lives affect us and vice versa. Examples should include a developed capitalist country, a socialist country, a developing African country, an Asian country and a Latin American country.

*Unit 2 People and resources*

*Objectives*

(i) To help pupils understand some of the effects of human activity on the earth's environment.

79

Projects and courses

(ii) To help pupils to evaluate their own life-styles in the light of some knowledge of the earth's resources and their distribution.

*Syllabus*

Approaches to the use and conservation of the planet's resources.
Environmental damage.
The energy debate.

*Unit 3   People, language and communication*

*Objectives*

 (i) To help pupils towards an understanding of the importance of language and culture as a political force.
(ii) To examine the nature and role of the mass media.

*Syllabus*

Case studies of nationalist movements based on language and culture, e.g. Ireland, the Basques, etc. A study of the book *Man and Language* (Cripwell, 1979).
A study of how news is gathered and presented.

*Unit 4   People and conflict*

*Objectives*

 (i) To examine the causes and effects of some of the conflicts and wars in the contemporary world.
(ii) To consider some alternatives to armed conflict.

*Syllabus*

At least three examples of war, violence, terrorism and oppression, their causes and effects, e.g. Ireland, Israel, Latin America, southern Africa. World development 'the new name for peace'.

## Setting up the Ely Materials on World Studies Project

The first year of the course relied heavily on outside interest and help. In particular, representatives of a number of agencies involved in curriculum development came to Ely to discuss the course and contribute a lead lesson. No durable new teaching materials were produced. In September 1977, however, a new group of twenty-two pupils was to start the course. Fortunately the Languages Department included an able and adaptable teacher, Alan Draper, who readily agreed to take on the new group. The question of resources, however, now presented a considerable problem. It was not possible to continue to sustain two groups on outside help and interest, and the school could not afford a heavy investment in those materials that were, by then, available. It was already evident that written materials such as traditional textbooks were not appropriate, even if suitable ones had been available.

The help of the Ely Resource and Technology Centre[6] was therefore enlisted with a view to producing some study units for the Ely Mode 3 syllabus. It was decided to apply for a grant from the Ministry of Overseas Development's recently established Development Education Fund, and to satisfy the terms of the funding the scope of the proposal was broadened to involve other schools in the area.

The application to the Development Education Fund was the first act in setting up the Ely Materials on World Studies Project. Funds were requested for the setting-up of a bank of resource materials which could be borrowed by any local schools wishing to teach a World Studies course, and also to finance the production of materials to supplement those in the resource collection. The rationale for the project was described as follows:

## Rationale

A number of factors hamper teachers of World Studies in secondary schools or inhibit them from adopting a World Studies course. These include:

- The lack of a related body of teaching and learning materials on which to base a course.
- The lack of access to a collection of specialist literature for background reading.
- The low priority given to World Studies in schools and a reluctance to allocate adequate funds for the purchase of suitable visual aids.

The project is designed to promote the teaching of World Studies in the following ways:

- By providing a series of materials produced locally which can be easily revised and updated as necessary, and which can provide a framework round which materials from other sources can be used effectively.
- By providing teachers with the support of a resource collection of loan items and background material.
- By involving teachers in a group of secondary schools in a curriculum development project, thereby enabling them to support and encourage each other.
- By involving appropriate individuals and agencies in the local community, thereby providing external support.

A meeting was convened at the end of the summer term 1977 to launch the project. Sylvia Stephenson, responsible for curriculum development at the Resource and Technology Centre, sent out a letter to the Heads of all local secondary schools with a request to pass on the invitation to all teachers whom they thought might be interested:

We are inviting you to participate in a local project trying out new materials on World Studies. We hope that you will be able to come to a meeting to discuss it and learn more about it.

Briefly the scheme involves the production of a number of study units for the World Studies CSE Mode 3 course now being taught at City of Ely College. The study units will comprise professionally designed and printed worksheets, together with slide sets and cassettes, on such themes as energy, poverty, population, alternative technology, basic needs, food and rural development. The first units should be available by December.

It is hoped that a number of teachers from neighbouring schools, such as yourself, will be prepared to use and comment on this material. A grant of nearly £2,000 has been applied for from the Ministry of Overseas Development, which should enable the materials to be made available free of charge to schools participating in the project.

Participation does not necessarily involve more than using those materials which you could use in your course, and reporting back. However, there will be ample scope for writing or devising materials and other involvement if you wish. Attendance at the initial meeting will provide an opportunity to decide on the order in which units are produced, purchases for the resource collection and also to give your ideas about a proposed World Studies Month planned for November.

A dozen people attended and it was felt that the project offered the classroom teacher four things, namely: resources, institutional support from the organisations represented, moral support by being part of a group of teachers, and leadership (Bridges 1978). The Development Education Fund made available £2,000 and a collection of resource material was purchased and housed with the Schools Library Service. A second meeting of the project group was convened early in the autumn term to discuss the writing and publishing of original materials. Five themes were adopted as being of interest to teachers of several subjects. These were poverty, energy, food, population and trade.

## The first materials

The initial intention was that the project should produce worksheets and that the issue to be tackled first would be that of world poverty. Discussion with those involved closely with the project revealed an uneasiness at adopting a problems approach to the issue. This approach outlines a problem and considers various possible courses of action to solve it (Starkey 1978a). In this case it was considered, however, that the act of defining something as a problem involved a value judgement inappropriate to materials advocating a global perspective. Moreover the simplification of the issues required to cover the topic within the constraints of the worksheet would be bound to lead to such distortion as to risk being intellectually dishonest.

The Ely Resource and Technology Centre had, in any case, a record of exploring new formats and there was a feeling that worksheets would be a conventional and unimaginative medium. Derick Last, the County Adviser for Curriculum Development Resources, in whose name the application to the Development Education Fund had been submitted, stressed this at the second meeting of the project when he said: 'Let's be sure that some of the things we do *are* innovatory, *are* pushing perhaps people's thinking a little bit further than their day-to-day concerns. It may be that an answer to a problem which has not yet been posed will answer many problems which are close to.' (Bridges 1978.)

Similar reservations were also applicable to those textbooks that were already available. Apart from concern about how a textbook can actually be used in an open-ended, discussion-orientated course, textbooks were seen to close down topics rather than opening them up. They often tended to be strong on analysis but weak on facts.

The solution to the editorial problem was to present facts, analysis and pictorial material, but in such a way as to raise questions rather than answer them. The format chosen was therefore that of a pack of 100 cards. Forty cards had a brief fact printed on a background of a striking globe motif. Forty more cards had quotations, with a human face as background. Finally, twenty cards had photographs illustrating the title of the material *The Rich and the Poor*. If the idea was a good one, the design and production work by Chris McLeod of the Ely Resource and Technology Centre, who had joined in discussions from the beginning of the project, at least doubled the impact of the materials. Clearly, with such new material, teachers' notes are very important. These are provided with the cards and suggest a number of ways in which they can be used for teaching (Starkey 1978b).

The proposed time-scale for production was very optimistic, and the cards were not in fact launched until September 1978. The first edition of 300 sets sold out within a year, and a revised edition of 200 sets was then produced. The sets were sold world-wide, to teachers and educationalists. It proved difficult to collect detailed examples of how the cards were used and so an example must be taken from City of Ely College.

The lesson, taught in November 1978, lasted seventy minutes. It was the fourth of a series using the cards and followed several lessons on a case study of a village in Bangladesh using the UNICEF slide pack *Shishir of Bangladesh* by Iain Guest (1978). Pupils were first asked to brainstorm a list of words to describe poor people and then a list for rich people. The lists were written up, without comment, on the blackboard. The class was then divided into groups of three and each group was given the twenty photo cards from the pack and asked to sort them into piles illustrating 'rich', 'poor' and a 'don't know' pile. This produced lively discussions. The groups were then asked to choose one card from each pile and write four or five questions about it and discuss them. Finally each group was given some of the fact cards, and asked to use the facts as captions to the pictures. Homework, which was writing an account of the lesson, produced the following quotations:

'When the things like unhealthy, docile and common were brought up, most people thought of poor people, but just because you are poor it doesn't mean you are thick, common and dirty.'

'From what we did in class (with the cards) (see fig. 4) we raised a few ideas. It seems that the people with money tend to waste it all the time. They don't spent it on constructive things.....'

Fig. 4  Ely Material on World Studies: the Rich and the Poor (after C. McLeod, Ely Resource and Technology Centre)

'Also in that lesson we wrote down some words describing rich and poor. Some of them I disbelieved and some I thought fitted. The one I disbelieved was the one on the poor side: stupid . . . look at a man in India who might be a very good farmer . . . but can't get his money.'

'The cards have made me think how disastrously the World is run, the terrible extremes in which people live ....This surely is not right and if it is not stopped soon somebody is going to fight back.'

The quotations clearly illustrate that the pupils have been able to reject stereotyped thinking and raise for themselves fundamental questions about the nature of the world in which we live. Whereas facts and analysis of situations learned at school will become dated as the world changes, the ability to ask questions and to reject received ideas is a skill that should last for life.

## Materials on energy

Although the topic on energy is just one of those mentioned in Unit 2 of the CSE syllabus, it is in many ways the ideal core topic for a World Studies course. Firstly, the events in distant countries, such as Iran, can be seen directly to affect daily life in this country. A revolution causes a cut in oil production, which causes the world price of oil to rise, which causes the UK price of petrol to rise, which causes families to cut back on motoring, which reduces the choice of weekend activities. Secondly, the distribution of world demand for energy reflects the economic inequalities in the world. Moreover, the topics of rapid social change, development, international trade, conservation of resources, environmental damage and many others are all likely to arise in a consideration of the topic of energy. Energy was therefore chosen as the topic for the second set of materials.

Two sets of material were finally launched in January 1980. A second set of cards was produced in the same format as *The Rich and the Poor.* The title this time was *Energy and People.*[7] More spectacular is a board game entitled *The World Energy Game* in which the players, representing countries, trade resources for technology and buy in the generating capacity to produce their energy requirements. They may choose any selection of generators from a range which goes from nuclear power stations to windmills. Each generating system has its advantages and disadvantages which are weighed up and discussed and also experienced in the course of the game.[8]

The game has proved very popular with pupils, and not only those following World Studies courses. Sixth-form students of geography and economics have also gained insights from the game, as have adult groups of teachers and Friends of the Earth. The game is open-ended and can be played in a number of different versions. Thus it really needs to be played a number of times and the different outcomes compared (Starkey 1979a).

## Conclusions

The Ely Mode 3 CSE World Studies course has shown that it is possible to provide a major course in this subject which 14–16 year-olds will enjoy, value and derive benefit from. It has indicated one area of the curriculum into which such a course can fit. It may be, however, that if the course is merely regarded as a convenient way for a particular department to fulfil its quota of teaching time, it will never be considered as central to the school's curriculum and it may therefore be particularly vulnerable to staffing cuts or a curriculum review. For a World Studies course to become a permanent and central part of the curriculum, intensive and extensive consultations and explanations with staff and parents may need to be undertaken, as was the case at Groby College, described in Chapter 4.

The developments at Ely must be regarded as experimental, but many positive results have emerged. Teaching strategies have been tried and evaluated. New kinds of teaching material have been produced, of a kind which commercial publishers would be unable to initiate and reluctant to adopt without the sort of trials provided by the project. Schools have co-operated with the LEA resource centre and a government funding body to ensure that a limited amount of funding produced useful and concrete results.

The project has also felt itself to be part of an international network. Contacts have been established and materials and information sent out to five continents. Close working relationships have been developed with a large number of individuals and groups in Britain. In the area around Ely new courses are being developed in several secondary schools. Primary school teachers have been encouraged by the Ely Centre to work on related themes under the general heading 'A world of difference'. Specific projects undertaken by a number of primary schools include clothing, shelter, explorers and energy. In-service courses and conferences have been arranged, as have sixth-form conferences and One World Week activities for the whole community (Starkey 1979b).

The materials produced by the Ely project have grown from the experience of developing and teaching a new course. They are an expression of the philosophy behind the course which is concerned with the most effective way to prepare pupils for tomorrow's world. The teachers' notes for *The Rich and the Poor* cards express this philosophy in a paragraph which succinctly sums up the project's concerns:

If World Studies is about preparing pupils for the future, and to understand the forces at work in the world in which they are and will be living, then it is not enough merely to look at the issues which today are defined as problems and at the solutions proposed for these problems. Tomorrow's problems may be defined in quite different terms. We must therefore not present pupils with problems and solutions already defined and categorised, but we must encourage pupils to ask fundamental questions which will help them to define their own areas of interest and their own problems.

## Notes

1. Diary extracts previously reproduced in Guest, I. (1978) 'Report to UNESCO, Geneva, on a pilot school linking project', unpublished.
2. For hire (lasts 27 minutes) from Christian Aid, P.O. Box 1, London SW9 8BH.
3. This theme was later developed and the materials published as Starkey, H. (1979) *Our Cup of Tea – Sri Lanka and the International Tea Trade*, Centre for World Development Education, London.
4. Available free of charge (lasts 37 minutes) from The Central Film Library, Government Buildings, Bromyard Avenue, London W3 7JB.
5. Approved by the East Anglian Examinations Board as a CSE Mode 3 syllabus.
6. Ely Resource and Technology Centre, Back Hill, Ely, Cambs.
7. Available from the Ely Resource and Technology Centre (see 6 above).
8. Available from the Ely Resource and Technology Centre (see 6 above).

# Chapter 6   Jim Dunlop
# The Jordanhill Project in International Understanding

## Education for international understanding: the need for a strategy of curriculum innovation

Curriculum development is a term which has been absorbed into the language of educationists during the last two or three decades. It remains, despite its increasingly common usage, a term with a slightly pretentious conjunction of terminology. Many would agree that education by its very nature is developmental, and recognise curricula, however imperfect they may be, as social tools which can effect change. Yet such curricular tools offer possibilities in attempting to achieve what may, in practice, be a difficult task of maintaining a dynamic state of tension between our perceptions of where we might be and where we are.

A distinction may be drawn between educational development which is evolutionary and educational development which is deliberate. Changes of practice can and do occur spontaneously within educational systems. In some systems, if not all, the teacher who is conscientious is constantly alert to the possibility of incorporating new ideas into school practice. Perhaps classwork will be modified as a result of the teacher's sympathetic response to children's interests; perhaps it will occur due to events which are external to the school. Regardless of the reason for change, experimental courses are tried, some of which succeed. Others may fail. Syllabuses, subsequently, are subjected to review. Articles are written with the aim of communicating experience, courses are organised and lectures delivered. New books are published. Thus practice changes. The rate of change is, however, gentle and, for the most part, manageable. It is evolutionary in character and of necessity slow to reveal its characteristics. The question which may be posed is whether the pace of evolutionary change in education is sufficient to match or keep abreast of the evolutionary pace of change within society itself.

## Curriculum innovation: socialisation or social change?

Until fairly recently, the task of education was to transfer to young people the skills and knowledge possessed by adults. A communication, perhaps, of the cultural heritage. Such a concept, although not entirely dismissed, is not currently regarded as being adequate. There are various reasons which may be offered to account for its inadequacy. The most obvious is the explosion of knowledge, notably in the fields of mathematics and sci-

88

ence. Society, certainly in the northern half of the Earth, has become inured to publicised discoveries in science, engineering and medicine and the technological application of these to social existence. One is no longer amazed, although perhaps still somewhat bewildered or disorientated, by the profusion of such innovations. One may also become resentful of the effects of some of these technological changes on society and inclined to comment upon the quality of change and upon the ability of society to adjust to one wave of innovations before the next flood rushes in. Social standards are weakened. Such changes do tend to make for stress and strain which may manifest themselves in a variety of forms. In this light it is legitimate to ask whether education can respond adequately or swiftly enough to come to terms with the discomforts of an uneasy society. The scale of this discomfort is world-wide. There is a school of thought which subscribes to the view that education is incapable of making the required response. This is a matter for debate; conventional responses certainly may be inappropriate.

As a result, the forms of knowledge that are proffered are susceptible to a loss of esteem because such knowlege is judged to be impermanent, less useful to the consumer, the young person, and soon to be superseded as the pace of change accelerates. It follows, predictably, that it is less important that all that was previously regarded as worth perpetuating requires to be transmitted to young people. The emphasis in education then shifts from preserving the status quo to being more concerned with what might be or, indeed, what ought to be according to one's values and beliefs. Put another way, it may be less important to know something than to develop the necessary skills to be able to find out about something. This argument – which has a certain weakness if carried to excess – is nevertheless one which favours the notion of adaptability. The adaptable man or woman could be seen as being more appropriate to the character of society in the last two decades of the twentieth century, a period which will continue to be characterised by quantitative and qualitative change.

## Problems of curriculum innovation

In the case of the curriculum, however, the direction of change, as well as the mechanisms which facilitate the process of change, is crucial. Whether initiated 'from above' by central government, for instance, or 'from below' by teachers, some forms of innovation have in-built strengths and identifiable weaknesses. There is the risk, for instance, that downward change could, while speeding the introduction of major curricular reforms as an expression of the drive and convictions of policy-makers and educational administrators, be counter-productive in the long term. Mandated innovations are seldom accepted by teachers who do not fully understand their nature or sympathise entirely with the interpretation they put upon their purpose. No major curricular reform can hope to succeed unless it wins the support of the profession that will have to put it into practice. Equally, upward pressure for change from the teaching profession itself, while being more creative and with a potential to bring about lasting change, is frequently unco-ordinated. Rarely does an individual school find the means to integrate the results of good practice into the fabric of its own organisation and far less to communicate adequately such experience to other institutions or into the system of which it is part. Teachers who are encouraged to become innovators frequently encounter frustrations unless curricular and administrative structures are able to accommodate the outcomes of successful programmes of work. Part of the difficulty here may lie in reaching some consensus as to the criteria which can be used to determine the extent to which the curriculum is 'balanced'. In this regard, it is widely accepted that there are three sets of claims on the curriculum, stemming from social, epistemological and psychological approaches to it, and in curriculum planning none of them can be discounted.

What, then, should be the strategy of curriculum innovation, as opposed to the tactics, which would favour the proper establishment of education for international understanding within educational systems? Cognisant of the differences in philosophy towards the pace and direction of influencing curriculum change, is it possible to identify the means by which a comprehensive programme could be introduced and, in anticipation of this, to erect a structure capable of supporting such a programme of curriculum reform? These are key questions. In arriving at some answers to such questions, the role of teacher education is of central importance. To what extent teacher education in the contexts of initial and in-service training is able to accommodate education for international understanding is a further matter which requires some examination. An exemplar of curriculum innovation in these areas in the Strathclyde region of Scotland is offered as a possible model for efforts elsewhere.

## The capability of teacher education to accommodate education for international understanding

### (a) Initial teacher education

Whereas for a long time – and for many people – it was accepted without too much question that education was a once-for-all experience, confined to ten or less years in childhood and to the classroom, there is now a great deal of support in many parts of the world for the view that education should be a continuing process spread over almost the whole of life. Amongst the practical manifestations of this comparatively new philosophy are the development of pre-school education, the extension of all secondary education, the expansion of further education and the growing importance attached to vocational retraining at one or more stages of a person's working life. Naturally, this change in attitude is a reflection of changes in the purposes which education is expected to serve. It is unlikely that 'education for its own sake' was ever a firm conviction of a majority of educationists, but in so far as this objective did attract support it has suffered erosion of that support (in the UK at least) in favour of a more fundamentally orientated education affecting the development and acquisition of skills, problem-solving, decision-taking and leisure pursuits.

The character and design of contemporary courses in initial teacher education are, in like fashion, constructed on the assumption that the in-service provision for teachers will become – if it is not already – a right to which practising teachers are entitled at regular intervals during their careers. (The nature of such provision and the manner in which it could accommodate and promote education for international understanding is described and discussed in part (b) of this section.) Thus, of necessity, pre-service or initial training is an incomplete first stage of the concept of training which must be extended to cover the teacher's professional life from the time he or she enters college (or university institute of educational studies) until retirement.

It follows from this that the content of pre-service courses should be reconsidered and that some elements of teacher education might have to be undertaken on an in-service basis. So far as graduates of universities and specialised institutes of higher education are concerned, a one-session training course concentrates solely on professional aspects of teacher education. In the case of college diploma courses in which prospective teachers receive concurrent academic and professional training, the situation is different and the period of time available to train teachers longer. The ability of either situation to accommodate the recognised needs of 'the potential teacher of education for international understanding' will, of course, vary according to circumstances in different countries. It would be unusual, however, vested academic interests being what they tend to be with entrenched positions guarding the status quo, that a new curricular area such as 'education for international understanding', 'World Studies', etc would be accorded more than a peripheral position. Such an accommodation as this in underselling the potential contribution that could be made is not particularly helpful; indeed it is undesirable. In-service education, being more flexible in many ways, may hold out greater promise in terms of its ability to accept on the basis of a sound argument being put, a new course of training. Otherwise it is only when an existing course leading to a professional qualification is under review that proper opportunities arise. Thus (UNESCO 1979), 'Member States are invited to include the application of the Recommendation notably at the time when educational reforms are taking place and to make available appropriate financial, human and material resources.'

## (b) In-service education

The UNESCO report of March 1976 recognises in paragraph 45 that the objectives of in-service teacher training vary from country to country in accordance with needs, but then in subsequent paragraphs (46–50) makes some useful suggestions on the ways in which in-service programmes could be developed and practice improved. That part of the report of March 1976 may, with the benefit of hindsight, exemplify a problem already referred to earlier in this chapter, viz. the way in which the pace of change in educational affairs as elsewhere tends to undermine the thinking of a previous period of time. That section of the 1976 report on in-service training is more of a commentary on a situation which obtained in 1976 (and so accommodated the thinking of preceding years) than what the future ought to·hold. Once again, there is a need for greater precision in terms of the overall strategy in order to promote education for international understanding so as to produce the optimum end-result. In a more cryptic form, perhaps, the Sofia Report (UNESCO 1979), and still more recently, the *Report on Education for International Understanding in the Context of Teacher Education, Helsinki* (UNESCO 1980), point to the need for a special effort in this area. It is as well to reflect for a moment on what is meant by in-service education and what forms it assumes.

The forms that in-service education can assume are many. A comprehensive list ought to include amongst others:
1.  Conferences and workshops of varying lengths;
2.  The provision of locally based courses for teachers which may or may not be held during school hours. Many of such courses are either school-based or school-focused;
3.  Consultancy on the part of college staff able to provide a service to schools;
4.  Correspondence or 'distance-learning' courses of various types;
5.  The establishment of award-bearing courses which, either as part-time or full-time courses, entail the release of staff from schools.

A case for the provision of in-service training does not have to be put here. There is broad international agreement on the need for it since it should enable teacher participants 'to monitor, to shape and to improve his (or her) professional competence and keep abreast of current developments. In turn this must contribute significantly to improvement in the performance of schools or functional groups within a school.' (HMSO 1979.)

Other factors likely to affect the volume and scope of in-service education can in this paper be identified and left at that. These include, *inter alia*: the *demand* from teachers (notably those involved in curriculum innovation and development as well as those seeking improved qualifications), what *role* specific *agencies* should provide in such in-service training and by what forms of *organisation* and, finally, there is the question of what is the *catalytic effect of reports* such as those emanating from governments or from international agencies such as UNESCO. The example of the Jordanhill Project in International Understanding (JPIU) may as, concrete experience of a school-focused action-research project, offer the type of curricular model identified in the report of March 1976 (paragraph 49) as being potentially useful.

## The Jordanhill Project in International Understanding

In September 1976 copies of the 1974 UNESCO *Recommendation Concerning Education for International Understanding* were sent by the Scottish Education

Department (SED) together with SED Circular 962 to official correspondents of colleges of education, LEAs and other bodies in Scotland. The SED circular, like its counterpart in England and Wales (Circular 9/76), invited a response in terms of measures taken to implement the recommendation.

The response of Jordanhill College, with the assured support of the Department of Education of Strathclyde Regional Council, was to put proposals to fund a major research and educational development project to the Advisory Committee on Development Education (ACDE) at the then Ministry of Overseas Development (ODM). Simultaneously, Jordanhill applied to the UK National Commission for UNESCO at ODM to become an institution linked to the UNESCO Associated Schools Project, which is a world-wide network of schools and colleges concerned with the promotion of education for international understanding. Subsequently, in the autumn of 1977, the ACDE gave approval for the allocation of financial resources, permitting the project, which relates closely to the 1974 UNESCO Recommendation, to begin.

The participation of secondary schools in the project since it began in 1977 has allowed emphasis to be placed on the development of approaches to the new Scottish Certificate of Education (SCE) 'O' Grade syllabus in Modern Studies[1] and, notably, the component known as the Special Study which is subject to internal assessment; and on the design of approaches to international understanding and their application in junior mixed-ability Modern Studies classes. The construction of interdisciplinary courses on topics appropriate to international understanding was envisaged as an optional and additional activity. In this instance, the core subject would again be Modern Studies, but attempts to engage the active participation of teachers of other subjects would be encouraged. Particular attention would be allocated to the needs of children with learning difficulties.

Since 1977, working groups of practising teachers from secondary schools, college staff and education officers from bodies concerned with development education have prepared and attempted to validate teaching programmes and materials on a wide range of topics whose origins are those of the 1974 UNESCO *Recommendation*, viz. 'Human Rights' (Apartheid, Minorities, Terrorism); 'Conflict'; 'Co-operation'; 'Interdependence'; 'The Development Process'; 'The Emergent Nation' (with special emphasis on Botswana and Jamaica) and 'Choices for the Future' (see Figs 5, 6 and 7). It was the intention of the Project committee that once the availability of programmes and such materials was assured, contact with additional schools and groups of teachers would be made to disseminate validated materials in order to generate enthusiasm and commitment to education for international understanding.

The latter stage in the project's programme was to harness audio-visual media in order to promote a wider interest in education for international understanding in schools and elsewhere. In particular, on a college basis, as part of the UNESCO Associated Schools Project, closed-circuit television (CCTV) programmes have been produced to extend effective development education throughout the secondary curriculum in Scotland.

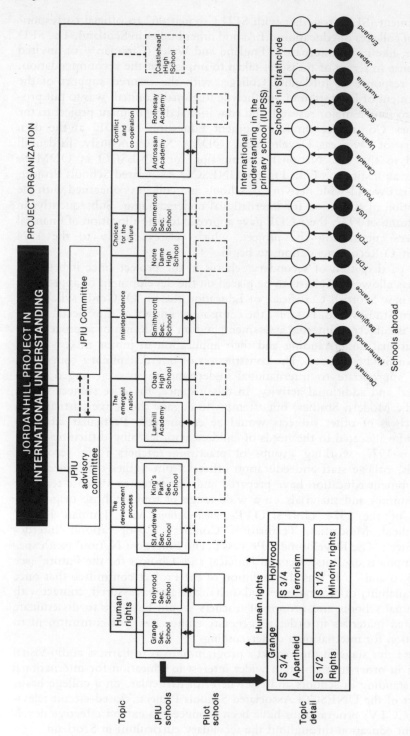

Fig. 5  Jordanhill Project in International Understanding; project organisation (after J. Dunlop, Jordanhill College of Education, Glasgow)

94

Over the three years since October 1977, when the inaugural meeting of teachers and college staff participating in the project took place at Jordanhill, twice-termly planning and policy-formation meetings held during the school day have been interspersed with visits by college tutors to the JPIU schools.

As a social and environmental course with a contemporary focus Modern Studies has been criticised by those who point to its dubious antecedents and also argue that it requires from young people an approach to questions of value and social ethics which only experience and maturity can bring. Its lack of 'pedigree' is of no real consequence; whatever it may lack in this regard is amply compensated by an irrepressible hybrid vigour. The criticism that Modern Studies requires from pupils a wisdom – particularly in social self-consciousness – which cannot properly be expected of them, can only be tested in practice. Certainly, some of the SCE examination questions posed to boys and girls of 16, 17 and 18 years of age have not yet produced answers from the grey heads of diplomacy, political science and political economy, and there is a case for avoiding the impression that there are answers to be found in textbooks and classrooms which elude leaders of nations and of thought. But there is also a case for bringing people into contact with the scope for social choice and the difficulties inherent in exercising such choice early rather than late – or not at all. Opinions harden quickly. Social attitudes once formed are slow to change and whatever can be done early in their lives to help individuals think rationally about social and political issues will bring a greater benefit than equivalent efforts later – when barriers of bias and bigotry will be even more difficult to overcome.

The syllabus in Modern Studies stresses on-going and emerging issues at home and abroad. In dealing with matters of concern such as the role of government, industrial relations, news presentation in the mass media, Britain's relationship with Europe, Great Power rivalry, race relations, the problems of developing countries, world population and food supply, the impact of technological change on society and the problems of the global environment, the content of Modern Studies is clearly the subject-matter of this day and age and mirrors those listed in the UNESCO Recommendation. The range of topics in the syllabus impinge upon each other at many points and the young person who develops an understanding of this has learned a most important aspect of a modern, complex society – an aspect which individuals and whole societies have at times overlooked and paid very heavily for the omission. The relationships between economic, ecological, social and political factors in a local, national and world community illustrate the point and are central to the subject-matter of Modern Studies as it is at the present time.

Teachers have given freely of their time and a considerable amount of creative and purposeful activity has been generated over the period. Educational spin-offs and unpredicted bonuses have been both numerous and significant. The BBC in Scotland, on the recommendation of the Schools Broadcasting Council, agreed to produce five VHF radio programmes in 1980–81 to complement JPIU materials. During the academic year 1979–80

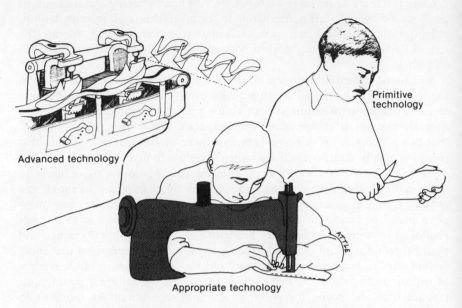

Fig. 6   Appropriate technology and the shoemaking industry (after P. Attle, Jordanhill College of Education, Glasgow)

a new and parallel pilot project: 'International Understanding in the Primary School' began and in a comparatively short period of operation achieved some noteworthy curricular achievements (Appendix A). As a result, plans for a modified and extended project likely to last until 1982 were drafted. This new project sought and received the co-operation of national commissions for UNESCO in specified member states in the European region and with a structure which takes account of differing education systems in the four countries, aims to document and report upon achievements with upper primary classes.

As a result of the activity which has been described in outline, many of the constraints to the advancement of education for international understanding have been tackled and in many cases removed. It has been this same activity in the in-service context which has more recently begun to influence curricular policy in the area of initial training alluded to in part (a) of this section.

It is an extremely difficult thing to say what was the precise combination of circumstances which helped such curricular momentum to build up in connection with the Jordanhill Project. A consideration of the alchemy is, however, important. Key ingredients from the time the *UNESCO Recommendation*[2] was published undoubtedly were:
1. The co-operative partnership between a large and autonomous institution concerned with all forms of teacher education and the local education authority in which it is located;

Fig. 7   Multilateral aid (after P. Attle, Jordanhill College of Education, Glasgow)

2.  Support 'from the top' – both from the SED which gave considerable professional support and advice and from the funding body, the ODM;
3.  The existence of the subject Modern Studies which, unique to the Scottish education system, had established a firm place for itself in the secondary school over a period of about twenty years and was eminently suited to tackle those issues identified in paragraph 18 of the 1974 UNESCO *Recommendation*. Post graduate teacher training at colleges such as Jordanhill guaranteed the professional competence of teachers to handle economic, political and other sometimes controversial social issues in the classroom;
4.  A cadre of essentially young, potentially innovative and well–motivated teachers who recognised the importance of the work they were to undertake voluntarily to their pupils, their subject and to the education process;
5.  Commitment to the ideal of education for international understanding from a small but significant group of staff at Jordanhill College whose co-ordinating and servicing role enabled the alchemy to work its particular magic.

School-focused in-service is a most important key in the coherent school we ought to be working towards in the context of education for international understanding as well as other areas, but these courses are notably difficult to devise, run and sustain without adequate structural provision and funding.

The strategy for the longer term which will continue to be dominated by short in-service courses such as workshops (or methodological aspects of international education such as human rights for instance) or school-focused activity in some form may have to take greater account of the need for an increase in award-bearing courses. Such courses would have as their main purpose one of helping prepare teachers to perform their professional duties more effectively. If education for international understanding consolidates, as has been suggested, its curricular base within the social subjects, then it is possible to recognise the benefits which would accrue from the construction and presentation of advanced level modular courses on issues such as those in paragraph 18 of the *Recommendation*. Whether by the application of distance-learning techniques or by sandwich-style in-service courses requiring the release of teachers from school duties for specified short periods so as to attend classes at a national or regional centre, it would seem possible that an important step in the creation of the teacher of education for international understanding could be taken. Particularly if member states were able to construct a modular system of courses with the backing of UNESCO this would go a considerable way towards dealing with the vast range of important world issues in the *Recommendation* and, by a credit system, enable teachers to take modular units appropriate to areas in which they lack academic and professional confidence. The creation of a teacher equipped with an armoury of competencies and capable of teaching in a multidisciplinary manner is what is needed above all.

These activities which have been described and which have an application within the area of in-service education had an eventual influence upon internal Jordanhill College policy towards education for international understanding. During 1980 a subcommittee of the academic board of the college was established to find out the amount of teaching that went on within the college in the area of 'education for international understanding' both in terms of specific undertakings and on assessment of the degree of permeation in everyday teaching.

After several months of deliberation its report was presented in November 1980 to the Board of Studies. A conclusion reached was that present initiatives were insufficient and that there were no grounds for complacency. As a result, Jordanhill College of Education boasts a Standing Committee on Education for International Understanding with a remit:

(a) to foster and encourage placements of students and staff outside the United Kingdom;
(b) to liaise with agencies such as UNESCO, UNICEF and the Council of Europe in order to promote the college's known role as an institution concerned with international education;
(c) to co-ordinate and to develop education for international understanding within the college.

As a result of this key decision, taken after three years of effort in the field of in-service teacher education, it may be legitimately claimed that one of the last remaining links in 'the pernicious circle of neglect' has been removed.

## Postscript

In a search for the means to promote most effectively international understanding one considers and takes into account several possibilities. The analogy with civil engineering comes readily to mind whereby foundations are established, functional structures erected and bridges built to span the offensive chasm which separates rhetoric and action. As one becomes professionally involved in the cause of international education, strategies set in the long term have an increasingly greater attraction than tactics likely to produce only an ephemeral and a superficial appeal. The experience of the Jordanhill Project is that qualitative progress in this crucially important educational field is most likely to be made when formal recognition and due priority is given to the need for professionally qualified teachers able to practise their multidisciplinary craft in an accommodating educational environment. Within secondary education, the manner in which the subject, Modern Studies, has enabled the desired curricular changes and new emphases to come about may be regarded as a model for efforts elsewhere.

## Appendix A

### Summary of the experience of schools participating in the pilot project 'International Understanding in the Primary School, Scotland'

*General aspects*

(a) Some schools had been able to communicate with their 'twin' schools in English whereas the majority had not;

(b) Some schools (a minority)had had a very positive experience in terms of a regular flow of correspondence and materials whilst others had not;

(c) Two schools had been able to make direct contact with the teaching staff and children at the linked school whereas others, because of factors such as distance and cost, of necessity placed reliance upon the effectiveness of a postal service;

(d) Materials from schools in overseas countries took a great variety of forms and varied enormously in educational value;

(e) The frequency at which such materials arrived varied greatly from packages which arrived every three to four weeks to the receipt of one letter in nine months.

*Specific aspects*

1. The inability of children in countries to speak, read or to communicate in English had not, contrary to earlier fears, proved to be a problem. (It was an advantage, however, to have at least one member of staff in the overseas school who could understand English in order to foster teacher–to–teacher exchanges in correspondence);

2. Teacher–directed material had been less frequently obtained (or sent) than children–directed material. In this latter context the range of items mentioned was wide-ranging and had included Christmas and Easter cards, handicrafts and artwork, photographs, audio-tape recordings of

songs and music, samples of advertisements, illustrated shopping lists from supermarkets, local newspapers, carrier bags and foreign language versions of 'Auld Lang Syne';

3. The opportunity of developing a method of how to look at other cultures in other countries had presented itself without giving sufficient time to resolve that problem;

4. The vast range of materials received by some schools offered a good opportunity to teach education for international understanding across the curriculum (e.g. in mathematics and in language arts. In the latter instance, Scottish children were noticeably more careful in written expression, knowing that their work was intended to convey a favourable impression of themselves and their country to foreigners);

5. The need to communicate an impression of their school or neighbourhood (or national) environment to others had developed in Scottish children a greater understanding of that environment;

6. Numerous opportunities had presented themselves over the previous eight months to broaden children's awareness of other cultures and environments (e.g. by visits which took class groups away from their locality; by having foreign visitors [students and others] come into the classroom). As a result of these developments, there was general agreement amongst those present that a real world existed beyond, say, Easterhouse in Glasgow, and this was having a beneficial effect upon children's attitudes towards 'things foreign' and things remote from their direct experience;

7. The school year proved inadequate to achieve the stated aims of the project which had been agreed by project schools in September 1979. Ideally, work ought to go on over a two-year period in order that the project should reach a satisfactory outcome. There were implications, too, for those secondary schools to which the children would transfer beyond P 7 (11–12 year olds). Some IUPSS schools (International Understanding in the Primary School, Scotland) had already established worthwhile links with secondary schools in their area, notably in having access to language laboratories and in having the help of modern languages teachers in translating correspondence. It was generally felt that some attempt might be made to ensure as far as it was possible to do that the momentum and interests built up in the primary school to foster education for international understanding should not be lost at the point of transfer to secondary education;

8. The frequency of deliveries (and despatches) of letters and parcels was not so important as knowing roughly *when* these might be due to arrive. One school had received a parcel of material at frequent intervals (three to four weeks), others once per term or even less frequently. The uncertainty affecting the arrival of materials – and to some extent the nature of these – created some curriculum management problems but, more than anything, dashed children's hopes and expectations;

9. Where there had been a frequent – if irregular – flow of material children's motivation and application was high. This was a point on which

all who attended the workshops were in agreement, but even where the deliveries were spasmodic at least one teacher commented that classwork on materials to be sent abroad had been enhanced by the purposeful training in research and communication skills. There was, however, a need to engage in correspondence with the teacher of the overseas school in order to co-ordinate professional activities and to provide some structure for possible future collaboration;

10. Quite unforeseen developments, stemming in part from the project, affected children's interests and interpretations of foreign affairs and events as portrayed on television and in the press (e.g. the siege in May 1980 of the Iranian Embassy in London). This was seen as a spin-off which, although not directly linked to the 'twinning' of schools in Strathclyde and those abroad, had implications for the broader aims, in terms of media presentation, of a project intended to promote education for international understanding.

A conclusion reached was that the experience gained in the pilot project ought to enable a new project, spread over two years, to be planned and implemented.

## Notes

1. Modern Studies can be defined as (Dunlop 1977, p. 163):

   a multi-disciplinary study of contemporary society. It deploys skills, concepts and knowledge drawn selectively from the social subjects to focus on social, economic and political issues of concern to individuals and groups at local, national and international levels.

   Through the study of contemporary society and issues, Modern Studies aims (a) to develop knowledge and understanding of contemporary society, its changing nature, its institutions and the influences acting upon them; (b) to develop the practical and intellectual skills necessary for the study and intelligent discussion of contemporary issues; (c) to encourage the formation of considered attitudes of an intellectual, humanitarian, social and political nature; and thus contribute to the candidate's preparation for full and active membership of society.

2. Copies of all UNESCO documents may be obtained from the UK National Commission for UNESCO, Overseas Development Administration, Eland House, Stag Place, London SWIE 5DH.

# Chapter 7    Barry Dufour
## West African study cruises

During the Christmas period of 1974 and of 1977, two West African study cruises were undertaken by sixth formers and teachers and were somewhat unique in their conception and organisation. It seemed the ultimate challenge to consider taking over 400 sixth formers to West Africa by air, sea and land with the object of providing an educational experience that was to be enjoyable and serious and to involve hundreds of people in the overall planning and execution of the enterprise (Owen *et al.* 1976).

Making it possible for pupils to learn about the world by experiencing it directly, as opposed to vicariously in the classroom, is a much-discussed but rarely practised educational goal. School courses which give an important place to pupil involvement in the local community or schools that arrange regular trips or bring in outside speakers as the basis of a more meaningful social education, are few in number. The restraints and administrative burdens of organising these kinds of activities generally overwhelm all but the keenest of teachers. So the idea of taking several hundred students, rather than a few dozen, on a journey, was challenge enough, but when the destination was to be the continent of Africa, and not the local factory or museum, the challenge assumed really major proportions. Yet the cruises took place. I shall describe and assess the two visits as if they were one because they varied only slightly in organisation and were identical in conception, but I shall refer to each trip specifically where there are unique events to recount.

The two West African cruises described here were originated by a few staff at the School of Education of the University of Leicester, but especially by John Baker who became the key organiser and inspiration of the whole venture. They were based on the idea of using the normal educational cruises run by British India (P & O Lines) but with a dramatic adaptation in their planning, operation and destination. Accordingly, British India (BI) was approached and agreed to our booking two-thirds of the pupil places *en bloc* on SS *Nevasa* on the first cruise and SS *Uganda* on the second in 1977. The bookings had to be made over a year in advance and the plan was to visit the countries that BI usually went to at Christmas, such as Sierra Leone, Gambia, Senegal and Morocco, with an average of two days moored at each coastal capital city so that trips could be made.

The planning team, known as the Central Team (mainly Leicester teachers and university staff), began operations two years in advance of each cruise. The wider party, who all participated in the planning and educational preparation before the cruise, was made up of – for West Africa '74

– 582 sixth formers, teachers from non-Leicester and Leicestershire schools (the total number of all teachers was 43, coming from schools in the Leicester area, London and elsewhere) and 50 postgraduate student teachers from Leicester University School of Education and Goldsmiths' College, London. There were also a few staff from other universities. The total for West Africa '74 was 688 persons. Over many months the Central Team negotiated with BI on various aspects of the cruise, including the desire to run our own shore excursions and to operate our own special shipboard timetable which would only partially link in with the normal school programme on board.

## Aims

The main aims of the West African study cruises were:
1. To enable sixth formers (and teachers and others) to gain first-hand awareness of Third World conditions in the context of study as a contribution towards understanding human existence in the global environment.
2. To make a first-hand examination of aspects of West African life against a background of study of topics and approaches from geography, history, and social sciences, biology and other subjects.
3. To enable everyone to gain experience of community living, to mix with new people and to see new places together.

## Preparation and planning

These aims were pursued through a variety of educational and organisational arrangements which took place before, during and after each cruise. Study booklets were produced for everyone by the Central Team and other teachers involved for use before and during the cruise. The titles included: 'People in West Africa', 'Religion in West Africa', 'West Africa: some basic facts', 'Housing in West Africa', 'Villages and Towns', 'Politics and Nationalism', 'Aid', 'Animals and Plants of West Africa', 'Manding Art and Craft', 'West African Literature'. In all the participating schools, in normal lesson times and during lunch-times and after school, these booklets, as they became available, and books, films and maps gathered together by teachers, were introduced progressively beginning over a year before the actual cruise was to take place. The educational work in each school was combined with regular meetings to sort out the constant administration that needed to be dealt with. Therefore, although each cruise was a superb holiday and an experience of a lifetime, its serious and intensive educational foundation was paramount throughout the enterprise and, of course, continued on the cruise itself with regular lectures, discussions and the issuing of additional special resources on each of the ports and countries we visited.

The Central Team met monthly to make decisions on every possible aspect of the cruise including the route, shore visits, educational preparation in schools, shipboard school work and activities, general administration, money, inoculations, passports and a thousand other items, educational and practical, all leading up to the final meetings before departure which were more concerned with pressing issues such as arrangements for the coaches to get everyone to Gatwick Airport to catch the chartered planes that would fly us all to Morocco. The participating schools away from the main Leicester/Leicestershire party, in places such as London, the West Midlands and elsewhere, had their own meetings and plans but they were in constant communication with the Leicester group at the centre of operations. After every Central Team meeting all the teachers would hold meetings with their sixth formers in order to relay the relevant details. By the time each cruise took place, all the participants knew a considerable amount about West Africa, the countries, their way of life and the problems of development in the Third World.

## The countries visited

To join the cruise ship, anchored at Ceuta (the Spanish enclave in Morocco), everyone flew on specially chartered planes from Gatwick to Tangier and took coaches through Morocco into Ceuta. Most people were exhausted at the end of this journey to meet the ship. Some had been travelling twenty-four hours:by car to the coach pick-up points in Leicester or London or elsewhere, by coach to Gatwick, by plane to Tangier and then on to coaches again for a fascinating but hot and dusty ride through Moroccan villages to Ceuta.

The itineraries for West Africa '74 and West Africa '77 varied only slightly and were as follows:

| 1974 | 1977 |
|---|---|
| Ceuta | Ceuta |
| Arrecife (on Lanzarote, one of the Canary Islands) | Casablanca |
| | Las Palmas |
| Freetown (Sierra Leone) | Freetown |
| Banjul (Gambia) | Banjul |
| Dakar (Senegal) | Dakar |
| Las Palmas (on Gran Canaria, one of the Canary Islands) | Ceuta – fly back from Tangier after a coach trip from Ceuta, through |
| Casablanca (Morocco) – fly to Gatwick from here | Morocco to Tangier Airport |

On West Africa '74, the cruise from Ceuta to West Africa and back to Casablanca took sixteen days with nine of these days, including Christmas Day, at sea. The longest period at sea was of course the journey, either way, between North Africa or the Canary Islands and West Africa, usually four days at sea. We spent an average of two days in each of the main ports of call: Freetown, Banjul and Dakar. As can be seen from the itinerary, there were slight variations at the Morocco end and elsewhere on the two cruises; for example, on West Africa '74, we were able to spend half a day on the volcanic island of Lanzarote. On both cruises, we spent a day at Las

Palmas (on the return in '74 and on the outward journey in 1977). This provided a striking contrast with our time in Africa. Our day in Las Palmas
was engaged in visits and meeting local pupils and teachers, but it also
allowed us the opportunity to witness the duty-free package-holiday antics
of visitors from the UK, West Germany and Scandinavia. This contrasted
starkly with the poverty, dignity and tradition of West Africa.

## The shore visits and fieldwork

The shore visits were the main objective of the cruise rationale for West
Africa '74 and '77, whereas BI's regular educational cruises placed a higher
value on shipboard life and activities. Consequently, much of our time
before the cruise and during it focused on the shore-party visits. The shore
parties were made up from mixed groups of sixth formers from different
schools. This meant that they got to know new people and shared a wider
experience than if the shore visits consisted of single-school parties. The
parties contained an average of twelve to fifteen pupils (from anything
between four to six schools) and also included one or two postgraduate
student teachers (who acted as assistant party leaders) and one or two staff
(called party leaders). In Freetown, Banjul and Dakar, the shore parties met
and spent time with African sixth formers, postgraduates and teachers. The
immense planning for this had begun over a year before each cruise took
place and had been arranged as the result of Central Team staff making use
of contacts they already had with African schools, colleges or universities.
These encounters were extremely important and were amongst the major
personal and educational successes of the West African cruises. There were
many exchanges of addresses after sixth formers and staff from the UK had
enjoyed the company of their African counterparts, which had in some
instances included visiting their homes and meeting their families. Some
West Africans came on board ship during our stay and entertained us or
were hosted by us. Some of these close contacts are still maintained today.

In addition to these personal contacts, there were more formally organised educational tasks and activities, some of which included our African
counterparts. There were town trails, village surveys amd many visits
either of a general nature or with a specialist slant, but all of them entailed
close examination of African life. Each such visit was assisted by the background briefing notes on each port of call and country which included maps
and general information.

## Freetown

In Freetown, as elsewhere, visits were made to markets, mosques, churches
and craft shops in the town, but there were also trips into the coastal and
inland villages where the people made us very welcome. We spent time on
the beaches and in the forests. One group visited the village of Leicester,
near Freetown. For the 1974 visit, Freetown had formed a special committee to plan our stay; Sierra Leone radio broadcast a message asking

everyone to offer friendship and assistance to the visitors from SS *Nevasa*; the Minister of Education gave an address to some of the visitors whilst others were welcomed by the Deputy Mayor of Freetown. Most of us enjoyed following the 'Freetown town trail' devised by a Leicestershire teacher (Smalley 1975) and consisting of a route map with questions to answer and suggestions on what to look out for. It began with the advice to 'absorb the sights, smells, sounds of the area. Sketches and drawings can be made, poems and prose compositions written, tape recordings made, paintings created . . .'. The trail meandered by some of the most interesting groups of people, streets, activities and buildings we had ever seen. The impact of Kissy Street was especially dramatic, offering us the sight of countless roadside market stalls, the noise of hundreds of brightly dressed Africans talking, laughing and bartering, and the contradictory smells of the fruit for sale and the open drains. It was not difficult to follow the advice of the town trail!

British India also arranged special trips, activities and tours. In Freetown, these included an organised visit (for all passengers) to the two-mile Lumley Beach where we all swam in the incredibly warm and buoyant sea, followed later by a display by national and local dance troupes, with acrobats and drummers pounding out complex rhythms. However, one of the drawbacks of these massed visits and entertainments, whilst enjoyable, was that they presented us to local people as superficial tourist-spectators clicking our cameras by the hundred at everything and everyone.

Nothing will ever erase our recollections of our arrival in Freetown in the early hours of the morning. The ship anchored well out of the town to await the pilot to lead the ship to its mooring. From the decks and cabins, we were acutely aware of the wet and muggy tropical atmosphere and over in the distance was Freetown, our first sighting of sub Saharan Black Africa, spreading up the hillside and covered in mist from the morning dew and the smoke of outdoor charcoal fires as people prepared breakfast.

## Gambia

The next visit was to Gambia, up the coast from Sierra Leone. Here the ship was played into its mooring to music from a local military band waiting on the jetty to greet us, along with dozens of cars and buses which were to take us on the first of our trips into Gambia. We were all intrigued by the economic and geographical features of this tiny country, no more than a strip of land on either side of the Gambia River, and much of it swamp with a high intensity of mosquitoes, so much so that the death-rate for white people many years ago earned it the title of 'the White Man's Grave'. The simple houses and the open drainage, useful in tropical areas but with obvious risks of disease, created a vivid impression on us. Such facts as the high infant mortality rate and the number of doctors for the whole nation (twenty in 1974) were a powerful lesson on Third World conditions. We had two days in Gambia spending the time between walks around Banjul and some planned trips to inland areas, including industrial and agricultural areas such as a rice territory organised by the Republic of China as a form of aid to assist Gambia in its attempts to move away from dependence on one exportable product – groundnuts (also the main product in Sierra Leone).

On the second cruise I was able to achieve something, alone, on an impulse, which would have been a superb adventure for the sixth formers if I had known beforehand that my little expedition would be less precarious than I had imagined. I left the ship early one morning determined to cross the Gambia River and travel inland to Juffureh, the famed village of Alex Haley's Kunte Kinte in *Roots*. I met a Canadian teacher on the ferry who was accompanied by half a dozen school pupils, all with the same intention of getting to the village, so we teamed up and hired a minibus to take us inland. On the way, we saw vultures, monkeys, an alligator pool and we stopped to look at giant anthills. On reaching the village, we were made very welcome in spite of an increasing flow of tourists, especially Black Americans flying in to try and trace their own roots. I met the actual old lady who had spoken to Alex Haley about his roots. She was a *griot*, a kind of historian in the oral tradition. She posed for pictures clutching a valued copy of the US magazine, *People*, the front cover which displayed her with Alex Haley. I spent the remainder of the day in the village school where I was made very welcome by the headmaster, his wives and one of the teachers. I was proudly shown what was described as the library: a wooden building with no furniture, bookshelves or books – there was no money for such additional refinements.

## Senegal

We left the Gambia and sailed for Senegal, spending another two days here, with the ship moored in Dakar, the beautiful capital of once French Senegal. Again there were a variety of visits and activities, many planned by the Central Team in co-operation with local contacts. Some of the party went to fishing villages, others elsewhere, the rest of the main group spent the day in Dakar. The next day, the programme was reversed so that everyone had a variety of experiences whilst there.

One of the most significant visits for all of us was the trip out to the island of Gorée which was a major centre for the slave trade in previous centuries. This encounter had a profound effect on all of us as we walked round the slave house which contained the slave dealer's quarters upstairs and tiny cells below either side of an open arched door leading straight out to the Atlantic Ocean.

More general impressions we gained were of the remarkable mix of races, cultures and religions and how these dispersed themselves geographically in Dakar. Near President Senghor's palace were the administrative buildings and police headquarters, no doubt organised with French efficiency by the former colonialists. Here were the Black and White élites and the mixtures of Catholic and Muslim faiths. Sleek Citroën saloon cars glided into driveways and garages whose doors were invariably operated by remote control. Contrast this with the modern ghetto for the Black working class especially constructed on the edge of Dakar. Dakar was the most obviously opulent of the West African ports we visited and, as a result, some of the cabin passengers from the ship were pleased to have arrived at 'Paris-by-the-sea' so that they could buy expensive perfumes and enjoy the more sophisticated shopping and night-life that Dakar offered. For the other cabin passengers, the sixth formers and staff, their pleasure was derived from different sources – from the mysterious beauty of the West African sculptures in the Ifan Museum to the excitement of the markets.

## Morocco

Our time in the Muslim world of Morocco was not as distinct as many had imagined. Although everyone had read beforehand about the powerful and extensive influence of Islam on Black West Africa, it was a surprise to many to witness the pervasiveness of the religion and its associated way of life in all of the West African countries we visited. However, Muslim North Africa was different. In Casablanca, for example, the vibrancy of the place was noticeable, as was the stark contrast between the sophisticated modern buildings and city centre compared with the traditional *medina* part of the city. All the passengers enjoyed buying souvenirs from Morocco because there was such a choice of attractive artwork and craft material at such reasonable prices, ranging through the leather goods, brasswork, clothing, slippers and shoes to the beautiful filigree jewellery.

Tetuan was the most striking place we visited because it was so visually medieval and untouched by 'progress'. The sixth formers were fascinated as they walked through the narrow streets jostled by donkeys and the Moroccan people dressed in their djellabas, with the women in purdah. Our behaviour had to be modified for our visit. All girls were told to dress with special modesty because there would be comments from Moroccan men – and there were. One teacher was offered a camel in exchange for one of the sixth-form girls! We were told to be on the lookout for pickpockets and to refuse offers of drugs for purchase. Mostly everyone was tolerant of the constant attention from street vendors persuading them to buy things and sometimes holding on to them or dropping articles in their bags so they would have to stop and feel obliged to engage in barter. I think the vast majority of sixth formers enjoyed this and some became brilliant at winning a bargain by clever bartering.

Two other visits were to leave a lasting impression on us. One was the long trip out to the mountains and remote villages by coach, never before done by tourists apparently, and the other was the visit to Rabat to see the royal palace and other buildings.

## Life on board

Since most of the time was spent at sea, it is just as important to reflect on the shipboard routines and events. These were a major part of the total

West African cruise organisation, although there were many unplanned and fascinating incidents to place on record. For example, just as we had come to learn about the rich–poor divide in the global village, so we encountered it also on the ship.

The daily life on board was very much governed by who you were, i.e. your status. To begin with, all the pupils on the ship were berthed well below decks in dormitories which were adequate but basic. The first introduction to this and the communal living shocked a few of the students and there were tears, but these reactions disappeared after the first couple of days on board. The pupils had their common rooms, discos, deck games and the lecture theatre on the main deck, but below were their sleeping quarters, the cafeteria and the classrooms. In contrast, all the adults were cabin passengers, whether paying the minimum sum of £500 for the cruise or teachers who all went free. The teachers had cabins, usually for three to four people, and the use of all the excellent facilities such as the ballroom, the bars (open till 2 a.m.) and first-class catering consisting of five-course meals with constant waiter service. The luxurious privilege of our life on board compared with that of the pupils or contrasted with that of the average food consumption of the countries we were visiting, embarrassed all of us and caused envy and gentle derision from the pupils. But the lessons in hierarchy – an added and unforeseen educational nourishment – did not end here. The crew were, of course, divided into officers and men: non-commissioned officers were not allowed to come on the cabin decks. But at the bottom of the ladder were the Asian stewards (from Goa on the 1974 cruise) whose presence on the ship had its origins in the British India Shipping Company's links with the Indian subcontinent during the last 150 years. These stewards waited at the tables, brought morning tea – we were always awakened at 6.45 a.m. on both cruises – and ran baths and did the laundry and other menial tasks on the ship. The British Empire was therefore still very much alive until the end of the 1974 cruise when SS *Nevasa* was taken out of commission and broken up due to rising fuel costs and its age, although many of those features continued on the SS *Uganda*. All of us on the ship were aware of the irony of these divisions which added to our reflections on the Third World.

Related to this were the problems created by the different authority structures on the ship. The 1974 cruise was especially memorable because the attitudes of the ship's educational team to sixth formers and the more liberal Leicester team were very much at odds. The tensions on ship were increased by the fact that we were trying this venture for the first time and only slowly finding our way. There were problems of communication. Furthermore, the gloom that was cast over the whole ship by the announcement during the cruise that this was to be SS *Nevasa*'s last voyage did not help matters. To all the ship's company, this message from head office whilst at sea came like a thunderbolt. The disagreement about rules eventually involved the captain of the ship in discussions with the leaders from the respective groups. There were none of these problems on the second cruise.

Life on board was generally more interesting and positive in its orientation than these incidents would suggest. All of us, staff and students, had a well-spaced daily routine. The ship was a floating school consisting of a tiered lecture theatre for talks and films; it had classrooms, a games area, a cafeteria, school office, a hospital and common rooms. It was staffed by a headmaster, two teachers, a matron and her staff. The school day was divided into four activities which took up six forty-five minute periods made up of main lectures, classroom sessions, deck games and private study. Everyone was involved in the programme which was very much a mix of work and leisure and administration such as checking maps and currency before each port of call. There were daily briefing sessions. In the evenings, we had feature films and a disco on deck. Some of the staff, young and old, enjoyed joining the students in this entertainment. Dancing on the open deck, lit by the coloured bulbs of the disco and the stars in the clear tropical sky, will be memories some of us will cherish. For most staff, there were the more sedate attractions of the ballroom, bars, writing room and lounges.

The Christmas period, with Christmas Day at sea, was a joyous occasion, helped along by good food, parties and entertainments. The students put on a variety of shows and fancy dress competitions for the staff and other cabin passengers. At Christmas dinner the captain and staff served the students. Obviously all of us felt sad being away from family and friends at Christmas, but these feelings were soon dispelled, lost in the revelries and communal spirit of Christmas. Perhaps some readers will be shocked at these admissions of good times had by all. I make no apology for this. Since most of our time was spent on the ship and since the Leicester group had to join in with the usual schedule and routines of the P & O educational cruises, it would have been churlish to adopt a high moral tone and disregard all opportunities to enjoy each other's company and friendship: one of the key aims of the cruise was to participate positively in communal living and co-operation, not just at Christmas but throughout the cruise. For example, amongst the staff and students there were many differing attitudes about discipline, education and political perspectives towards the Third World, yet we did, in a successful manner, learn from each other and were able to live with and benefit from contrasting viewpoints which sometimes infuriated us individually.

## Evaluation

Looking back on the cruises, it seems fair to say that both had positive and negative features. Firstly, the notion of the cruise needs to be examined. Since most of our time was spent at sea, the shipboard activities figured large. We enjoyed ourselves socially and ate well, the latter fact a constant source of reflection, irony and embarrassment (although not enough to force us on to a diet of bread and cheese!). But what must be emphasised is the persistent and overriding dominance of the educational programme which took up every day, except Christmas Day. Furthermore, the preplanning, the on-board programme and the shore visit system made the Leicester West African cruises dramatically different from the usual P & O educational cruise. Generally, few schools arrange the kind of intensive briefing that was a hallmark of the Leicester concept and few schools produce the kind of educational resources that we did. Few schools take sixth formers – most are much younger pupils. On shore, with only the most rudimentary preparation, children and teachers tour round the ports of call in the Mediterranean or Baltic, the major routes of the P & O cruises. Our approach was to provide the most thorough preparation, cruise briefing and even follow-up: we held a public West Africa Exhibition and social event at the University of Leicester in March 1978 which attracted large numbers of people locally and was attended by cruise participants of West Africa '77 from many parts of the country. It could be said that the two cruises supported a continuing educational programme which lasted from 1972 to 1978.

One tangible example of the educational impact was the account written for *Teaching Geography* by a few of a group of thirty-three sixth formers from eighteen different schools who, on 27 December 1977, went on a field trip to the Kasewe Hills in Sierra Leone. The trip was organised and led by a member of the Central Team, Patrick Bailey of the University of Leicester School of Education, with the help of Des Bowden of the Geography Department at Njala University College, Sierra Leone. Detailed briefing took place on Boxing Day and on the following day everyone was taken by coach and deposited in small groups at eight different villages. Each group studied their village for the whole day using carefully prepared questions and with the help of undergraduates from Njala who acted as interpreters. The personal accounts of the sixth formers on this expedition have been published in two places (Bailey 1979), and I suggest readers go to these sources, but what is impressive about these descriptions is the extent of the learning from these encounters and the acute observations that were made in a wide geographical context. They describe their meeting with chiefs, the chattering children excited at the visit, the welcome and hospitality given by the adult villagers, some of whom had spent a week preparing a shade to protect the guests from the midday sun. The sixth formers also refer to the lack of medical care for people, the way the houses were constructed (corrugated zinc or thatched roofs and wooden frameworks filled in with mud), the crops of rice, ginger, groundnuts, cassava and pepper. They looked at the system of cultivation, the layout of the village, the work of the craftsmen such as blacksmiths, weavers and so forth. In short, there is ample evidence here of vivid recall and learning about almost every aspect of life and routine in this region of rural Sierra Leone.

This brief citation from one outcome, one piece of work, cannot do justice to the experience and learning in the different countries of the 700–800 people who in total took part in the two cruises. Each person had different encounters, different interpretations and stories to tell, but no person will forget the assault on the senses that West Africa offered us and the mixed responses of admiration for West African life and environment and sadness or anger towards the crushing problems confronting the countries we visited.

The variety of people we met and with whom many of us formed friendships gave us a greater insight into this life than if we had only participated in standard mass tours. Staff and sixth formers met African university lecturers, politicians, civil servants, teachers, sixth formers, trades people, villagers and other people. We were invited into their houses, often simple huts in the villages, but sometimes smart houses in the towns complete with servants. We came to appreciate in stark reality the many aspects of life we had only read about before, such as the climate or the problems of just living in an underdeveloped country. But this was balanced by the exuberance of the people and the friendliness, which I mention without being patronising. The poverty we knew about beforehand from our neatly assembled statistics on mortality rates, life expectancy, income per capita and so forth, but the reality was a better educator because it showed something else which the statistics could not depict, and that was the way in which people made the best of difficult and sometimes distressing conditions, by being resourceful and often triumphing over obstacles which would have defeated many of us.

My major criticism, in retrospect, is that we did not prepare enough materials for focus on the colonial aspects of history and the related problems of the North–South divide, the gulf between rich and poor worlds. We did include these vital areas, but there could have been more of a systematic and deliberately provocative attempt to present the many alternative viewpoints on development and underdevelopment in the wider non-African context, although when we did highlight these issues in the West African area, the concepts and trends were not difficult to illustrate. For example, our BI guest lecturers on the cruises, Professor Hodder on the first and Professor Harrison-Church and Professor Hopkins on the second, drew special attention to the distortions in the economy caused by the increased tourism in the area from people from Scandinavia, the UK and West Germany. However, I would still want a bold curriculum which reflected more strongly the view outlined by Dave Hicks (1977b) when he stated that:

many of the North – South problems we face today, many of our perspectives in fact come from the impact of colonialism, that brief period of imposed white rule which is now nearly over. Davidson's *Africa in History* (Paladin) shows this clearly whilst Killingray's *A Plague of Europeans* (Penguin Education) provides excellent classroom material from which one could begin to examine concepts such as the exportation of European culture (language, religion, etc.), patterns of economic exploitation, the destruction of indigenous culture and industry, the creation of a belief in white superiority, the creation of unrealistic boundaries and economics geared to the production of raw materials to be processed in the North.

We learned about all of these things and saw the results of many, but I think more emphasis could have been put on these trends.

In any future venture, which seems highly unlikely because of the escalating costs and the problems of transport (P & O no longer attempt the West Africa route because of problems and it does not attract sufficient cabin passengers), we might spend more time in just one country, say Gambia or Sierra Leone, the latter certainly the most popular place of the whole trip.

To sum up. It is impossible, as I suggested earlier, for me to generalise about the many unique experiences of so many people. Each has his or her own special memories, moments or adventures that would be highlighted, but I can say that no other method apart from the cruise idea would have given so many such a deep appreciation of African life and problems. No teaching device in the classrooms of the UK would have communicated so much about the cultures of other peoples, and no amount of maps and films would have taught so much about the environment of West Africa. If our task as teachers is to extend pupils' knowledge about the world, either its physical or social dimension, and if we are trying to assist them in the formation of their attitudes and understanding of the human condition, including the inequalities of the world, the immense variety of ways of being, ways of seeing and ways of living, the different cosmologies which may unite or divide us, then there can be few alternatives to the cruises as an organised and extended educational experience, notwithstanding spending a long period of time in one of the West African countries, which few have the chance to do. This was the best we could offer for the price[1] in providing an experience-oriented curriculum whose span lasted two years and which guaranteed an indelible learning opportunity. For the future, any schemes such as the UNESCO Associated Schools Project or visits organised by enterprising teachers[2] should be supported and encouraged in the hope that in these small ways the world will grow closer and more people in the UK will demand that the West, which is responsible for some of the problems of the Third World, through colonial and neo-colonial exploitation, should work towards initiatives aimed at reducing the North–South divide. The single awful fact of our time is that we have solved the problem of sending people to the moon without solving the problem of why two-thirds of the world goes to bed hungry.

## Notes

1. The 1974 West African cruise cost each sixth former £100 and the 1977 cruise just over £200 per head.
2. Third World study visits are of course part of a continuing tradition in the 1970s. One of the most detailed accounts of the impact of such a visit on teachers can be found in Stig Lindholm's (1975) *Seeing For Ourself: A Report on an Experiment in Development Education.* This analyses the perceptions of a group of Swedish teachers to Chile just before Allende's downfall. It is published by the Swedish International Development Authority, Information Division, S-105 25 Stockholm. David Wright (1978) has also described study visits to Tunisia in his 'The Third World at first hand: an experience for student teachers', *The New Era*, 59(4). Practising teachers have recently been on study visits to Ghana, India and Colombia as a result of extremely enterprising in-service work by the Development Education Centre in Birmingham. This work has been written up as *Learning About Africa:*

*Dilemmas, Approaches, Resources* and *Birmingham and the Wider World: A Report on an In-service Course*. Both reports are available from the Development Education Centre, Selly Oak Colleges, British Road, Birmingham B29 6LE.

The author wishes to extend thanks to John Baker and Patrick Bailey for their comments on the draft of this chapter.

# Part III
## Teacher education

# Chapter 8     David Hicks
# Global issues in initial teacher education: an overview

The initial education of teachers can, and should, play a crucial role in the growth of 'global literacy'. Whether it does or not will depend on various factors including the perception that those working in initial teacher education have both of its function and of their own role in society. It has been argued that teacher education institutions 'are potentially the greatest source of educational change in an organised, orderly society' (UNESCO 1976b) and, if this could indeed be the case, it accordingly becomes extremely important to focus on their activities.

## The context

The initial education of teachers inevitably takes place within the context of changing values in society generally, as well as changing perceptions of the teacher's role in that society. Colleges thus have to consider the role that a teacher may be expected to fulfil including the possibility that he or she will be amongst the agents of change. Taylor (1969) has also drawn attention to the 'newness' of the social framework within which teachers work:

... it is all too easy to take for granted the characteristics of our world that stem from industrial growth and technology, and see these as a kind of natural state in terms of which all other undeveloped rural societies are abnormal...although an urban existence, surrounded by the apparatus of technological invention, is rapidly becoming the norm ...it is still a very new pattern of life in terms of the length of man's span on earth...

It is this very 'newness' and the concomitant rate of change that pose all sorts of critical questions for teacher education, for children increasingly need to understand all sorts of new economic and social pressures, new modes of thought and new patterns of behaviour. It has been argued that, in considering the overarching goals of teacher education, a strong case can be made for criteria directly related to the fact that we live in a period of rapid change. Vickers (1973) thus talks about 'future history' – 'those assumptions about the world in which today's young will live as adults, which affect the preparation they should have now'.

Obviously both the influences on college curricula and the demands made in curriculum decision-making are complex. The rapid obsolescence of knowledge results in fundamental changes in the social circumstances against which the curriculum must be measured and it can be argued that college curricula show a serious time-lag in relating to societal change. Thus (Calthrop and Owens 1974):

117

colleges are not concerned with the major issues of contemporary society: survival of the human race, poverty, famine, the population explosion, pollution and the environment, nuclear/biological/chemical/germ warfare, urban disaster, the miseries of factory life, the ethics of the stupendous changes taking place in the biological sciences (transplants, AID, definitions of death, mind control, the control of pain, the creation of life in the laboratory, euthanasia),the clash between races or the profound changes in the family structures and relationships between the sexes. Underpinning all these issues is the political/economic factor: the concentration of wealth, property and power in the hands of relatively few, and the increasing bureaucracy, impersonality and tyranny of most of our 'democratic' institutions. Many of these problems demand political answers – and politics appears to be anathema in our colleges.

This chapter sets out to examine just such claims and describes a survey aimed at establishing how serious an interest in global issues there appears to be at initial teacher education level in the UK. It is important first, however, to clarify the theoretical perspectives from which one might approach such questions. Are teacher education institutions potentially a great source for educational change, as suggested previously, or do they ignore the major issues of contemporary society and thus point education away from the dilemmas of the real world? A radical perspective on both schooling and the curriculum would argue that education generally perpetuates existing social patterns and only serves to reinforce existing inequalities. Far from liberating students, education thus serves to perpetuate the ruling ideology and to protect the status quo. On this analysis, schooling, and we can include here teacher education, acts as a conservative force moulding the very thought processes by which we approach issues (Bourdieu 1960) and making what is seem 'normal' and right rather than only one possible version of reality.

Real concern over contemporary global issues may therefore in fact raise too many fundamental questions, questions about hierarchy, stratification, power, exploitation and the use of knowledge. The traditional issues of educational reform, i.e. teaching styles, curriculum development, innovation, can accordingly be compared with the concerns of the radical critic: 'the patterns of relationships presupposed in the educational system, the premises which teachers unconsciously bring to the educational system and which affect their ways of operating, the messages which these very ways of operating and the educational system itself send out to learners' (Smith, M. 1977). Global issues are certainly complex and controversial, thus on a radical analysis we might expect them either to be ignored in the college curriculum or, if dealt with, to be examined in a superficial way.

## The survey

Previous to this survey interest in global issues in initial teacher education had been minimal. Indeed only three very impressionistic surveys existed and all resulted from initiatives coming from outside the formal sector of education. Thus the International Committee of the Association of Teachers in Colleges and Departments of Education reported in 1961, and again in 1966, on the teaching of world affairs in colleges (Lyall 1967). A tendency was noted at that time for courses to reflect an interest in world affairs.

In 1968 the Voluntary Committee on Overseas Aid and Development, arising out of replies from just over a third of colleges, reported that there seemed to be a reasonable awareness of the need to teach about global issues. Burns (1975), in her survey of higher education and Third World issues in industrialised countries, also felt that UK teacher education was more concerned with these issues than, for example, the universities.

It was against this rather meagre background that a more detailed investigation into the role of contemporary global issues in initial teacher education was recently made (Hicks 1977a). It mapped in outline the scene as it was in 1977–78, very much a period of change and contraction in initial teacher education. The survey thus came at a critical point in time, since it caught several innovative courses that were a response to the global crises of the 1970s but which, due to college cutbacks, were not necessarily going to survive into the 1980s. Important developments in course design were thus highlighted and may also offer some sort of yardstick for the needs of the 1980s.

Not only were all institutions concerned with initial teacher education approached but also, in order to ascertain their various contributions the following subject areas: geography, history, environmental education, religious education, contemporary studies and education. Nearly 300 replies were received, a response rate of 54 per cent which, given the traumas of closure and merger at the time, was considered acceptable and certainly higher than the other surveys mentioned previously. The picture which emerged from the survey was probably a fairly representative picture. Naturally not everyone was sympathetic to the issues under discussion, and as one Head of Educational Studies replied:

We do nothing in the field of world studies, and I wonder even though this might have been debated at major UN conferences that is sufficient justification for including it in initial teacher education? I have been under the impression that one of the criticisms of initial teacher education stems from the fact that we are all trying to do too much, too badly and too superficially, and it seems that one of your assumptions is that anything can be included.

## Overall findings

The proportion of respondents actually teaching about global issues in any way was 58 per cent (164 courses in all). This varied considerably between colleges (63% of courses) and university Postgraduate Certificate of Education Courses (PGCE) (30%). Since the survey was primarily interested in the longer B.Ed. courses, one can in fact say that nearly two-thirds of those respondents taught about global issues in some way. Table 3 shows how the various subjects contributed to such teaching.

*Table 3*  Global issues: subject contributions (%)

| | |
|---|---|
| Geography | 27 |
| History | 20 |
| Environmental education | 17 |
| Religious education | 13 |
| Education | 7 |
| Contemporary studies | 6 |
| Other subjects | 10 |
| | 100  (N = 164) |

The likelihood of different subjects teaching about global issues is shown in Table 4. Courses with a specific emphasis on the contemporary world have been grouped together under the heading contemporary studies and obviously they all teach such issues. The table clearly shows the strong position of geography followed by environmental education.

*Table 4*  Importance of global issues by subject

| | % of courses |
|---|---|
| Contemporary studies | 100 |
| Geography | 77 |
| Environmental education | 74 |
| Religious education | 49 |
| History | 49 |
| Education | 28 |

Not only is geography very likely to teach about global issues but it also makes the largest contribution as shown in Table 3. Contemporary studies, although very likely to teach about global issues, makes the smallest contribution overall.

Seventeen main areas of study were offered as likely to be included in courses and their importance, or popularity, is shown in Table 5.

Whilst Table 5 certainly shows what was being taught, it cannot tell whether the ranking reflects the popularity, the acceptance, or the relative perceived importance of topics. It is probably a combination of all these; thus world poverty and world population were seen as the most important contemporary global issues within the context of teacher education, whilst resources, urban problems, food and environmental issues have gained varying degrees of acceptance. It is notable that the major international conferences during the 1970s on employment and the role of women received little media coverage, and that these topics are in the lowest grouping, as also is some consideration of solutions, i.e. alternative life-styles and future studies.

*Table 5*  Overall ranking of areas of study (%)

| | |
|---|---|
| World wealth/poverty | 67 |
| World population | 67 |
| World resources | 61 |
| Urban problems | 59 |
| World food | 56 |
| Environmental issues | 51 |
| Role of technology | 45 |
| Problems of industrialised countries | 45 |
| Trade and aid | 43 |
| Ethnic minorities | 41 |
| Peace/conflict/war | 40 |
| Alternative technology | 34 |
| World health | 32 |
| Alternative life-styles | 31 |
| World employment | 20 |
| Role of women | 15 |
| Future studies | 10 |
| (N = 164) | |

Table 6 shows how important, or otherwise, some of the key concepts from peace research, development education and World Studies were seen to be in these courses.

*Table 6*  Overall ranking of some key concepts

| | |
|---|---|
| Underdevelopment/development | 74 |
| Social justice/injustice | 51 |
| Dependence/self-reliance | 47 |
| Alternative life-styles | 43 |
| Liberation/oppression | 34 |
| Global village | 29 |
| Alternative futures | 28 |
| Participation and action | 24 |
| North/South | 22 |
| Conscientisation | 14 |
| Structural violence | 11 |
| (N = 164) | |

A radical perspective would argue that this rank order needs broadly reversing as the more frequently used concepts (underdevelopment, social justice, dependence) are more to do with symptoms than the causes of problems. The lower-placed concepts (structural violence, consciousness-raising, participation and action) on the other hand point more directly at the need for fundamental structural change from the grass roots up.

## Subject approaches

It is not possible here to describe in detail the approaches found under each subject. It is possible,however (a) to comment briefly on *some* of the development within each subject area that could provide a global perspective, and (b) to describe briefly some of the more interesting things that were found to be going on.

## Geography

Whereas the new geography of the 1960s saw a revolution in the use of models and quantification, the subject may now gradually be shifting towards a 'geography of concern', which is increasingly preoccupied with ethical questions. This dates from the late 1960s in North America and a considerable literature has now developed on what is sometimes referred to as 'radical geography'. This is in fact a revolution of social responsibility for it calls for a greater professional involvement in matters of contemporary social concern such as poverty, hunger, the environment and issues of human welfare and social justice, which in turn may lead to a basic re-evaluation of the scope and subject-matter of geography. Such a move queries the positivist approach of much 'establishment' geography as merely being supportive of an unjust status quo (Peet 1978).

Nearly three-quarters of the geographers who replied were involved in teaching about global issues. Courses tended to focus specifically on the Third World, but in the comments made and the texts referred to there was little evidence of the perspectives of radical geography having had any influence on teaching. Course outlines varied from the Eurocentric, based on notions of industrial 'take-off' and problems of the tropical environment, to the more innovative which set out to dispel common myths and stereotypes. One rationale stated:

We are all aware of locations – the inner city, the older industrial regions of Britain, Southern Italy, the so-called Third World – which are seen as 'problem areas'. This status is earned by the evident disparities between these areas and more favoured zones – the outer suburb, the South-East of England, the Ransted, the industrialised affluent countries. The course investigates these contrasts, the processes that generate them and the sorts of political responses stimulated by these enduring 'North–South' tensions.

One respondent also commented: 'My general impression is that students are far more interested in the so-called "environmental crises" than in the details and niceties of spatial patterns, which appear to be the preoccupation of many geographers today.'

## History

History, as other fields of study, has been going through a crisis of identity related both to its role and its purpose, whilst the concern for a more international context in history teaching has largely arisen out of the realisation of the narrowness of much teaching in the past. As Ballard (1970) points out, the idea that school history is properly national history runs very deep: 'History has been used as a subject by which children are indoctrinated in patriotic and military virtues...it yearly becomes more clear that history teaching must break out of the narrow nationalistic strait-jacket in which it has lived for so long.'

The arguments in favour of world history are thus very strong, for it should work against narrow nationalistic outlooks and Eurocentric points of view, such as the assumption that Africa did not really matter before the Europeans arrived (McNeill 1970):

The ease and rapidity with which European empires spread across the world seemed only to confirm the validity of this viewpoint. Europe, it seemed, was the seat of progress, the rest of mankind had been left behind, but through the efforts of missionaries, merchants, administrators and soldiers would soon be privileged to share in the benefits of modern, progressive civilisation.

The consequences of such assumptions are discussed by Hannam (1970) when he considers the role of history teachers in relation to prejudice. He suggests that a history syllabus entirely centred on British history 'will only reinforce those ethnocentric attitudes and foreigners, who only appear on the scene to be defeated, enslaved and exploited for the glory of one's own group, will hardly be seen more tolerantly when encountered in another context'.

Nearly half of the historians were teaching courses which looked at the twentieth century and thus had a strong global perspective. From such rationales came statements such as:

We think it important student teachers should be aware of the problems of poverty outside Britain and should investigate to what extent colonial rule is responsible for them.

To correct the Eurocentric nature of most history teaching.

To provide a point of departure for developing insights into the values, institutions and aspirations of other cultures in the hope that this will help the student to understand him/herself and the interdependent societies (national and world) to which he/she belongs.

*Environmental education*

The rise of environmental education from the late 1960s and into the 1970s was in part prompted by the growth of public environmental awareness. This was directly related to international conferences on the environment, population, world food and dire warnings about the likely effects of uncontrolled industrial growth. The 'limits to growth' debate focused attention on the finite nature of the globe and many of its resources.

Whilst much environmental education concerned itself with local and national issues, the global dimension was continually kept in the public eye by reports, conferences and the media. What had, in part, arisen out of the earlier rural studies movement to become an interest in conservation and the environment could now be directly linked to global issues. The debate, however, was often seen to be rather limited (Harper 1972) and:

restricted to polite discussion of well-thumbed topics, controversial issues have been played down and ideologically sensitive areas have been neglected altogether. In my view, this is to contradict the very purpose of environmental education, which cannot fulfil its function if it does not tackle politically and ideologically 'hot' topics. Effective environmental education is not a 'nice' subject. It has conflict, controversy and uncertainty in its very bones.

The references to conflict and controversy pin-point the real, and therefore often avoided, dilemmas of environmental education. What may start with environmental concern may lead to social and political issues, which are seen as being outside the scope of the subject. For example, how many environmentalists would agree with Gribbin (1977) that 'the problems of world food and population are not technological problems but almost entirely political'?

More than three-quarters of the environmentalists were teaching courses that dealt with global issues. Some courses were based on a particular disciplinary viewpoint whilst others focused on particular issues. Amongst the aims of some of the latter courses were:

To increase the awareness of students of the human condition.
To promote attitudes of commitment and involvement, leading to active participation in events . . .
To create sympathy for, and understanding of, different environments.
To give students some insight into the resources and pollution problems that the population explosion and material affluence in the developed nations are now presenting the world. To enable students to appreciate the functioning of human life supporting systems and to become aware of the change occurring mainly due to man, with reference to possible consequences.

### Religious education

During the last two decades both the aims and the subject area of religious education have also undergone fundamental reappraisal. Religion is thus not an optional extra in the interpretation of life. It is, rather, a dimension of the whole of experience.

Smart's phenomenological, or 'undogmatic' approach, which has had a major impact, requires a sympathetic portrayal of *any* viewpoint without bias. In an increasingly multicultural society the task of religious education may well be 'to broaden and deepen this "universal perpective" so that it becomes one of "universal understanding"'.

Young people today...need help in developing their *own* perspective from which to examine the claims, demands and values of the 'technological society' *and* the 'alternative society'. Only if they are able to exercise personal discrimination and make informed choices, especially in matters of belief and action, will they be in a position to prevent themselves from being exploited (Grimmitt 1973).

Teaching *about* world religions, with its emphasis on social and cultural patterns, will also in its way contribute to an awareness of the diversity of human life in a global context. What is increasingly happening, however, is that religious education is being seen as education in attitudes to life.

Nearly half of the respondents felt that their courses touched on global issues in some way. Some focused on world religions and were concerned to explore 'other religions and alternative lifestyles that have been adopted, the influence of eastern religious movements on the West, the hippie culture, etc. In short, our rationale is that we need to put before students alternative possibilities to religious and moral orthodoxy.' Others stressed the implications of Christian commitment in the contemporary world:

1. Christian theology developed in Latin America has identified a political/revolutionary dimension.
2. This political involvement is total, i.e. concerned with economics, population, resources, etc.
3. The theological underpinning of this involvement is worthy of investigation.
4. One major development from this could be (I think is) a fresh approach to education.

A third focus emphasised understanding human nature and pointed out:

The need to understand the different functions of empirical investigation, conceptual analysis, value judgement and theological insight in formulating an overall view of human nature.

And from aims:

1. An understanding of the principal ideological forces in the modern world both religious and non-religious, with special attention to Marxism.
2. An understanding of religious systems and philosophies and their relation to social structures and activity.

*Education*

It has been suggested that, in the face of current rapid social change, 'school can and should take an active part in assessing the worthwhileness of contemporary culture and promoting what it takes to be educationally desirable changes in that culture' (Skilbeck 1975). Thus, if understanding and coping with contemporary global issues is as urgent a matter as it seems, education must prepare children and students for *future* living (Skilbeck 1975):

This means that teachers require more sociology, social psychology, politics, economics, environmental science, contemporary history and more experience of problem-solving, critical enquiry and creative activity in their training...it will be no less important for teachers to come to view themselves as agents of change and renewal and not as transmitters of settled or slowly changing bodies of knowledge.

Musgrove (1973) sees the challenge as offering preparation for 'a life which must be ever less linear, increasingly episodic and open-ended' and suggests that the 'counter-cultural' curriculum might in fact become the most appropriate:

In the cognitive domain, the main elements are these: extensive biological–physiological knowledge, especially for its bearing on foodstuffs, additives, impurities, vegetarianism and drug use, chemical–geographical knowledge, especially with regard to the environment and pollution, psychological knowledge...political philosophy – not only Marx and Marcuse but the seventeenth century Diggers and Levellers, Eastern Philosophy and Comparative Religion, Anthropology, and, of course, Astrology...

Only just over a quarter of the education courses claimed to touch on global issues in any way. Sometimes this was as part of curriculum studies because:

In teacher education concern for issues such as these is often left to Special Subject areas, and then they will only find a place if a particular tutor is interested in this area. Therefore, we must find a way of involving all students in an awareness of world concerns and their role in developing this awareness for their pupils.

Alternatively, it was as part of a comparative education course and amongst the aims of such courses were:

– To encourage teachers to think more deeply about some of their assumptions by showing that things do not necessarily have to be the way they actually are.
– To introduce the student to the basic problems of development as they affect education or are affected by education in the developing and developed world.
– To provide an opportunity for students to encounter the educational thought of certain influential Third World figures – in particular Freire, Nyerere, Ghandi, with particular reference to the ways in which education can contribute to social change.

Two of the most innovative education courses to involve a Third World perspective were in fact a result of initiatives from Oxfam and they have been interestingly written up by Richardson and Poxon (1979).


*Contemporary studies*

Only a very small number of courses had this, or a similar, title. However, they are important simply because their *prime* concern was contemporary global issues. In other words they were courses that had been designed from a social science perspective with the express intention of exploring complex contemporary issues with a global dimension. From such rationales came the following statements:

– The need to provide a world dimension in an otherwise UK-centred degree course. This provides an opportunity to grapple with momentous issues.
– To help students acquire a general knowledge of the nature, causes and likely development of problems facing the world. No current issue can be appreciated from a single discipline alone. Students need to put both their main and educational studies into a world context.
– This section of the course is future-oriented, i.e. it asks questions about the sort of future our children will grow up in: 'How do we prepare children for a future which will certainly be different from the present?' 'Can we get any clues about preferred alternative futures by looking at contemporary world

affairs?' Four reasons for looking at such a complex field might be: making sense of the news . . . preparing for the future . . . choosing an individual life-style . . . commitment to change.

## Some comparisons

It is important to remember that the subject sketches outlined above particularly drew attention to developments within each area which *could* legitimate the study of global issues and then quoted some of the most relevant statements from courses. The emphasis, perhaps rightly, was on what *is* and what *could* be. Later, emphasis will be given to what is *not* going on.

Geography, environmental education and contemporary studies make the largest contribution to a global dimension in college curricula and it is interesting to note the different emphases they give to the topics listed in Table 4. Thus geography ranks seven (poverty, food, population, health, employment,urban problems and role of technology) as more important than any other subject does. Contemporary studies ranks three topics (trade and aid, problems of industrialised countries and future studies) as more important than in any other subject. Whilst environmental education ranks four topics (world resources, environmental issues, alternative technology and the role of technology) – the latter highest in both geography and environmental education – as more important than in any other subject. In fact different emphases are apparent here over the role of technology, with geography stressing intermediate technology in a Third World context and environmental education more concerned about the exponential use of finite resources in relation to the negative impact of technology on the environment. Contemporary studies is revealing in this context because it stresses one of the most important links between North and South, i.e. trade and aid, and also spends more time looking at the problems of the North, as well as stressing the need for investigation of alternatives, whether in technology, futures or life-styles.

To summarise, very briefly, some of the main differences found between subject approaches, it is possible to say that geography frequently dealt with contemporary global issues, with the stress on Third World matters or on particular global problems. A strong disciplinary approach was combined with an apparent reluctance to get very involved in conflicting value positions. Issues were, however, central rather than peripheral. History only looked at global issues in just over half of the courses and tended to present a traditional appearance. It had a strong disciplinary approach in which issues were central. Three-quarters of the courses in environmental education were likely to deal with contemporary global issues which were central and often related to resource problems. Approaches were strongly inter/multidisciplinary.

Over half the courses in religious education were concerned with contemporary global issues, but these were central only in those relating to Christian commitment in the world today. Education courses were least likely of all to deal with contemporary global issues. The role of women and ethnic minorities received more attention here than elsewhere. Contemporary studies was most likely of all to deal with contemporary global issues, but only represented a small number of courses. There were fewer low-ranking themes or concepts than in any other field of study. Approaches were strongly inter/multidisciplinary. There was a willingness to explore conflicting attitudes and values.

## Some conclusions: What *sort* of global perspective?

Nearly two-thirds of the college respondents were involved in teaching about global issues. This figure applies to three and four-year courses at colleges and polytechnics. Much less was done, partly because of the brief time available, in the unversity PGCE courses. The subjects most likely to teach about contemporary global issues were contemporary studies, geography and environmental courses. In numerical terms the main contributions came from geography, history and environmental courses.

The most commonly taught themes overall, in order of importance, were: world wealth and poverty, world population, world resources, urban problems and world food. The most common important concept to be used was underdevelopment/development.

The most neglected themes were: future studies, the role of women, and world employment. The least-known concepts (from peace research but nevertheless crucial in dealing with contemporary global issues) were structural violence and consciousness-raising.

### What is the quality of available courses?

The courses encountered in this survey ranged from the very traditional to the very innovative, but some attempt also needs to be made to assess the variations in quality. One could suggest some sort of broad centre –periphery continuum, with the most aware courses at the centre, and the least aware courses on the periphery. Cullinan's 'stages in awareness' (1975) could be used here to categorise courses in terms of their perception of the real issues of global development; so courses might teach about: (a) wanting to help in the Third World by giving aid, (b) helping people to help themselves, (c) a concern for justice rather than charity, (d) realising we are all involved in structural injustice, (e) the need for real liberation through consciousness-raising and (f) that the first and fundamental response must be within oneself.

In terms of course approach to the Third World, for example, there are similar stages. Thus many courses merely teach *about* the Third World or about issues, others may do this and also look at traditional 'liberal' *solutions* to problems. Some will *link* underdevelopment in the South with over-development in the North, perhaps in terms of standards of living. Only a few courses attempt to show actually that this is really about justice and oppression, or even conscientisation, needing *reflection* and *action*, which lead to analysis of our own motivations and perspectives and consideration of real alternatives.

It was impossible to place courses in any detailed fashion on such a continuum, but a generalised breakdown into three broad groups was possible. Thus the peripheral group of courses involved those respondents who gave too little information really to learn much about their courses and courses which made little real assessment of the complexity of global issues. The group of courses which lay between the centre and periphery were those which did attempt to explore the complexities of contemporary global issues in some way. The group of courses which could be placed at the centre were those which represented real innovation in this field, or radically came to grips with the social, political, economic and personal issues concerned.

About half of the courses tended towards the periphery category, about a third of them came in the midway category and the remaining 15 per cent (about one in eight courses) came in the critical central category.

## What were the restraints on course quality?

This is using the term 'quality' in the sense of a radical approach, which is both critical, reflective and committed to social change. If all that is required of courses is a global perspective of some sort, then this was being partially achieved. The restraints partly lie in traditional disciplines only being prepared to acknowledge contemporary affairs from their *own* perspective, and their consequent wariness in handling controversial issues.

The restraints are inherent perhaps in the tensions between what have been called the 'conservative', 'liberal' and 'radical' voices (Richardson 1974a). Richardson has described the 'liberal' position as growing strong in Europe and America in the late 1940s and early 1950s. Adding a decade or so for this really to permeate higher education, the 'liberal' position has become increasingly influential in educational planning. It considers there is a 'need for changes in the content of courses in school and colleges, changes which will, it is hoped, lead to changes in attitudes and loyalties amongst the young' Richardson (1974b). Obviously most of the courses fell into this category.

The radical critique, however, argues that this view does not go deep enough, and only treats the symptoms rather than the causes. Only when one also takes into account the structural violence of political and social systems do further insights occur (Richardson 1974a):

The first is that the focus of analysis should not be primarily on the behaviour of sovereign governments, acting in what they perceive to be their national interests, but on the dominant economic and social *élites* of nation-states, acting in their own material and psychological interests. Elites may have more interest in common with each other than with the majority of people whom they claim to represent.

The focus of courses should thus also be on structural change and commitment to action in order to create a more just global society. The balance of courses on such a centre–periphery continuum reflects these three positions, two of which in fact actually lead to the depoliticisation of global issues. Their distribution is reinforced by the nature of teacher education itself which reflects the status quo, but is at the same time painfully and slowly trying to change to cope with a fast changing world.

## What are the future prospects?

Two current trends now need to meet up more clearly in initial teacher education. The first trend has already been described in Chapter 1 and related to the various 'global literacy' initiatives that were made in the 1970s. The second trend can be seen in the radical perspectives found within each of the subject areas discussed. Thus each has its leading radical edge, whether in the geography of social welfare or in a Christian commitment to consciousness-raising. In these terms the one in eight innovatory courses are not merely the work of a few committed individuals but part of the leading radical edge as it manifests in teacher education. This edge always represents the minority who go on ahead, paving the way to deeper analysis. It consists of those who *can* cope with future shock and assess the most immediate needs of the present for the future. All else that happens, in contrast to this, represents a cultural time-lag which is always several years behind. The list of the most important topics illustrates this, since the top five received particular media coverage in the late 1960s and early 1970s.

Despite the difficulties, whatever the future, a radical edge will always remain. It may not increase its hold on traditional educational structures, but instead draw the pedagogy of teacher education into increasing confrontation with reality. As Lawrence (1975) has suggested in another context: 'New groupings will be born continually, and others will die if the need for them ceases. This may seem Utopian, but already it is beginning to happen. This is not an age for founding institutions to endure for generations...but rather for sudden experiments, which flow and fade quickly, yet not before they have scattered their seed.' Or as Smoker (1976) suggests, it may not depend on numbers if 'the critical mass required for establishing an effective peace culture requires dispersion and pattern rather than concentration and size. Given an appropriately dispersed 'critical few' the crucial social processes could be reinforced and magnified.' If this is true the task for the 1980s is clear and the case studies which follow provide some pointers along the way.

# Chapter 9    Bill Kelly and Tony Ghaye
# The Third World: a geographical interpretation

The invitation to reflect upon the evolution of a global dimension to undergraduate work in geography at Worcester College of Higher Education was received with some amount of trepidation. With reflectivity and analysis over a decade of developments would it be a case of the same 'old' medicine being put into new bottles? When each course was shorn of its particular labels would we find that the content and learning experiences remained little changed?

We knew that we could not produce a neat and tidy response to the challenge. The most that we can claim is that we have produced a paper which makes explicit certain potentials and problems that have confronted us in the planning and implementation of a global dimension in the curriculum. We illustrate this with sustained reference to developments in one part of the B.Ed. and BA degree programme between 1977–80. We acknowledge the messy bits and pieces and the loose ends. We have endeavoured to present things as they are, in ragged–edged actualities.

What follows is the result of a multiplicity of external and internal developments, conflicts and pressures, operating over time. These have caused us to examine and question the correctness and desirability of a global dimension in the curriculum. This has been the challenge of change. The nature of our response to this invitation is explicated below and is broadly analogous to one conception of development in that our response describes attempts to move towards a more desirable state. It represents a process of moving towards rather than arriving at.

## Influences on course structure

Two basic considerations have governed the structure of the courses shown in Figure 8, these being the nature of geography and the nature of the institution. With regard to the former, the global dimension in the undergraduate geography courses has reflected changes in the nature of geographical knowledge (Johnston 1979). Figure 8 indicates a move from a sustained and explicit use of the regional paradigm to a multiple and to some extent competing paradigm situation. Changes in geography which are identified as being particularly significant are:
(a) the emphasis on a nomothetic rather than on an ideographic style of explanation for spatial patterns, processes and relationships, and (b) an increasing emphasis on matters of contemporary social concern which invite commitment to the study of relevant issues of the real world. In our

131

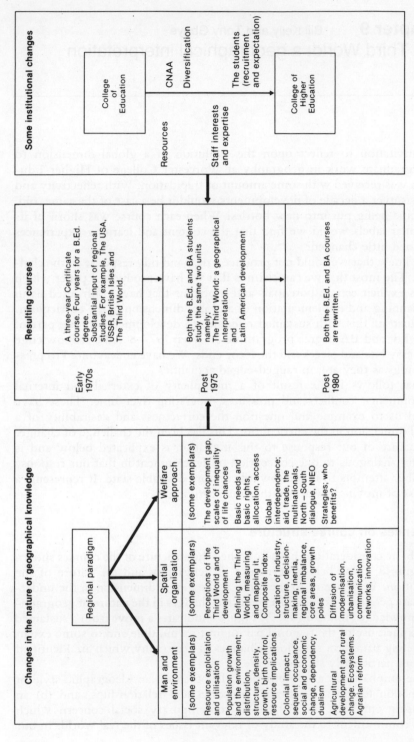

Fig. 8   Some influences on course structure

course planning we have been increasingly concerned that we should provide students with the opportunity to explore the notion that these patterns of inequality or whatever reflect not just the environment that is, but the environment as it is perceived by the agents acting in it. In other words we felt we needed to give our work on 'development' a phenomenological dimension (Buttimer 1976). The nature of geography has been subject to a radical reappraisal and this dynamic situation of restructuring and of changing emphases is still continuing.

An implicit assumption has been and still is that it is both necessary and desirable for geography undergraduates to familiarise themselves with the concept of 'development' and for some to appreciate its significance in curriculum planning and for classroom practice.

The other major consideration is concerned with institutional changes. These are reflected in the geography strand of the 1975 B.Ed. (Hons) submission and the revision of this degree programme which took place in 1979–80 in the context of national changes in teacher education. There have also been academic developments and much diversification within the college. The introduction of a BA degree in Combined Studies in 1977 is relevant here.

## Planning the unit

To illustrate the nature of curriculum change, namely the evolution of the global dimension, this paper focuses attention on one term's work common to both the B.Ed. and BA degree programmes. 'The Third World: A Geographical Interpretation' is ten weeks of study and will hereafter be referred to as the unit. As a broad guideline, the unit consists of approximately 120 hours of study time, although many students do considerably more. Six hours of tutor–student contact is timetabled and available each week.

The unit presents the tutor with the task of helping students search for a clearer understanding of the rich–poor gap which dominates the world and to help develop student awareness of the complex interrelationships which exist between the relatively more advanced and the less developed nations. The concept of global interdependence is utilised and efforts are made to tease out the common bonds between the 'haves and the have nots'. The teaching of this is often coloured by our conviction that those already in the lifeboat have some sort of obligation to those who are still adrift in the sea of poverty and despair (Smith, M.D. 1977).

Many questions are continually raised regarding the utility of this unit. For example, how does it foster student attitudes towards development issues which are responsible and critical? What teaching strategies and styles need to be adopted so that the issues presented to the student act as catalysts to help make explicit group and individual ideology, judgement, opinion, stereotype and value? How does it provide opportunities for students to organise and structure information on development issues in a coherent way; a way where knowledge can be stored and recalled when needed?

Table 7   The Third World: A geographical interpretation. The unit structure

| Topic | Selected references (examples for the 1.1) | Resources (for unit 1.1) | Workshop assignments (unit 1.1 and 1.2) |
|---|---|---|---|
| 1.1. Defining the Third World Human geography and the development dimension. The concept of development; what do we mean by it and what is it meant to achieve? How meaningful is the term 'Third World'? the selection and use of indices to delimit the Third World. Images and perception of poverty | Todaro M.P. (1977) Economic Development in the Third World. Longman Mountjoy, A.B. (1978) The Third World, Problems and Perspectives. Macmillan Donaldson, P. (1973) Worlds Apart. Penguin Smith, D.M. (1979) Where the Grass is Greener, Pelican Smith, D.M. (1974) Who gets what, where and how? A welfare focus for human geography, Geography 59, Nov. | The United Nations Demographic YearBook 1980 The United Nations Statistical YearBook 1980 World Development Report 1979; World Bank Concord Film Council; Five Minutes to Midnight | Measuring development; selection, weighting and ranking of indices to 'produce' a composite index Choropleth and topological mapping of patterns of inequality Perception exercise; ranking of a variety of explanations of underdevelopment Possible essay title (one of a possible ten titles based upon each topic of the course) What is a less developed country? Consider the criteria used and discuss the problems involved in establishing a satisfactory definition of a less-developed country |
| 1.2. Inequality: global, national, regional and group levels | Streeten, P. et al. (1978) 'Basic needs: some issues', World Development 6 (3) Francome, C. and Wharton, R. (1973) 'An international social index', New Internationalist, 7 Sept. Mountjoy, A. B. (1981) World's without end, Third World Quarterly 2 (4) | | BA Assessment (1) 2,000 word essay 40% (2) Synoptic examination 60% |
| 2.1. The historical process of emergence | | | B.Ed. Assessment (1) 2,000 word essay 50% (2) Workshop assignments 50% |
| 2.2. Explanation of underdevelopment. Classical growth theory versus historical–structuralist approaches | | | |
| 3.1. Prescriptions for socio-economic development and the spatial dimension in development | | | |
| 4.1. Population perspectives | | | |
| 5.1. The rural problems and trends in rural impoverishment | | | |
| 5.2. Rural change; agrarian colonisation, the Green Revolution and land reform | | | |
| 6.1. The problems of industrial-led growth; import-substitutions, multinational corporations. | | | |

134

With regard to the teaching of this unit in the B.Ed. programme, the assumption is that students need opportunities to reflect upon the nature of 'development' geography and the degree to which it is essential and appropriate learning for the pupils they may teach. In particular how far it meets or fails to meet the needs of different categories of learner in a variety of school contexts. A further significant concern is the way we encourage students to make public the assumptions and related values implicit in the use of certain models of development, forms of analysis and published resources (Watson 1977).

We are sensitive to the observation that there are few areas in the affective domain about which there is so much talk and so little action as there is with values. One observable trend in recent years has been our increasing use of dialectic teaching for this unit; in other words, a form of teaching which encourages discussion because it challenges students to formulate, to communicate and to react to contrasting ideas.

The unit is value-charged. It is controversial in the sense that it requires discussion of issues such as poverty, caste and contraception which involve value judgements.

In order to examine ways of improving human well-being, of explaining global problems of contemporary concern such as modernisation, justice, security, energy balance and prosperity in a world of increasing interdependence, more opportunities are being afforded to students for value clarification. This we regard as a conscious effort to move away from the dangers of moralising and inculcating The objective of this strategy is to enable students to sort out their own values. The assumption is that it is important that students who complete this course of study know how they feel about such real world problems as exploitation, unemployment and hunger (Huckle 1978). Three examples of the value-clarification activities we use in a workshop context are briefly presented.

## 1. *An alternative search activity*

Here students are encouraged to examine a problem (e.g. that of increasing agricultural productivity in West Africa) and to consider a range of alternative strategies at different scales to overcome specified problems. Details of three projects are given:
(a) large-scale commercial rice-farming,
(b) agricultural extension to local subsistence farmers involving improved crop husbandry,
(c) bullock-ploughing training schemes.
The student assumes the role of an agricultural advisor, selects and then proceeds to justify his choice. This kind of approach helps students to appraise development projects and may make them more aware of the appropriateness of certain forms of innovation and the need for progress to be conceived in terms which peasant farmers can understand and be able to implement. The activity may help students appreciate more fully that people may think or act in the same manner or in different ways to try to resolve problems of development.

*2. Value-voting activity*

This requires students to indicate their feelings and thoughts publicly. Through a debate they have to voice an opinion about the ecological impact of a rapidly expanding Latin American city. Some students are asked to represent the 'government view' whilst others represent an 'ecology group'. The students are invited to think of some other people who might speak in the debate and are encouraged to try to argue from that person's point of view, when the motion is being discussed. Normal debating procedures are adopted.

*3. Rank order activity*

Here a village health project in India involves students in making decisions and judging the consequences. The health problems facing the villagers are presented in the form of a vicious circle together with a list of activities such as health education, sanitation and pest control. The students are invited to assume the role of the person who has the responsibility for the Health Care Project. Using a list of eight activities they arrange them in an order of priority, and they have to justify their order and suggest how their health care programme helps break the vicious circle. Students compare their thinking with others in the group. Compatibility leads to reinforcement, whilst differences can lead to fruitful re-examination of their own thinking.

These three activities serve to illustrate the personal nature of development.

There are plenty of advantages and opportunities associated with such value-clarification activities. For some students it is the long-awaited opportunity to discuss issues and defend a variety of positions with evidence. It is an opportunity for all to shed their own cultural bias momentarily and see the world from someone else's point of view. There are opportunities for the discussion to be channelled into enquiry, for the exploitation of heuristic learning objectives, creativity and inventive problem-solving.

One of the greatest difficulties in organising a unit or series of units of work in development education is creating a coherent structure. The problem seems to be that the whole can only be understood if we understand the constituent parts, whilst the parts in their turn can only be understood if we understand the whole. The search for a 'coherent structure', a 'conceptual schema' or 'analytic framework' is an expression of a desire to probe for the essentials that are the basic ideas, the principal issues, the concepts and related skills. It also implies an effort to redefine the educative value of the unit.

Over the last three years we have been wrestling with this problem of coherence. It is a problem which seems to stem from at least two sources, namely the nature of the material and the nature of the learner.

Development is an elusive concept. It is multi-faceted. Many might argue that difficulty is an intrinsic quality of the material to be studied in a course which tackles development issues (Buchanan 1974). But difficulty also stems from the quality of the relationship between the learner and the material; it is a phenomenological attribute. The challenge has been for us to formulate a coherent unit structure compatible to both B.Ed. and BA programmes. The problem is that the students who follow the one or other degree programmes differ significantly in their sense of need and purpose. The B.Ed. student is a different 'animal' from the BA student in one important respect, that of expectation. For the B.Ed. student the coherence of his degree is based upon the theme of developing professionality.

Table 7 describes a sequence of instruction and represents a personal response to the problem of coherence. The sequence shown has two qualities, order and time. The elements of the sequence are ordered with certain development issues presented to the student before others. It is a sequence largely based on a pragmatic premise. The topics are arranged on the basis of generalisations from experience. For the past three years it has been regarded as fulfilling a need to provide a vehicle by which the study of individual and seemingly dissociated ideas are carried to a meaningful, synthesised focus.

## Unit structure

The unit structure is presented to the student group from the outset. It presents:

(a) the major development issues to be explored,
(b) a carefully selected reading list,
(c) some idea of the variety of non-book material that is available for student use,
(d) a range of assignments which serve to focus and sharpen student thinking.

Marking student work nearly always poses problems. Marking criteria need to be carefully explicated. Students have to respond to a problem, therefore purely descriptive work is discouraged. Insight based on informed analysis of the problem is important. In both seminar and essay work plausibility and logical consistency are important criteria for success. Students are also given opportunities to explore issues and problems in workshop sessions.

The unit structure shown in Table 7 presents some of the major development issues such as inequality, rural development, medical care and aid as a series of advance organisers. These organisers are then progressively differentiated. In other words the issues are increasingly refined. There is research to suggest that concepts, like 'development', form more quickly and with less error when the learners know in advance what they are looking for. Knowing what to look for infers the use of advance organisers. These organisers are early warning systems consisting of an initial generalised reference to an idea before elaborate discussion, exemplification and application of it.

For example, development is a core concept when beginning any study of the Third World so the question is posed: 'What do you think devel-

138

opment means?' Here we look for statements from students beginning with, 'I think', or 'I feel' or 'in my opinion' and so on. We are establishing from the outset an open classroom atmosphere and asking open questions. In just a short time an interesting 'development web' often begins to emerge (see Fig.9). How it is presented on the blackboard or overhead projector (OHP) screen is unimportant. What is important is that it serves to sensitise the students to the multi-faceted nature of the concept; each facet can then be sharpened up as the unit unfurls.

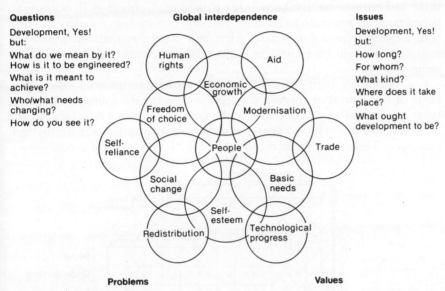

**Questions**

Development, Yes! but:

What do we mean by it?
How is it to be engineered?

What is it meant to achieve?

Who/what needs changing?

How do you see it?

**Global interdependence**

Human rights · Aid · Economic growth · Freedom of choice · Modernisation · Self-reliance · People · Trade · Social change · Basic needs · Self-esteem · Redistribution · Technological progress

**Problems**

**Issues**

Development, Yes! but:

How long?
For whom?
What kind?
Where does it take place?

What ought development to be?

**Values**

Fig. 9   The development web

The 'development gap' is another advance organiser which students can begin progressively to differentiate by exploring the degree to which a gap exists of varying spatial scales, the utility of the notion of development as a linear gap which is closed by the developing nations catching up with the developed ones. Further, students can explore the reasons for its existence, especially the degree to which it is acceptable and necessary, and to what extent and in what sense it is possible or desirable to reduce the actual or perceived development gap.

The re-submission of the 1975 B.Ed. (Hons.) degree and the imminent rewrite of the BA Combined Studies degree has once again provided us with an opportunity to reappraise and modify the global dimension in our geography courses. We are looking at the problems of coherence and structure again and exploring the potentials and problems for teaching and learning of material presented as a sequence of interdependent concepts and related skills.

The current objective is to develop more rigorously modes of thinking, as well as to convey knowledge through a sequence determined by the logical analysis of the structure of the discipline; this to be the new basis for

Teacher education

unit construction. With the information explosion it seems more imperative than ever to seek continuously for better organising principles for curriculum planning.

The unit is now beginning to be conceived in terms of an analytic framework (see Fig. 10). It is not characterised by its store of knowledge, by coverage, but tries to emphasise the importance of processes leading to the gaining of new knowledge. It is a concept skill-focused teaching which inevitably starts from data and not conclusions. The aim is for students to make and not just receive knowledge structures. Concept-skill acquisition is facilitated by reference to specified focusing ideas within a particular context. Explicit reference to 'who', 'what' and 'where' suggests that patterns and processes will be viewed in terms of their relevance to human well-being.

Concepts have both classificatory and associative qualities. By using some of the central organising concepts within the discipline we hope to bring greater order and coherence to the unit. Well-chosen concepts can act as nucleic growth crystals, aggregating phenomena to reveal patterns and processes. Thus the sequence shown in Fig. 11 is based on a conceptual

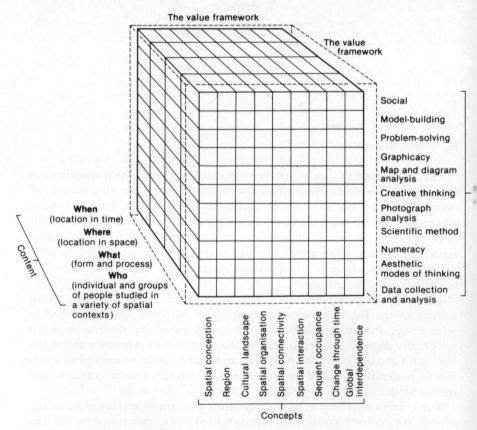

Fig. 10 An analytic framework

140

premise. A ten-week teaching programme can be devised using the analytic framework as shown.

We still need to decide whether we prefer the concept of 'continuous progress' to that of 'sequence'. Continuity comes from the Latin word meaning 'to hold together' and implies concern with how the parts of the unit hold together to build something of worth. Sequence means 'follow', the concern being with the best order of development issues for achieving a specific goal. Does the emphasis on continuity in learning allow for greater flexibility and variety in curriculum development than emphasis on sequence?

The continuity–sequence dichotomy is both an inter- and intra-unit problem as shown in Fig. 12.

## Thoughts on the future

Our long-term objective is to develop a major course (nine units) in Third World Studies for the BA Combined Studies degree which utilises the experience and expertise of other subject departments in the college. Thus to produce a multidisciplinary programme which might provide a more holistic and meaningful course of study. In a climate of educational cutbacks and tertiary reorganisation, this goal, with all its potential and opportunities for field research, remains on the drawing-board.

At the dawn of a new decade we can also look forward to more fully utilising the varied contribution that the computer can make to development studies. Our aim is to use, where appropriate, the growing collection of computer programs in our work. The objectives set for Computer Associated Learning (CAL) such as 'enriching learning', 'deepening understanding' and 'fostering intuition' are enticing.

When reflecting on our classroom practice over the last few years, the message that has come through with some considerable strength and clarity is that if a course of study in development geography is flexible enough to respond to the mood of the student group, if it adopts an open-ended exploratory approach and if it is backed up with sufficient tutorial support, the students are not only willing but on the whole eager to explore the issues involved (Walford 1979).

It is agreed amongst those who teach the units identified in Fig. 12 that student response is an important criterion of the worthwhileness of those units which serve to foster a global dimension in the curriculum. Student response reflects a measure of its value and relevance to them. However, this response has to be a positive commitment to debate the issues and to search out alternative strategies. To achieve this it is simply not enough to deliver a set of impersonal lectures and hand-outs or to present formal assignments. It is necessary to become personally committed to the course and to the students on it, striving continuously to develop a sense of co-operative enquiry in an atmosphere of mutual respect and trust. Thus as geography has changed to take more cognisance of contemporary social issues (Peet 1978), so must our teaching styles.

| A Chosen organising concepts (ideas) in geography (logical sequence?) | B Relatively lower order concepts (ideas) derived from A (logical sequence?) | C Some examples of the variety of expressions of each concept. Derived from B | D Teaching might stress one or more system | | | | Some of the | | |
|---|---|---|---|---|---|---|---|---|---|
| | | | Motor (symbol system) | Language | Maths | Visual | Data collection and analysis | Aesthetic modes of thinking | Numeracy |
| Perception | Spatial conception | Quality of life, stereotyping, poverty, the development gap | | | | X | | | |
| | Region | Where is the Third World? How do we recognise, measure and map it? | X | | | | X | | |
| Location | Cultural landscape | Built environments, townscapes, architectural styles | | | | X | | X | |
| | Spatial organisation | Inequality, core and periphery, land tenure co-operatives | X | | | | X | | X |
| Areal association | Spatial connectivity | Infrastructure, growth poles, information flows, access | | | X | | | | X |
| Interaction | Spatial interaction | Vicious circles, spread and backwash effects, rural-urban migration | | X | | | | | |
| | Sequent occupance | Colonisation exploitation | | X | | X | | | |
| Change | Change through time | Technological change, stages of growth, mechanisation, agrarian reform, planning, demographic transition | | X | | X | | | |
| World mindedness | Global interdependence | Trade, aid, self-reliance, NIEO | | X | | | | | |

Fig. 11 A teaching programme derived from the analytic framework (see Fig. 10)

A. The role of perception in promoting efficient and lasting concept attainment is not overlooked and is included in the programme. The five organising concepts are linked by a sixth, underlying concept namely that of causality. The inclusion of causality is to remind students and teachers to continue to ask the question 'why'? More specifically why do the observed patterns and processes change in space and through time?

B. The understanding of one concept is enhanced by the prior understanding of other concepts. The nature and extent of student exposure to each concept varies according to each teaching context. Progress through the programme is based upon adequate understanding rather than mastery of these concepts.

C. This serves to illustrate that there are several expressions of the same concept.

D. Presenting knowledge in a variety of forms inevitably means utilizing a number of symbol systems.

E. This represents some of those skills which are central to geography and provides the student with an opportunity to practise skills used in other fields as well as in geography. The aim is to encourage stu-

| E — major skills that might be utilised. Derived from: A – D | | | | | | | | | F — Some examples of context. Derived from A – E | | |
|---|---|---|---|---|---|---|---|---|---|---|---|
| Scientific method | Photograph analysis | Creative thinking | Map and diagram analysis | Graphicacy | Problem-solving | Model-building | Social | Who | What | Where | When |
|  | X | X |  | X |  |  | X | 1,2, 5,7. | The 'funny peculiar' | Indonesia, Egypt, England. North – South gap | I |
| X |  |  | X | X |  |  |  | 5,6, 7. | Qualitative and quantitative parameters | Africa SE Asia | I |
|  | X | X |  |  |  | X | X | 3. | Urban morphology, shanty, New Towns | Singapore, Hong Kong Cairo, Djakarta | I, III. |
| X |  | X |  |  |  | X | X | 4,5, 6. | Selected economic and social data | Brazil, EEC, Ghana | I, III. |
|  |  |  | X |  |  | X |  | 4,5. | Railways, roads, airways | Nigeria, Namibia, Amazonia | I, III. |
|  |  |  |  |  | X | X | X | 2,3, 4,5, 6. | Health care programme | Senegal, India, Dacca | I, II. |
|  | X |  | X |  | X |  |  | 2,3, 4,5. | Agricultural systems, economic base | Indonesia, West Africa | IV. |
|  |  | X | X | X | X | X |  | 2,4, 5,6. | Selected economic data | Ghana, India, Latin America | I,II, III, IV. |
|  |  |  |  | X |  |  | X | 2,5, 6. | Selected commodities, funded projects | Malaysia, S America | I,II, III. |

dents to learn how to learn. To do this they need a variety of tools with which to inquire. They need a rich repertoire of skills to help them come to know the world.

F.    This makes a distinction between content proper (concepts, ideas, propositions) and the kinds of examples which may be used to illustrate them (the context).

Who?    The individual and groups of people studied in a variety of spatial contexts.
1 = the individual               5 = the nation
2 = the village                  6 = international
3 = the town                     7 = global
4 = the region

When?    I = at one point in time               III = over time. Up to 10 years
II = over time. Up to 5 years          IV = over time. More than 10 years

It is important to note that the teaching programme exemplified here is only one of a variety of programmes that might be derived from fig. 10 to explore 'The Third World: a geographical interpretation'.

143

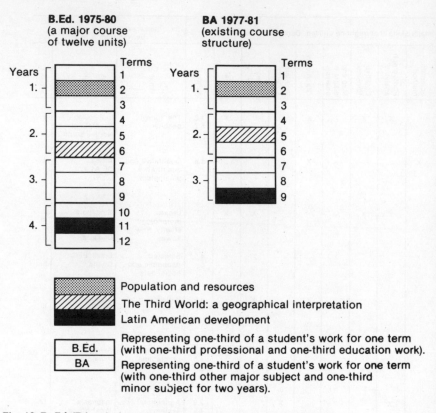

**B.Ed. 1975-80**
(a major course
of twelve units)

**BA 1977-81**
(existing course
structure)

Population and resources

The Third World: a geographical interpretation

Latin American development

| B.Ed. | Representing one-third of a student's work for one term (with one-third professional and one-third education work). |
| BA | Representing one-third of a student's work for one term (with one-third other major subject and one-third minor subject for two years). |

Fig. 12 B. Ed./BA units in geography representing a global dimension

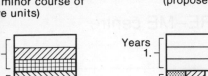

**B.Ed. 1981 till present**
a minor course of
ive units)

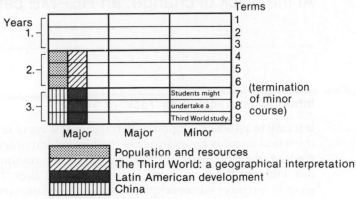

**BA 1982 Geography Human Studies**
(proposed course structure)

Terms

Years

1.

2.

3.

1
2
3
4
5
6
7
8
9

(termination
of minor
course)

Students might
undertake a
Third World study.

Major          Major          Minor

Population and resources
The Third World: a geographical interpretation
Latin American development
China

Population and resources
Problems of development on a global scale
Regional inequalities
Regional planning and policy
B.Ed. Representing one-third of a student's work for one term
(with one-third professional and one-third education work).

# Chapter 10     Brian Gates
## At the quick of change: an RE–ME centre

---

### Introduction: religion as 'rock' or 'rocker'

It is easy to associate religion with traditional ways of life and establishment, the world over, as for example in the hierarchical order of medieval Christendom, the caste basis of Indian society or the routinised life of an orthodox kibbutz. Religion, then, is as the rock of ages. Nor is it difficult to identify instances where religion has had a revolutionary impact on the lives of individual people or whole nations, from Jesus of Nazareth to Simon Kimbangue, Muhammad to Malcolm X, or Prince Siddartha to U Thant. What is much harder to appreciate is how such different webs of meaning can be spun out from common origins to take either revolutionary or conservative forms (Lewy 1974).

The explanation, in part at least, of this ambivalence is that religion has to do with the very questions of the sources and ends of human life which are fundamental to any form of social order. Just as the relative emphasis on the prophetic and the mystical varies from one religious tradition to another, and even within a tradition, so too does the degree of emphasis on this-worldly or other-worldliness, introversion or extroversion, and of post-mortem prospects or present vocation (Smart 1981). Whatever the emphasis, however, basic questions about the direction or directionlessness of life are involved, about its worthwhileness and its contingency (Richmond 1970).

The transforming, rocking thrust of religion past and present deserves special mention at the outset of this chapter, as a counter to any lurking inclination to reduce it, without argument, to nothing but underlying physical and material needs. Precisely because its horizons are set on the heights and depths of human experience, as on the origins and ends of time, religion is the archetype of global concern. Indeed the limits are pressed beyond not just the immediate neighbourhood, to the nation, the continent and the global world, but to the total universal context of any being. Nor are the limits those of individual roles played by each person in their divers social contexts, but the pondering and wondering depths of each person in their private I-ness. Global perspectives from religion route into the most final boundary questions of human being, at both macro- and microcosmic levels (Bowker 1973).

The point can be illustrated pictorially by reference to mythological language, which has been generated by religious traditions. Creation stories from whatever source, biblical, Ancient Near Eastern, African, Indian or

146

other, represent a struggle for ordered existence as against disorder and nothingness. Cosmos and global order are under threat from chaos and global irresponsibility (Eliade 1959). Similarly, stories of the end times redound with tendencies towards integration or disintegration of all that is (Robinson 1968). In both, there are personal and private poles of response, as well as organic and collective ones. Global perspectives may still be picayune if closed off at outermost and innermost limits.

## Religious education and moral education: last bastions and rival concerns

The alternating stress on religion as transforming or as rigidifying is also apparent in the history of the provision for religious and moral education (RE and ME) in England and Wales. Christians, individually or in groups, through their provision of church schools have had an innovatory role in pioneering popular education (Pollard 1957). At the same time, many of these church schools have also had a traditional catechetical allegiance, which has sometimes gone hand in hand with a more general conservatism in the classroom; indeed, their popularity with particular middle-class groups of parents on these grounds can be an embarrassment at a time when school rolls generally are falling.

Another example of contrary emphases can be seen in the 1944 Education Act's legal support for RE and the act of worship in schools. Thus, even with the 'conscience clauses' guaranteeing withdrawal rights, in practice the presentation of biblical Christianity was preserved by law. Yet, by intent the Act was insisting that 'personal and spiritual values' (words used by R. A. Butler and others in the parliamentary debate recorded in Hansard) (Niblett 1966) deserve special attention in schools, if boys and girls are to be able to recognise and resist a Nazi-type threat to individual freedom should one ever again arise. So important for the health of society is this independent-minded core of concern that it should be legally guaranteed within the programme of post-war educational reconstruction. Again, there is a mixture of the conserving and transforming aspects of religion.

The conjoining of beliefs and values in church tradition or in an agreed syllabus for RE has lately been the occasion of much righteous indignation. Baroness Wootton and certain curriculum philosophers have complained that, where this link is made in school, its consequence is adolescent delinquency and barbarism: since childish belief in God is outgrown, the moral and social constraints, which were made to appear to depend on this belief, are also rejected. Let us campaign instead to replace RE with a rationally based ME. Others have made a plea for a return to biblical morality: the provision for religious instruction in schools should be strengthened precisely because its weakness is at the root of the nation's current plight.[1]

Neither of these prescriptions has gained acceptance from the weight of professional opinion. Back to biblical or ecclesiastical authority may have the attraction for some as a point of security in a world which to them

147

seems otherwise to be falling apart, but diversity of belief and unbelief is manifestly the world-wide human condition, and living on a British island provides no escape from it. Morever, within the Christian tradition there are different views on the same major moral issues, from capital punishment and abortion to nuclear deterrence and energy programmes.

To separate out moral values entirely from any religious reference in practice proves equally unrealistic. The evidence of secularisation and ecclesiastical decline may be thought to point this way, as also may the number of teachers who themselves are doubtfully committed to Christianity. But the argument plays down the ambiguity of the evidence on secularisation (Martin 1978) and most certainly takes little note of the impact of immigration on the religious life of the nation (Morrish 1971). The now considerable diversity of religious belief in our society variously informs individual life-styles and value judgements. At the same time the principles of autonomous morality may themselves be variously derived, in for instance utilitarian, intuitive or de-ontological vein, and applied, so that a moral consensus is not much more easily arrived at than a religious one. Just as religion is not reducible to morals or morals to religion, neither is RE to ME or ME to RE.

## Proper partners

Theoretically, other solutions might in principle be possible, but the end-result would be to impoverish our national tradition of public education which has been gradually extended to represent the curriculum of a participating democracy. The USSR pattern of atheist instruction and moral training may be harder-headed in its discipline, but largely at the expense of alternative belief systems and individual judgement (Price 1977). The USA pattern of leaving religion to the parent communities outside the school protects the area of beliefs and values from the public scrutiny that is encouraged on other fronts, and all manner of curiosities may flourish unquestioned as a result (Needleman and Baker 1978).

Constitutionally, in the UK, freedom of beliefs and values is an established norm for the whole society. The emancipation of Jews and atheists, as now of other minority groups, has been only slowly achieved since the seventeenth century, but their position is guaranteed by rule of law, as is that of rival political parties and pressure groups. Similarly, in education, the areas of RE and ME have been successfully opened up to nurture boys and girls in the matter of beliefs and values, presented not in any closed-minded, unilateral way, but sensitive to the richness and depth of human concerns which variously inform them.

This, at least, is the licence assumed by the Standing Advisory Councils on RE[2] which have produced such agreed syllabuses and handbooks as those of City of Birmingham (1975a, b) and Hampshire (1978; Laxton 1980), or the ILEA guidelines on assemblies (ILEA 1980). This, too, is the basic assumption around which the National RE Council was formed ten years ago, comprising representatives of each of the professional teacher associations with interest in RE and of each of the major belief communities found in the country, including the British Humanist Association.[3] It is also reflected in published DES utterances on RE and ME, such as those contained in *Curriculum 11–16* (HMI 1977), and *Framework for the School Curriculum* (DES 1980).

Sufficient work has been done at the level of curriculum theory to vindicate both RE and ME as belonging in schools on educational grounds. The most appropriate procedures for implementing this may still, however, be in dispute – as subjects separate from each other, and each with its own timetable slot? or, one as separate subject, the other 'across the curriculum'? For the resolution of these questions much depends on available expertise and the particular school context and curriculum model. It has become nigh impossible, however, to justify the immorality of leaving either or both entirely to the 'ethos' or 'hidden curriculum' of the school or of allowing them to be subsumed in some primary theme or project work, or a secondary humanities programme, which may in effect integrate RE and ME out from deliberate line of enquiry.

In sum, RE is directly concerned with cosmic sense of being and the development of global perspectives. Any religious tradition itself serves as a framework within which the believer interprets his daily life and the significance of his location in the universe. The content of RE, even where still biblical, rather than dealing with Christianity as a whole, let alone other religious traditions, still has global perspectives. In so far as the full Christian tradition is dealt with, the horizon is world-wide; beginning in Palestine/Israel, the Christian community is beyond, as well as within Europe from the outset. Alongside this, the Buddhist and Hindu, Jewish and Muslim traditions are finding a place within RE throughout the land, and so, more occasionally, is African traditional religion (Gates 1980). To engage in trying to understand any one of these traditions, or counters to them, entails developing the child's own global and synoptic view of life and death in the world, and if no headway has been made with this within compulsory schooling, RE will have failed.

Similarly, ME is aware of the global, as well as the local context for value judgements and action. It is able to draw on models and resources, near and far, for life-styles, and the attitudes and motives that variously inform them. The classroom approach may be direct teaching to develop recognition of moral concepts and reasoning, or practice in the skills of moral judgement and evaluation (Wilson 1972). It may also, or instead, be the gradual development of sympathetic attitudes towards the needs and feelings of others through work on personal relationships done in regular form periods (Baldwin and Wells 1979), or cultivated indirectly by general exposure to the 'ethos' of the school. The likelihood is that poor tuning on this emotional wavelength will make it much harder for any child to be open enough to receive global signals when transmitted in more remote conceptual terms.[4]

To do any of this work effectively, the demands made on teachers are enormous. They are so, partly because of the content shifts in RE which have taken place in the last ten years, considerably enlarging the international orientation. The need to clarify the matter of individual commitment in regard to religion is also demanding. It may take some time for any teacher to get used to the idea of separating private religous conviction and doubt from public and professional commitment, to take seriously the religious experience of mankind so as to encourage better understanding by pupils. Rather fundamentally, however, such a distinction is a necessary preliminary for genuine appreciation of global perspectives by anyone who would be a teacher.

Likewise, sensitivity to the different modes of moral reasoning which a school may contain – in teaching, assembly, playground, staffroom, or wherever – will require mature self-knowledge, as well as the clear reading of others. Moreover, the greater diversity of folkways found in the family backgrounds from which the children come, as well as the splintering consensus on such matters as strike action, sexual morality and nuclear power, can each make sudden demands for thoughtful comment and response. Professional attention to these matters is personally demanding, yet directly related to global prospecting.

## Daunting difficulties in teacher education

The government's reduction in the total number of places for the initial education of teachers has had the effect of guaranteeing for at least the next decade that a relatively small proportion of RE and ME (primary and secondary) in schools will be in the hands of those specifically trained to take it on. Already the teaching profession suffers from a serious shortage of RE specialists and it is doubtful whether more than a tiny minority can claim any formal experience of method work in ME.[5] Given the massive changes just outlined which RE has seen in recent years and the new developments in ME, the need for RE and ME in-service support and guidance for teachers generally is enormous. Unfortunately, the closure of many colleges of education has significantly curtailed the availability of local resources for this kind of in-service work. The reduction in student-teacher numbers in remaining colleges has also led to the closure of several religious studies departments, in the interests of maintaining viable numbers in other subject areas. This has had the further consequences (already apparent in one-year graduate courses in many University Departments of Education (Marratt 1979) of reducing or eliminating the expertise available to help with professional work in RE and ME – as vital for all first-school and middle-years students as to the secondary specialists.

## St Martin's College, Lancaster as an RE – ME centre

It is against this background that the work of St Martin's College as an RE–ME centre is now described. St Martin's was established as a college of education in 1963; this teacher emphasis remains, but extends to include BA courses, Community and Youth Studies, as well as adult education. Sited in a former barracks, the college was dubbed St Martin's by the first principal, to indicate an institutional change of role, imitative of its patron namesake, who exchanged military armour for the power of the word in teaching. The college's claim to be an RE – ME centre stems from a core of educational and theological concern, to which we will return. In practice, it expresses itself in the full range of courses and resources which the college affords in RE and ME, Religious Studies and Social Ethics. Global dimensions emerge from the curriculum content, as well as from the supporting resources. Although all these different strands are interrelated, for clarity and coherence sake they are now described in turn.

## Initial teacher education

All students, whether on B.Ed. or BA courses, do subject studies, and Religious Studies is available as a main subject within the B.Ed degree, or a minor within the BA. The common BA/B.Ed. one-year Part 1 course introduces students to the scope of religion in the world and to the disciplines which define Religious Studies. Three examples of the variety of contemporary religious and atheistic thought are given special attention: Christianity, the Indian religious tradition, and secular humanism. In addition to the use of book, videotape and film resources, fieldwork observation and documentary study of religious groups (e.g. Sikhs, Quakers, Celtic remains) in the northwest of England are built into the course. High priority is given to developing sensitivity to the treasures of human experience, by encouraging the direct contact with different religious communities and the expressions of each faith in visual and bodily forms, as well as in story and systematic theology.

Part 2 courses diverge. B.Ed. students have the opportunity to follow up the full range of Religious Studies. The Christian tradition is studied directly in the second- and third-year course on the New Testament and the Rise of Christianity and in the fourth-year options on Christian Doctrine and Christianity and the Arts. Less directly it is also treated in the term 4 course on the Old Testament, the course on Ethics later that year, and in the fourth year Religious and Atheistic Thought option. Other religious traditions are studied in Year 2 and the Judaism part of the Old Testament and Jewish Tradition course, in the Year 3 Hinduism course, and in the option of Buddhism or Islam in Year 4. The interplay and encounter between secular philosophies and religious beliefs is studied most directly in the Year 4 Religious and Atheistic Thought option, but again it is present also in the Ethics and Doctrine courses. BA students concentrate expressly on the many facets of Christian tradition, including its global responses to alternative claims to religious truth, thrown up by other faiths and philosophies. In consequence, whether on a BA or B.Ed. course, it is very difficult to do Religious Studies without personal horizons being considerably stretched.

151

The B.Ed. Honours course in Religious Studies provides an academic base for secondary specialist teaching of RE and equally a reference point for a primary teacher. For the intending teacher on the BA course, however, there is an additional strength available – should he or she intend to specialise in RE and ME teaching – the Major or Minor in Social Ethics.

**Social Ethics**

This is nationally unique as a degree course and for teaching provides the academic underpinning for ME which Religious Studies provides for RE. The Part 1 draws on law and moral philosophy to define the terms of reference for the course as a whole, and introduces students to the ethical analysis of particular problem areas – in family life, sexuality and uses of alcohol. The variety of urban placements at the end of the first year ensures experience of a different environment from what the students have previously had. The Part 2 extends the case-study work to cover medical issues, work and leisure, discrimination (animal, racial, sexual), revolution, war and peace. It also involves two other strands; psychology and philosophy courses on human behaviour and the nature of moral judgement, and, from a comparative point of view, courses on religious (Christian, Indian, Semitic) and humanistic (utilitarian, Marxist, existentialist) perspectives. Again, the centrality of global concerns is immediately obvious. In association with the major in Social Ethics there is opportunity in minor courses to study, e.g. Development Education within the Geography minor, Youth Work and Community Action, and, for ordinary degree students, Science and Society (see fig. 13).

**Educational and professional studies**

Secondary method courses (B.Ed. or PGCE) in RE and ME are available for those specialising in Religious Studies and/or Social Ethics. All other students, whether first-school/middle-years B.Ed. or middle-years PGCE, take basic method courses on RE and ME. In these attention is given to children's religious and moral development, including their capacity for global understanding, as well as to classroom teaching schemes and resource supports. Educational Studies courses (B.Ed. and PGCE) themselves include substantial work on values in education, and, in the case of the BA minor in Education, a separate course on the theory of ME. In addition, for all students there are optional courses on Minority Groups and Multicultural Education, which build on the same first-hand experience as the rest of our work. In a substantial way therefore, the RE–ME ingredients in initial training at St Martin's pushes students to extend the limits of their thinking and valuing to take in global problems and cosmic apprehensions.

**In-service provisions**

A very strong case can be made for a college's involvement in in-service

**B.Ed. (Hons.)**

| Year 1 | Year 2 | Year 3 | Year 4 |
|---|---|---|---|
| Education in theory and practice | Teaching practice/School experience | Educational Studies | Educational Studies |
| | | Professional Studies inc. RE and ME | Advanced Professional Studies |
| Old Testament and Jewish Tradition | | New Testament and the Rise of Christianity | Two courses, selected from: Religious and atheistic thought, Christian theology and other religions, Islam, Christianity and the Arts |
| | | Christian Ethics | Hinduism | | |

**BA (Hons.)**

Social Ethics major · Religious Studies minor

| Year 1 | Teaching practice/School experience |
|---|---|

Religious Studies
Introducing basic disciplines.
Christian, Indian and secular traditions.
Religion in NW England

Educational Studies Community and Youth Studies/art/English/French/geography/history/maths/music/science

Social Ethics
Basic terms; values, questions in family life, sexuality, and a minority group

Social Ethics first subject · Religious Studies second subject

**Year 2**

Comparative Ethics: I Christian; II Indian, Semitic and Secular
Values and teachings derived from particular beliefs

Case studies
Medical ethics, discrimination, poverty, war and peace

Psychological issues
Attitude formation, aggression, self-concepts

Philosophical issues
Relativism    Is/ought

New Testament and the Rise of Christianity

Christianity and the Arts
Literature, music and architecture

Christian Doctrine: I Christ and man; II Attitudes towards other religions

**Year 3**

Comparative Ethics: I Christian; II Indian, Semitic and Secular
Values and teachings set in the life of particular communities

Case-study methods
Research techniques and skills of interpretation

Science and Society

Local Community Decision-making

Christian Doctrine: I Christ and man; II Attitudes towards other religions

New Testament and the Rise of Christianity

Psychology of Religion

Fig. 13 Religious Studies and Social Ethics in St Martin's BA and B. Ed. degrees

153

provision, simply in the interests of helping enrich initial education. We have no doubt that the direct engagement with teachers, in and out of their school contexts, has fed back into college experience which has been appreciated by tutors and students alike. It has done much to break down the suspicion with which the college tutor may be regarded from afar. This is especially important in the areas of RE and ME where perhaps a great gulf can otherwise seem to gape between what teachers may have previously expected of them and what the students themselves have been exposed to.

A greater incentive to the college to press forward the cause of in-service RE and ME provision comes from another source – sheer professional need. Since, because of cuts, it is the teachers already in service who will continue to have the greatest responsibilities for RE and ME, a deliberate effort has been made to lay on courses which will help them. These include short courses and conferences, as well as named awards. A feature of the shorter courses (five to eight two-hour sessions after school) and day conferences, is that most of them are taught away from the college, in school or teachers' centres. This has the double advantage of making them more accessible to the teachers and on their own professional ground. Themes offered in any one year include: 'Developing Primary RE', 'Developing Primary ME', 'Biographical Resources for RE and ME', 'Assembly Workshop' (Christian, secular and multi-faith).

There are three named awards. There is the MA in RE, a one-year full-time (or two-year part-time) course, jointly taught with the University of Lancaster. This includes taught courses on the Religious and Moral Development of Children and Key Issues in the Theory and Practice of RE and ME, as well as one in Religious Studies. This award attracts teachers and lecturers from throughout England and from overseas (e.g. Australia, Greece, Hong Kong, New Zealand). Secondly, there is the Advanced Certificate in RE, a course of one day a week over two years; it comprises both subject studies and professional work in RE and ME. Thirdly, there are Certificates A and B in RE, year-long courses half a day a week. Together they make up the equivalent of year one of the Advanced Certificate, but they also stand on their own, as awards planned with the local Anglican and Catholic dioceses and with the needs of teachers in church schools particularly in mind. This ecumenical dimension is an indication of the centre's interest in Christian ecclesiastical horizons, and again it feeds back into initial training.

## Resources

In line with its claim to be an RE – ME centre, and to service the various courses in Religious Studies and Social Ethics, RE and ME, the college has developed a range of support facilities and resources. The main college library is stocked to support the studies in religion and ethics as well as the theory of RE and ME. With the help of Job Creation Programmes (JCP) and Special Temporary Employment Programmes (STEP) projects funded by the Manpower Services Commission, subject indexes have been prepared, systematically abstracting from the books and journals for students', teachers' and community workers' use. Similarly a compendium index of organisations and agencies active in all the areas of our concern has been prepared, with summaries of the services they provide and illustrative files of materials they produce. A reference collection of school textbooks and slides, records, school broadcast materials, kits, etc. on all aspects of RE, ME and school assemblies has been put together and is continually updated. For loan purposes to registered students most of these materials are duplicated within the College Teaching Practice Library and Resource Centre and explorations are afoot to develop a system of loan boxes of materials that may be left for a week in a school for staff to browse through before passing them to another school.

In addition to advice on resources available from the specialist staff appointed to teach Religious Studies and Social Ethics, RE and ME, colleagues in other areas also lend their support. Thus counselling, development education, political education and health education are all sections which are comprehensively resourced.

Three further agencies also relate directly to the college or RE – ME centre. One is the SHAP Working Party on World Religions in Education, a ginger group that has striven for more than ten years to broaden the base of English education by reference to Christianity as a world religion and the faiths of other folk.[6] Jointly sponsored with SHAP is an annual four-day residential conference for teachers, the themes of which have so far been 'Jesus as a Jewish and a Muslim Prophet'; 'Christ and the Buddha in History, Art and Ethics'; 'Jesus, Muhammad and Marx in Conflict and Congruence'. They combine scholarly presentations with active classroom preparation and again attract teachers from throughout the UK.

The second is the Social Morality Council (SMC). Implementing its plan for ME (SMC 1977), St Martin's is the National Information and Resource Centre. This SMC centre is able to draw on the expertise and resources of the college as an already existing RE – ME centre, but its staff and additional resources have been independently funded by a grant from the DES. The SMC sponsors the *Journal of Moral Education*, published for them by the National Foundation for Educational Research. The SMC has also sponsored several working parties which have produced reports on different aspects of ME, including broadcasting, drugs, and primary RE and ME.[7] Happily, in its broadly based constitution, which acknowledges the importance of diverse viewpoints (including secular humanists) in the task of ME, the SMC's approach is complementary to that of the college.

The third link is with the Schools Council, and in several ways. The council has given limited funding to the college to provide an RE Enquiry Service, to follow on from the Primary and Secondary RE Projects, which had also been based in Lancaster from 1969–78, under the direction of Ninian Smart at the University. St Martin's own involvement with RE went hand in hand with the history of those projects and, in the absence of any new projects or major continuation elsewhere, we receive visitors and respond to teachers' letters and phone calls seeking information relating to the projects. This service has been extended to provide advice on all aspects of RE, especially resources.[8] A similar service is also available on ME, following up the Oxford, and then Cambridge-based Schools Council Moral Education Projects.[9] In addition, in joint sponsorship with the Rowntree Trust, the Schools Council has established a *World Studies 8–13 Project*, with one base in Bristol and the other at St Martin's. Its concern with peace and conflict matches well with existing strengths and interests, and once again is entirely in keeping with the college's designation as an RE – ME centre. In all these regards, by association the Schools Council is able to demonstrate consistency and continuity in its curriculum development in both RE and ME, thereby to meet the charge that it lacks sense of longer-term extension and consolidation.

In all our thinking on resources we are determined that they shall never be reduced to a particular collection of materials tied to a particular location. That there are such is part of St Martin's claim to be an RE – ME centre, but more important is the fact that we are a large team of resource persons, ready to interpret and travel out with the materials which might otherwise be a treasure trove of very limited circulation.

## This RE – ME centre: a theological rationale

The educational justification for St Martin's as an RE–ME centre arises from the developments described at the outset of this chapter. Economically it can be afforded by the college because care is taken to ensure that courses are arranged only if numbers are viable. What, however, has so far gone unsaid is how properly the centre belongs within a Church of England College of Higher Education, which St Martin's is. These arguments are now given, successively more theologically explicit.

One of the inspirations of the dual system by which Church and State contracted to provide education for the nation's children is a determination on the part of the Church of England (the RC position is somewhat different) (National Society 1980) to affirm the importance of education for all, to take a share in the costs of providing it, and to try to ensure that the schools and colleges which it sponsors achieve the best education possible at the time, In this respect, this RE–ME centre attempts to provide the courses and resources which on educational grounds are needed to enrich the nation's schools.

Thanks to the Taylor Report, it has become more fashionable to acknowledge the importance of parental participation in education, for example by their serving as school managers. Undoubtedly, more could be done to involve individual parents in particular institutions. Nevertheless, church schools and colleges have this principle already built into them, in the sense that they are actively sponsored by the parental religious community. The St Martin's RE–ME centre has this Church parental interest invested in it. These interests extend from the local and parochial to the ecumenical and global.

Thirdly, it is intrinsic to Christian theological endeavour that there must be continual conversation between the faith inherited from of old and the contemporary world. Christianity would cease to exist as a world faith if it talked only to its own followers and on their own premises. Thus just as a college, St Martin's is open to students of all faiths or none, so the provision of the RE–ME centre contains within it an appreciation of the diverse starting-points that illuminate personal belief and values. This exposure of the Christian heart to other viewpoints, as to the rawest facts of life that scientific inspection of the human condition can reveal, is a pre-condition for a Christian theology which is genuinely global. In turn, from within the cumulative Christian tradition there are sources and reserves that can give hope and vision for a future for humanity that may yet be forged differently from our present. As a working necessity, St Martin's as an RE–ME centre is at the quick of change.

## Notes

1. The campaign for Moral Education, active in the late 1960s, had the support of Paul Hirst, then of the London University Institute of Education, the National Secular Society and British Humanist Association; its Secretary was H. J. Blackham. The Order for Christian Unity has been more recently active with the claim that Christian teaching in schools is under threat from 'so-called Religious and Moral Studies'; it invites Christians of all denominations to pledge themselves to uphold Christ's commandments. The chairman is the Marchioness of Lothian.
2. Section 29 of the 1944 Education Act makes provision for the preparation, adoption and reconsideration of agreed syllabuses and empowers a LEA to constitute Standing Advisory Councils to deal with this and related matters. The details of the constitution are given in the Fifth Schedule. In recent years the clause which authorises that 'such religious denominations as, in the opinion of the authority, ought, having regard to the circumstances of the area, to be represented' has been taken to include, where appropriate, both minority faiths and secular humanists (cf. Hull 1975.)
3. The chairman is H. Marratt, Deputy Principal, West London Institute of Higher Education, Isleworth, Middlesex TW7 5DU. The two honorary secretaries are James Thompson, 123 Green End Road, Hemel Hempstead, Herts HP1 RRT, and John Sutcliffe, CEM, 2 Chester House, Pages Lane, London N10.
4. The materials produced by the Schools Council Moral Education Projects under the direction of Peter McPhail were built on the findings of interpersonal psychology that motivation for learning and behaviour generally follows from feeling and perceiving that something is significant. High priority is therefore given to enabling pupils to understand and interpret the various cues in any relationship or social context.
5. The shortage of RE specialists is documented in the RE Council's 1978 *Report on the Development of RE* and was admitted in parliamentary debate (Easter 1980) when Dr Rhodes Boyson stated that 500 new secondary RE teachers would have to be recruited annually in the 1980s if minimum provision for the subject is to be met. Provision of direct method work in ME in initial teacher education is even less substantial than that for RE. The Social Morality Council's 1973–74 questionnaire to colleges and UDEs exposed the diffuse nature of the provision for ME throughout the country.
6. The SHAP Working Party takes its name from the location of its first meeting in 1969; coincidentally SHAP is an acronym of the founding co-chairmen, Professors Smart, Hilliard and Parrider. The secretary is John Rankin, West Sussex Institute of Higher Education, Chichester.
7. The working parties have been broadly constituted to reflect the range of religious belief and unbelief in the country, and of professional expertise (SMC 1970, 1973, 1975). Edward Oliver is the Secretary-General of the SMC and its London office is now at 23 Kensington Square, London W8 5HN. The Lancaster centre is under the direction of Dr Birman Nottingham.

8. Elizabeth Cook, formerly a Primary RE Project Officer, is responsible for primary school enquiries, John Hammond for secondary enquiries and John Ewan for general resource advice (telephone 0524 63446, ext. 40).
9. Michael Cross, the Research and Information Officer of the SMC centre in the college, is generally responsible for ME enquiries (telephone 0524 63446, ext. 31).

# Chapter 11    Roger Morgan
## African Studies: issues of course development

The aim of this chapter is not to make any universal statement regarding courses on global change at the post-secondary level. It is more an attempt to look at one institution, a college of education, and its move to set up a course in African Studies as part of its diversified programme.

The brief analysis attempted here does not in any way try to discuss the establishment of an ideal course. It is more concerned with the reality of establishing within the constraints (organisational, conceptual and financial) a new course which examines a continental area still mainly regarded in Third World terms. It is therefore a report that offers suggestions for the discussion of the mixed disciplinary elements of the course structure and the validation procedure which would have formed the next stage.

### Course origins

The origins of the course proposal lie in the James Report and White Paper (HMSO 1972) in which it was stated that a range of intellectually demanding two-year courses would be a critical element in achieving greater flexibility in higher education. We can with some hindsight argue that these plans implied an organisational rationalisation of teaching resources in higher education which have since been savagely reinforced by the predicted teacher-training figures involving a considerable overall cut in the numbers of students in initial training (Lodge 1976). The idea, however, of an African Studies course was formulated prior to the application of the cuts and when these placed pressure on Rolle College to look for new and different courses to fill student places, the proposal had already developed sufficient impetus to be considered in detail.

The original idea for the course stemmed from two members of staff from the History and Education departments who already had teaching interests on Africa (one teaching a course on West African History, the other a course on Education and Development in Africa). Considerable African expertise also existed in a number of other departments within the college, Religious Studies, Geography, English and Science, where the main interest was in anthropology. Approaches to these departmental lecturers brought a favourable response and, following a call from the College Academic Board for the submission of plans for new courses, a planning team was set up to look into the viability of establishing a course in African Studies. The planning group had no official status, being interdepartmental.

The traditional academic structure, however, in no way restrained the team's work and the departmental members reported general progress to their departmental heads who provided advice regarding their own departmental perspectives. Ultimately the team also reported directly to the Policy Committee which was the body set up by the college to deal with all planning of new courses.

## Planning issues

The African Studies planning team felt that there should be maximum flexibility and thus an attempt was made to devise an ideal course which would administratively, as well as conceptually, form a cohesive unit. Because of this the group became aware at an early stage in the planning that a number of issues would need to be resolved:

1. If the course was to focus on Africa from a variety of perspectives what kind of course structure would be appropriate and what combination of subjects would be ideal?
2. What administrative arrangements would best serve the needs of such a course at a planning and organisational level?
3. What could an institution such as Rolle College with limited expertise and resources offer that was genuinely different from that offered at a larger institution?
4. Would there be enough students sufficiently interested to come on such a course and would there be sufficient employment prospects for them after obtaining the final qualification in the employment-conscious climate in which tertiary-level courses were being developed?

Prior to attempting to answer these questions an examination of the college's resources was undertaken. Eight members of staff, including the college principal, had personal experience of Africa and of these, five were involved in teaching courses on Africa within their own departments. The existence of such courses meant that within departments, library resources already existed which focused on Africa. In addition, Exeter University library, situated ten miles away, contained a specialist Ghana collection. A variety of Rolle/African contacts had already been established, resulting in a number of visits to Rolle by African educationalists and individual students, some of whom participated in certificate and degree courses.

With these resources in mind the planning group was able to turn its attention to the four main procedural issues stated above.

1. The group noted that by involving a variety of contributing disciplines a mixed-disciplinary approach would need to be established. The exact form would be decided upon later, but there was general agreement that the course structure should start from a wider mixed-disciplinary base leading towards greater disciplinary specialisation as the course progressed. It was argued that if the course structure took the form of a two-year Diploma in Higher Education (Dip. HE) course followed by an additional one or two years leading to the award of a degree, the later

years might be undertaken at Rolle or might involve transfer to a variety of specialist institutions.

2. Administratively, discussion showed that two critical factors had to be taken into account. It would be necessary to provide some degree of continuity throughout the course; more important, because of the contribution of a variety of disciplines, the position of course co-ordinator would be rotated after a fixed period to ensure that the course was not biased in any one direction.

3. The third question facing the planning team was a critical one. It was felt that the innovatory form of the proposed courses would be the most crucial factor in determining if the college could attract students at a time of declining student numbers in higher education. Consequently, the following criteria were determined:

   (a) *Flexibility*. In an institution with limited resources (staff, finance and material) there was a need for transfer of students between the college and institutions which could provide specialist facilities. For this reason it was decided to adopt two types of terminal qualification – the Dip. HE obtainable after two years' study at Rolle, and a degree in African Studies after a third year at Rolle or a third, or possibly a fourth, at a linking institution.

   (b) *Student choice*. The course would involve a focus on Africa but would depend upon an introduction to a variety of disciplined perspectives. It was felt appropriate, therefore, to provide some opportunity for the students to choose what they wished to focus their attention on towards the end of the course either at Rolle or elsewhere.

   (c) *Field experience*. At a time of calls for increasing relevance of courses, it was felt that there ought to be the opportunity for a variety of field experience which students could have the opportunity of sampling according to their interests. It was decided that this ought to fit into the first two years of the course. It was suggested that this could be academic, making use of particular facilities in existence in the UK. It might also involve a period of attachment to academic or commercial institutions in the field in Africa.

   (d) *Vocational as well as academic coherence*. To an extent the vocational element of the course would build upon an academic base, but preparatory courses and actual experience in the field could be linked with commercial enterprises in the field. Academic coherence would be provided not only through the integration of mixed-disciplinary contributions but also within the disciplines themselves to allow later specialisation.

4. To ascertain the viability of the whole exercise an attempt was made to examine the range of similar courses that existed in institutes of higher education and to establish linking course arrangements with these institutions. Student interest was to be ascertained by approaching all secondary and further education establishments in three LEAs, whilst an

analysis was undertaken of the response to the proposed course outline by 100 major companies dealing with the developing world.

## Planning procedure and course structure

To ensure that progress would be as rapid as possible, the group decided to undertake planning on three fronts simultaneously. The analysis of potential employers and students and institutions offering similar courses would form one avenue of planning strategy, whilst another would involve the attempt to develop links with other institutions who could offer Dip. HE courses. The third front would involve developing the course structure itself, incorporating the major criteria already suggested and obtaining validation and financial support from the appropriate bodies. Strategy and progress were determined by and reported back to the planning group who continued to meet regularly to discuss course development. The college's Policy Committee subsequently passed on the recommendations with a few minor structural suggestions to the college's Academic Board, where the course was accepted as one of three main alternative degree programmes to the B.Ed. which would form the college's main programme of diversification.

Up to this point no detailed identification of the form of integration in the course structure had been undertaken, as members of the planning group were clearly aware that constraints would be placed on the planning of the initial part of the course by linking institutions. They would expect that at least in part students who might be transferring to their courses would have undertaken a considerable amount of work comparable to that of their own students.

A general structure was then considered and agreed on a four-unit basis to make it comparable to the B.Ed structure of the college to enable some students to take selected B.Ed. units as part of their foundation work in African Studies. The initial year would involve a mixed-disciplinary element providing an African perspective, followed by a general introduction to a number of introductory disciplinary courses with an African focus.

The last term of the first year would be a mixed-disciplinary study of a particular African region with the first term of the second year completely given to field experience. The second and third terms would be mainly synthesising ones in which discussion about the various field experiences could take place in seminars; the students would be expected to produce a written report which in part would act as a basis for assessment of the fieldwork undertaken. The third year, forming the conceptual apex of the course, was to be given over to more specialised disciplined approaches to the study of Africa, which would have been also initiated by study in year two after the student had returned from field experiences (see Fig. 14).

General comments about the content of the various elements of the course had by this date, 1978, been included in the planning documents,

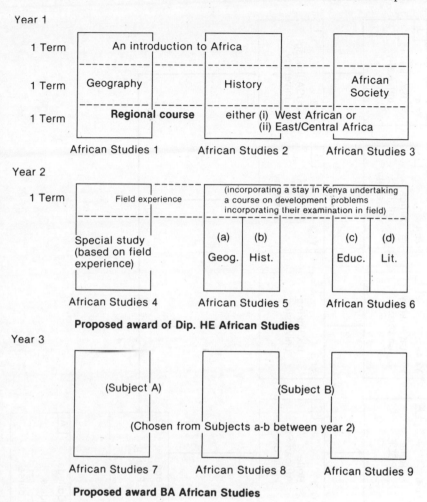

Fig. 14 African Studies: course structure

and the questionnarire response to the course had been analysed. This showed that there were a considerable number of prospective students, and two universities in the UK had expressed an interest at an informal level in establishing links. Negotiations had also been undertaken with two universities in the United States and three in Africa which would also have liked to involve themselves in a course interchange network. In addition there had been an informal suggestion from within the college of a link between the Diploma element of the course and the B.Ed. Honours course, indicating that the Diploma would have been an excellent base for a B.Ed. course which would have mainly focused its attention on cultural pluralism including an exchange teaching practice with an area with

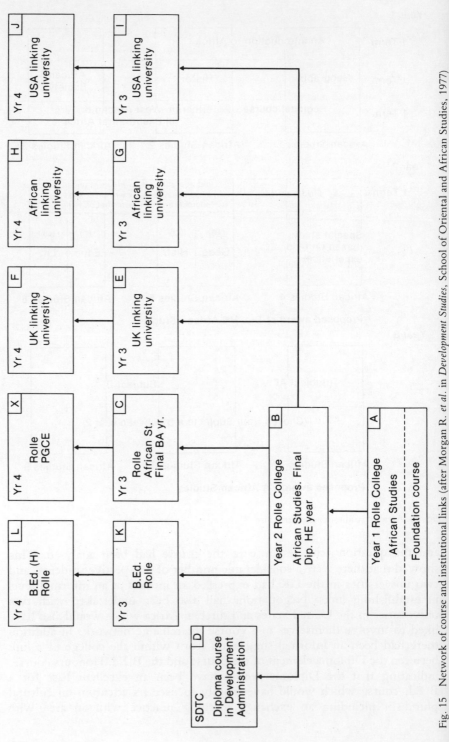

Fig. 15  Network of course and institutional links (after Morgan R. *et al.* in *Development Studies*, School of Oriental and African Studies, 1977)

multicultural schools. The intention here was that prospective student teachers who already had an interest in teaching in such areas in the UK would undertake the two-year diploma course enabling them to obtain a substantial awareness of the cultural background of one minority group. As the diploma course took two years it was suggested that the minimum period that could be given over to teacher preparation would be two years, which from a grant point of view would demand an Honours qualification at the end of the course. This also implied an additional difficulty for students undertaking the final two years of such a course – what main subject should they take as no B.Ed. African Studies main subject existed in the college at that time? Despite these difficulties, planning proceeded, but the planning group became aware that perhaps in terms of teacher preparation the opportunity for intending teachers to undertake a PCGE one-year course at Rolle that was completely professionally orientated with options in multicultural education after their degree was the best option. The general pattern of all these intended linkages is shown in Fig. 15. The establishment of such links, however, could have had considerable implications for the group's attempt to structure the course especially in terms of the mixed-disciplinary elements. The course was then submitted as a proposal in outline to the University of Exeter for discussion hopefully leading to validation and also to the local body responsible for financing courses, but considerable detail had yet then to be worked out.

## Planning problems

To an extent the group consciously chose not to provide course detail as they were aware that considerable alteration would have been required by the various faculties at the university. Also difficulties over planning were caused by absence of staff on study leave and the pressure of normal college commitments. For this reason a number of issues still faced the planning group:
1. What form of integration could be undertaken in the suggested mixed-disciplinary units of the course?
2. What would be the composition of the board that examined the proposal at the university for validation? Would the course be passed from one faculty to another or would it be allowed examination by a joint or interfaculty board? The answer to this question was to be critical for the production of a mixed-disciplinary degree which requires coherence between and within disciplines.
3. Would the college decision-making structure (itself changed since the summer of 1976) allow the establishment not only of the interdepartmental planning group but also of an interdepartmental administrative group who would have as much say as the departments in terms of course staffing? In other words, would the individual be able to opt for a proportion of his or her teaching time to be given to both the African

Studies and departmental discipline courses? For obvious professional reasons none of the staff involved wished to commit themselves completely to the course at this time until career recognitions were likely to be given for such involvement (GRIHE 1975):

The University teacher judges his expertise and receives his esteem and rewards for the most part within the framework of one subject. His courses and examinations belong to the traditions of that subject, his publications are judged by other teachers in that subject, he attends its annual conferences and if he is successful he is promoted through a small and fairly familiar peer group to a chair from which he continues to organise the teaching of the same subject. There are great penalties attached to breaking out of this cocoon into an insecure world of fewer posts and senior posts, fewer peers, and fewer conferences, and the best and most confident of teachers is quite justified in looking hard at what sort of prospects the system offers him if he once casts aside his subject label.

The first of these three issues is perhaps the only one which can warrant attention in a chapter in this publication, and in so doing it is worth noting a statement made regarding the mixed-disciplinary elements in the group's last submission document: 'There are many connections and points of contact observable between the different disciplines involved in the following syllabus; it is envisaged that these will become more obviously identifiable during the practical teaching of the course and a degree of adjustment will be both possible and desirable as the course proceeds' (Rolle College 1976.)

In essence the planning group suggested that a mixed-disciplinary structure could not be predetermined in detail. Considerable involvement in teaching the mixed-disciplinary element would be necessary before the 'bugs could be ironed out'. The group has also been aware that the success of this teaching will depend on the degree of compatibility between the personalities of the teachers. This was noted by Sathyamurthy (1975) when referring to the interdisciplinary teaching of politics at York: 'where failure occurred the main reason seemed to be a compound between personality factors and a related unwillingness to engage in continuing dialogue about differences'.

With these factors in mind the African Studies planning group attached importance to providing a framework for integration, a point also noted by the Group for Research and Innovation in Higher Education (GRIHE 1975) in their final conclusions: 'Interdisciplinary teaching necessitates greater explicitness about aims, teaching methods and assessment'.

It was with these comments in mind that the mixed-disciplinary elements that could be identified within the course concerned the planning group:

(a) The first/second terms Year I – Contemporary and Traditional African Society
(b) The third term Year I – Regional Studies
(c) The first term Year II – Field Studies

The planning group had up to that date, 1979, not decided on the detail of these mixed-disciplinary units, but had taken a decision about the form of discipline mixture – multidisciplinarity. This could be regarded as a logical step in keeping with the recommendations of the Development Studies continuum (previous section) and is in keeping with the report of GRIHE (1975) on 'Interdisciplinarity': 'A common approach it seems is to aim for a modest degree of integration at first, a 'Multidisciplinary' pattern, and to work towards a tighter whole over a longer term'.

As suggested here, and in the statement which preceded the outline syllabus submission, the adoption of a multidisciplinary position would not then have precluded the development of interdisciplinary teaching if and when the course structure demanded it. The group's decision to build in a multi- rather than an interdisciplinary emphasis was influenced by the advice of the 'college planner' (a post established to oversee the college course diversification) who suggested that there would be little likelihood of validation support being obtained for such a 'radical' shift from disciplinarity to interdisciplinarity.

The constraint was clear – the structure of the three mixed-disciplinary elements involved discrete disciplinary contributions to common issues rather than a complete conceptual and teaching integration. This raised the question of how the planning group could structure the two mixed-disciplinary elements (African Society and Regional Studies) when the third element would involve a multidisciplinary analysis of contemporary African issues, particularly in development problems in the field.

In structuring these elements a number of questions were considered:
1. Would the course elements start from a macro- or micro-level looking at the tribe or nation?
2. Would the study involve the notion of change or development at either macro- or micro-level?
3. Would the approach be an area one (e.g. Ghana and its problems) or would common issues such as rural/urban migration form the focus of attention?
4. It would only be after determining the actual approach that the group would ultimately be in a position to discuss individual discipline contributions and the possibility of sequence (e.g. will the geographer start off by delineating the physical and ethnic boundaries of the area under study to be followed by the anthropologist?).

Considerable discussion about conceptual and disciplinary sequencing had still to be undertaken and it was recognised that, although coherence should exist between the disciplinary elements, it would not pre-empt the sequence of concepts to be taught in disciplinary terms. It was recognised that this kind of debate was a protracted one which would extend to discussion after the course started between members of both staff and students. It was also recognised that it would involve considerable and perhaps even radical reconstruction of the course as it proceeded. This was likely in the proposed African Studies course in particular because it not only had to reconcile the disparate interests within the college but also the college interests and those of linking institutions. The latter, it was recognised, would

**Linking Institutions**

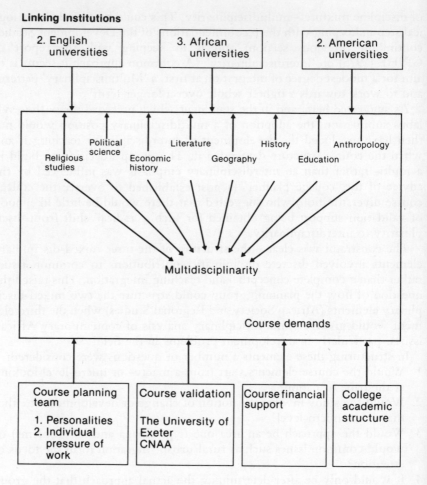

Fig. 16 Constraints on course planning (after Morgan R. *et al.* in *Development Studies*, School of Oriental and African Studies, 1977)

demand evidence of successful learning for student transfer to be effected. (See Fig. 16)

## Further constraints

The course, then was an attempt to look at Africa in a multidisciplinary manner in which certain problems of development were only to be examined explicitly in the field experience course element. It was hoped also that an awareness of many Third World problems would develop and that this emphasis on a multidisciplinary approach should enable the student in the early part of the course to obtain a broader base of knowledge.

An added bonus would stem from those students who choose to transfer to the college's B.Ed. structure and also go on to postgraduate education courses. They should add to the nucleus of young teachers who would have a greater awareness of problems facing developing countries and, by extension, of some of the problems faced by minority groups in this country.

In addition, to reinforce the strength of the proposal, Rolle College since 1976 has undertaken to provide a special course for Kenyan teachers which enables them to obtain a degree in two years after agreement of one year's remission for their existing qualification. This meant that by 1979 there were over forty-five Kenyan students in the college and the scheme had been enlarged to include ten Africans from other Anglophone countries by that time. This additional resource was by then a factor of the college's student intake and it was also hoped that a staff exchange programme could be established to include an African academic member of staff, whilst having the participation of one Rolle member of staff in the field every year to ensure the updating of research interests.

At the submission level the course proposal has not been so successful. Although the proposal has been successful in obtaining agreement of financial support from the DES, academic validation has caused problems. In the first instance, the University of Exeter was unable to provide a sufficiently strong validating committee with African expertise which represented all the contributing disciplines. Also informal discussion with the Council for National Academic Awards (CNAA) in which a special informal panel of African specialists has examined the course proposal (now reorganised following initial advice) has seriously questioned the college's resource to mount such a degree. It was argued that the amount of resources which the college will require to commit itself to in establishing the course may in the long run be the factor which prevents its establishment.

The course proposal at Rolle College represents one of a number of initiatives in global education which developed in the 1970s in the higher education sector, as indicated in Chapter 8, but from our experience we would suggest that in the planning of such courses in the future we would undertake the following action. We would still:

(a) undertake a detailed analysis in a sample area of potential student interest and prospective employer attitudes towards such a course, as we found the findings of this analysis essential in substantiating our claim for the need of such a course to validators and funding bodies;

(b) undertake the process of course development at three levels, developing course structure and content and assessment procedures, approaching linking institutions and validating bodies at the same time, thus establishing a complex but organic planning infrastructure.

However, we would as a team be more aware of the constraints (resources/financial/administrative) of the course institution and adopt a more realistic expectancy of progress that was possible in such course planning.

The course proposal in 1979 still had a long way to go before the academic exercise could be translated into an organic teaching course and, as others had found, its complexity led to many problems (Wright 1972): 'The list of difficulties was long by now: conflicts among lecturers, between lecturers and students, conflicts between lecturers, students and schools, to say nothing about the conflicts within ourselves as consultations about American Studies took more and more time'.

Reference, it is argued, ought to be made more to the Nuffield Group for Research and Innovation in Higher Education (GRIHE 1975): 'Interdisciplinary work takes time: time to hatch the basic ideas, time to plan the course and learn from one's colleagues, time to prepare the right materials. Not everything can be settled in advance; the course may need several years to sort itself out'.

There are indications that it is going to be a long, but not necessarily unsuccessful, exercise, even if it only involves the communication of our experience to other interested institutions.

# Part IV
Resources and sources

# Chapter 12

Charles Townley

# Resources for developing global perspectives

## Introduction

The secondary school curriculum in Britain is currently subject to pressure from several sources. The last decade saw the appearance of several new subjects on school timetables with many more, often supported by national curriculum development projects, claiming their share of curriculum time. As well as moral, social and political education, claims have emerged from advocates representing such diverse fields as education for industry, consumer affairs, health, sex, values and legal education. These must now be added to World Studies and the development of global perspectives which have been advocated since the 1930s. In addition to all these pressures, the 1980s are witnessing a dual pressure from the DES, to rationalise the curriculum in the light of falling rolls, and to develop a core curriculum for all pupils. It is therefore unlikely that many schools will have the opportunity to develop completely new courses.

In these circumstances it is all the more important to note that many of these 'new' subjects not only share features in common, but also overlap several subjects which are already widely institutionalised. They are interested in similar issues, they use a common set of concepts and they advocate a particular pedagogical style. One of the implications is that teachers may find resources in a variety of subject areas both new and established. Dave Hicks (see p. 121) has referred to developments in history, geography and RE, while David Selby (see p. 57) has indicated the importance of the conceptual approach in his own course and has identified concepts such as interdependence, co-operation and function. Robin Richardson (see p. 32) has also stressed the significance of concepts, though he focuses on culture and justice. David Bridges (see p. 37) has emphasised the place of values and Hugh Starkey (see p. 72) has stressed the pedagogical importance of involving the pupils in their own learning.

In this chapter I shall make a brief (and necessarily superficial, in the space available) examination of the relationship between resources and the curriculum, and indicate some of the resources available in the fields referred to above.

There is a reminder about 'home-made' resources and their organisation and finally, a list of organisations which teachers would find helpful.

## Resources and content in curriculum theory

### Resources: means or ends?

For many years theoretical approaches to curriculum development tended to emphasise the importance of aims and objectives as the starting-point in curriculum design. Thus Bobbitt (1924), Tyler (1949), Taba (1962) and Wheeler (1967) all suggest that aims should be clarified and stated before thinking about content. Content, according to this approach, is viewed as a means of achieving these aims. More recently, however, content and resources have come to be viewed as legitimate ends, in their own right. They have received both theoretical and empirical recognition as legitimate starting-points for curriculum development. In a theoretical debate on curriculum design, Stenhouse (1970, 1975) believes quite firmly that the curriculum can be organised satisfactorily by a logic other than the means–end model. History, science and literature, for example, illuminate other areas of life and can be justified intrinsically. His work on the HCP is a good example. At a more empirical level, Philip Taylor (1970) examined the way teachers do, in fact, plan their curricula and discovered that, in practice, many choose what they want to teach and the way they wish to teach it, as their starting-point. At this stage in planning, their aims are implicit and only emerge explicitly after the content has been stated. Thus for many teachers, the starting-point is 'what they want their pupils to know'. For them the curriculum is largely a question of knowledge, and resources tend to be viewed in this light – as a source of knowledge.

Keddie (1973) has labelled this view of schooling as a 'vacuum ideology' which emphasises the 'objective', non-problematic nature of classroom knowledge and the hierarchical, didactic nature of classroom relationships. It is based on an epistemological view of knowledge and offers a view of schooling which legitimates the status quo. It is a view which sees learners as passive recipients preparing to take their place in an adult society as we know it.

Yet the rationale which underpins the development of global perspectives in the curriculum is one which not only accepts that we are preparing learners for the future, but is one which views learners as preparing to take an active part in the creation of a world that is partly theirs, not given, but to be made. This social constructionist view of knowledge implies that we should not treat resources merely as knowledge to be learned, but as 'evidence' or 'data' which is to be examined critically. That is it should be examined in the light of alternatives in a manner which facilitates choice and, ultimately, action.

### Resources for two domains: cognitive and affective

Whichever view of knowledge one takes it is clear that resources must offer more than facts. In terms of Bloom's *Taxonomy of the Cognitive Domain* they must take our pupils beyond mere 'knowledge', the first level, at which so many teachers stop. They should enable pupils to develop intellectual abilities and skills by progressing to the higher levels of 'comprehension', 'application', 'analysis', 'synthesis' and 'evaluation' (Bloom 1956). At the final level pupils should be able to make judgements about the value of ideas or prescriptions or solutions to problems of, say, international tension. Thus the resources we employ must offer more than one view of the issue and should promote debate about cause and effect.

Perhaps it is even more important in this field that resources should stimulate pupils in the affective domain. Having 'received' a stimulus from our resources we hope our pupils will 'respond', 'value' and 'organise' their responses and values to the point where they 'characterise the value' of, say, justice, or empathy, or tolerance or open-mindedness (Krathwohl 1964). At this final stage, however, we are concerned not only with the internalisation of particular values, but with the development of a whole philosophy of life or ideology. Thus resources will need to raise a complex of related values like sensitivity, tolerance, co-operation and commitment and to use resources from a variety of media. Children learn through all their senses and it is important to remember, for example, the emotive impact of music. So, a song like John Lennon's 'Imagine' draws its power not only from the message in the lyric, including lines like:

Imagine there's no countries                    You may say I'm a dreamer
It isn't hard to do                             But I'm not the only one
Nothing to kill or die for                      I hope someday you'll join us
And no religion too                             And the world will live as one
Imagine all the people
Living life in peace . . .

which may even seem limp when written on paper, but from the appeal of the melody, the arrangement and the performance. If the song is played after looking at photographs of Hiroshima and Nagasaki (perhaps to the background of Richard Addinsell's romanticised 'Warsaw' Concerto) and after reading poems like R. N. Currey's The Poetry of War or those of Robert Graves, several issues will have been raised and the related values are likely to be internalised more deeply.

## Three modes of representation

The resources we use to stimulate response and development in the affective domain serve as a reminder that children learn in three different ways – through action, through images and through symbols. Sadly, teachers frequently concentrate unduly on the symbolic mode and neglect the other two. Yet the iconic mode may be the most powerful of all. 'It is still true that a thousand words scarcely exhaust the richness of a single image', (Bruner 1966) and few teachers can match the potential of film and television. However, it may not be necessary to go to the expense of film or video; often a single still photograph can encapsulate a great deal.

There are, too, some things that we can only learn by doing, for example, tying knots, riding a bicycle and learning to swim. But that same technique is a powerful tool in providing pupils with opportunities to experience situations, albeit vicariously, through games, simulations, role play, drama and exercises, which are not available through the other modes. Anyone who has role-played a rejection exercise will know of its impact; and anyone who has played Starpower will know what potential it has for illuminating societal structures, inequality and human nature.

**Process**

There will be many occasions in developing global perspectives when teachers will undoubtedly wish to use resources as finite, conclusive data. Income per head in different countries, rates of migration, the incidence of disease or dates of treaties are common examples of unproblematic information. Yet many of the issues to be raised in the classroom will be value-laden, political and open-ended. Debates about the use of natural resources, investment in the Third World, inequalities between nations, justice, poverty or pollution provide pupils with issues which are problematic and open-ended. They are in sharp contrast to much of the learning in mathematics, science and traditional history and geography where the emphasis is on the learning of objective facts or procedures. Here pupils can be offered the opportunity to seek information and opinion, to evaluate their findings and to form their own conclusions. All too frequently, however, pupils are denied the opportunity to raise questions which *they* feel are important, to speculate, to enquire and to form opinions. But in an era when knowledge doubles in a decade, it is impossible to decide what children 'ought to know' and it becomes important to foster in them the skills of intelligent enquiry.

The area of global perspectives is a good example of a field where the dictum that 'knowing is a process, not a product' clearly applies. If we wish to develop in our pupils some degree of global literacy, perhaps via economic, political and social literacy, then not only should the resources we employ stimulate such enquiry but the methods we employ should also encourage it. Bruner (1960) suggests that: 'The schoolboy doing physics is a physicist and it is easier for him to learn physics behaving like a physicist than doing something else.' In this case, students developing global perspectives are to a large extent entering the province of the social and political scientist and the methods we employ should be consistent with these disciplines. In practice this means developing resources to be used as 'data' and allowing students to enquire into them by observation, research and discussion. Students follow the process of traditional scientific research by observing, speculating and hypothesising, seeking further information and then testing the hypotheses in the light of the data obtained.

Putting students into a didactic, authoritarian relationship is hardly conducive to development into the higher levels of the affective domain. An increased consciousness of the relationship between self, society and the global system will not be achieved by denying the existence of self in the classroom, or of the open-ended nature of so many of the issues raised there.

Indeed the classroom and the school context are important resources in themselves. They provide a common set of first-hand experiences which can serve as the basis for that form of spiral curriculum, advocated by Taba (1972), which begins with the child's own experience and moves outward, in a series of concentric circles through the study of 'myself', family, neighbourhood, community and state, to a consideration of the whole world.

It is possible with older pupils, for example, to explore the existence and consequences of the 'hidden curriculum'. All of them have experienced it, but at different levels of consciousness. After identifying its essential features, power, authority, hierarchy, conflict, obedience, loyalty and acceptance, it is possible to discuss its consequences first in terms of the pupils themselves and then in wider terms. For example, to what extent is it the main means by which the social relations of production in all societies are reproduced? The next logical step is to consider alternative structures and methods of working, including those which are based upon sensitivity, mutual respect, equality, co-operation and critical examination. It is a challenging and, for many teachers, a threatening exercise, but it is one which leads to an understanding of ideologies, philosophies or belief-systems and the values which underpin them. It is an important exercise because, in using the classroom as a resource, it starts 'where our pupils are at'. It has a better chance of avoiding the danger of irrelevance which leads so often to alienation and rejection. Instead it provides an opportunity for the learner to obtain satisfaction through participation and identification. This, in turn, provides a sound 'concrete' base on which to develop an understanding of political structures as well as the moral and the political nature of global issues.

Throughout this exercise the emphasis will be not only on the concepts and data employed but on the process of enquiry, exploration and evaluation. 'Mastery of the fundamental ideas of a field involves not only the grasping of general principles, but also the development of an attitude towards learning and enquiry, towards guessing and hunches, toward the possibility of solving problems on one's own....To instill such attitudes by teaching requires something more than the mere presentation of fundamental ideas' (Bruner 1960).

## Structure, concepts and the spiral curriculum

The choice of resources, both for transmitting information and for stimulating the process of enquiry, needs to be based upon the consideration of further criteria. Assuming that one can, with integrity, teach any subject to any child at any stage of development, one needs first to understand the fundamental nature and structure of the subject. 'The curriculum of a subject should be determined by the most fundamental understanding that can be achieved of the underlying principles that give structure to that subject.... The task of teaching a subject to a child at any particular age is one of representing the structure of that subject in terms of the child's way of viewing things' (Bruner 1960). In practice this means that we should choose resources which illustrate basic concepts, the most fundamental ideas without which one could not understand the subject. Concepts are the basis for the development of generalisations and higher levels of understanding. They are tools which assist in transfer and in further learning.

The list of concepts around which resources could be developed and collected, in order to cultivate global perspectives, might well run into dozens, or even hundreds. The following includes some of the most fundamental: Capitalism, colonialism, Communism, conflict, co-operation, culture, dependence, democracy, ecology, ecosystems, ethnicity, ethnocentrism, exploitation, government, ideology, independence, inequality, institutions, interdependence, justice, law, minorities, nationalism, peace, population, power, prejudice, race, religion, repression, resources, revolution, socialism, Third World, treaty, underdevelopment, unity, values, war, wealth. Which ones would you choose as the most important?

Having identified those which you consider to be the most fundamental it is important to remember that education is a continuous process and concepts are not 'discrete' items which are encountered, learned and left behind. On the contrary, when Hilda Taba developed her Program in Social Science (1972) she wrote: 'The concepts must be visualised as threads which appear over and over again in a spiral which is always moving to a higher level. As the student's experience broadens and his intellectual capacities develop, he is provided with repeated opportunities in a variety of contexts to develop an increasingly sophisticated understanding of the Key Concepts'.

In thinking about resources, therefore, we need, as Jim Dunlop pointed out on p. 90, to take account of the whole period of schooling, from reception class or kindergarten through the infant, junior, middle and secondary school years to the period of post-compulsory education in further and higher education.

Each experience cannot be considered separately, for each has more or less effect on succeeding ones. When experiences are perceived as discrete and unrelated, the student loses any sense of order or purpose, and consequently his learning suffers. In the progression from one idea or set of ideas to another there must be some continuity in development, so that the later experience bears an inevitable relation to what has gone before (Wheeler 1967).

## The nursery slopes – resources for the early years

Few teachers enjoy greater autonomy and freedom, and thus the potential for incorporating global perspectives into their work, than British primary schoolteachers. They take their class virtually all day for five days a week and frequently undertake project work of one sort or another. It is not uncommon for projects to focus upon social issues such as pollution or housing, people of other lands such as the Native American, or topics which lend themselves to the study of problems on a global scale such as food, water and clothes. Yet, as a recent survey (DES 1978) has shown, such work was superficial in about 80 per cent of the classes. 'In many cases it involved little more than copying from reference books.... Much of the work tended to be superficial and there was often little evidence of progression.'

This work could be made much more rigorous if teachers were to identify concepts like power, conflict, justice, values, communication, similarity/difference and causes/consequences and choose resources which reflect them. In the infant years such resources could be fairy-tales, myths and legends. These are already institutionalised in schools, but teachers rarely choose to use them in order to develop an awareness of other societies or of particular concepts. Thus they rarely follow them up with other stories or activities which illustrate, for example, group pressures in *The Emperor's New Clothes*, scarcity in *The Three Wishes*, or stratification in *The Princess and the Pea* (Summer 1976). Edith King, of the University of Denver and the Institute of Worldmindedness, has developed this approach further (1971, 1973).

There is an ample fund of such material available to British teachers. Some useful titles are:

Appiah, P. (1967) *Tales of an Ashanti Father*. André Deutsch
Appiah, P. (1969) *The Pineapple Child* (Ashanti). André Deutsch
Arnott, K. (1962) *African Myths and Legends*. Oxford UP
Asbjornsem, P. (1969) *Popular Tales from the Norse*. Bodley Head
Avery, G. (1971) *Red Letter Days* (British). Hamish Hamilton
Beier, U. (1972) *When the Moon was Big* (New Guinea). Collins
Bell, A. (1967) *Fairy Tales of Ludwig Bechstein* (European). Abelard-Schuman
Bere, R. (1973) *Crocodile's Eggs for Supper* (Uganda). André Deutsch
Briggs, K. (1965) *Folktales of England*. Routledge and Kegan Paul
Brockett, E. (1970) *Persian Fairy Tales*. Frederick Muller
Broome, D. (1963) *Fairy Tales of the Isle of Man*. Norris Modern Press
Brown, M. (1971) *Sea Legends*. Hamish Hamilton
Colwell, E. (1972) *Round About and Long Ago* (English). Longman
Elgin, K. (1955) *The First Book of Mythology* (Greek and Roman). Franklin Watts
Haviland, V. (1970) *Favourite Fairy Tales Told in Czechoslovakia*. Bodley Head
Haviland, V. (1971) *Favourite Fairy Tales Told in Denmark*. Bodley Head
Haviland, V. (1970) *Favourite Fairy Tales Told in France*. Bodley Head
Haviland, V. (1970) *Favourite Fairy Tales Told in Germany*. Bodley Head
Haviland, V. (1970) *Favourite Fairy Tales Told in Ireland*. Bodley Head
Haviland, V. (1970) *Favourite Fairy Tales Told in Italy*. Bodley Head
Haviland, V. (1970) *Favourite Fairy Tales Told in Japan*. Bodley Head
Haviland, V. (1970) *Favourite Fairy Tales Told in Norway*. Bodley Head
Haviland, V. (1970) *Favourite Fairy Tales Told in Poland*. Bodley Head
Haviland, V. (1970) *Favourite Fairy Tales Told in Russia*. Bodley Head
Haviland, V. (1970) *Favourite Fairy Tales Told in Scotland*. Bodley Head

Haviland, V. (1970) *Favourite Fairy Tales Told in Spain*. Bodley Head
Haviland, V. (1970) *Favourite Fairy Tales Told in Sweden*. Bodley Head
Jacobs, J. (1970) *Celtic Fairy Tales*. Bodley Head
Jacobs, J. (1968) *English Fairy Tales*. Bodley Head
Manuel, E.A. (1968) *Folktales of the Philippines*. Routledge and Kegan Paul
Noy, D. (1968) *Folktales of Israel*. Routledge and Kegan Paul
Picard, B.L. (1961) *Tales of the British People*. Kaye and Ward
Pino-Saavedra, Y. (1968) *Folktales of Chile*. Routledge and Kegan Paul
Ransome, A. (1916/1971) *Old Peter's Russian Tales*. Nelson
Reeves, J. (1970) *Snow White and Rose Red* (German). Oxford UP
Seki, K. (1968) *Folktales of Japan*. Routledge and Kegan Paul
Shah, A. (1969) *Arabian Fairy Tales*. Frederick Muller
Sperry, M. (1971) *Scandinavian Stories*. Dent
Squire, R. (1972) *Wizards and Wampum* (Native American). Abelard-Schuman
Steel, F.A. (1894/1973) *Tales of the Punjab*. Bodley Head
Steinberg, B.H. (1969) *The Magic Millstones and other Japanese Folk Stories*. Oxford UP
Thapar, R. (1961) *Indian Tales*. Bell

## American elementary school materials

As yet there are few curriculum development projects at the primary school level in Britain which focus directly on global perspectives, and those projects which have been established are only now preparing to disseminate materials for the classroom. Thus the project, International Understanding in the Primary School, Scotland (see pp. 99), has encouraged schools to establish 'twinning' arrangements, facilitating an exchange of correspondence and materials between the schools involved, rather than promoting the development of materials on a centre–periphery model. The project *World Studies 8–13* is now preparing to disseminate its products.

There are, however, several American curriculum packages which have been developed for children of primary school age. They all contain several pupil books, separate teachers' editions and, usually, supplementary multimedia kits.

(*i*) *Man: A Course of Study*, Curriculum Development Associates, Washington, DC

*Man*, or MACOS as it is sometimes known, is the only American curriculum to have been implemented widely in Britain. It provides a good example of the way the principles outlined above have been implemented in a curriculum package which offers the opportunity to develop global perspectives in children at both primary and secondary level. The course has three main concerns, or organising questions:
What is human about human beings?
How did they get that way?
How can they be made more so? (Assuming that this is desirable!)

In the words of the developers, 'The content of the course is man: his nature as a species, the forces that shaped and continue to shape his humanity. We seek exercises and materials through which our pupils can learn wherein man is distinctive in his adaptation to the world....' The relevance of this course for a teacher wishing to foster global perspectives lies in the emphasis on the common features of humanity which bind us.

The aims of the course, as articulated by the developers, are twofold:

First, we wish to stimulate children to think about the nature of man.... By comparing man to other animals and by studying man in a cultural setting different from our own, they may reflect upon the deep structure of human experience, the common impulses and ways of coping with life which unite man as a species beneath the surface diversity of culture.... Second, we hope that through this course children will come to understand that what we regard as acceptable behaviour is a product of our culture. In judging others, particularly those from different cultures, children must learn how their judgements, and the judgements of all men, are shaped by the culture in which they live, and they, in turn, can shape their culture. (*Man: A Course of Study*, 1969, Teachers' Guide No. 1.)

In pursuit of the three organising questions, the course explores five humanising forces: language and communication; toolmaking and technology; social organisation and culture (arising from interdependence); child–rearing and the management of man's prolonged childhood (because of its importance in understanding learning and culture); and man's urge to explain the world through belief-systems. The content and resources provided for this exploration are a series of animal studies and a substantial unit on the Netsilik Eskimos. The animal studies serve the dual purpose of (a) introducing and developing concepts such as life–cycle, structure, function, innate and learned behaviour, territoriality, conflict, interdependence, social organisation and culture; and (b) providing contrasts which serve to highlight several features of human life. So, even when they are studying animals, pupils are learning about mankind.

The Netsilik units follow a nomadic family for a year of their traditional way of life. Because of the way the resources are organised, students come to develop great respect for the Eskimos and the culture which enables them to survive in the most extreme climatic conditions. The concepts employed include socialisation, division of labour, technology, belief-systems, co-operation and culture. Finally, the course ends with a look at the changing lives of the Netsilik today and the price of technological development and social change.

The resources themselves are extensive, including more than thirty pupils' booklets, several filmstrips and records, maps, photographs, posters and games. However, all these are really supportive of the major resource on which the course is based, a series of twenty-two films, most of which are natural sound films intended to provide the basis for the process of enquiry. They provide a good illustration of the belief that the curriculum is an enterprise where the borderline between resources and method becomes increasingly indistinct. Thus one finds amongst the pedagogical aims of the course the intention:

1. To initiate in youngsters a process of question-posing (the enquiry method)
2. To teach a research methodology where children can look for information to answer questions which they have raised....
3. To conduct classroom discussions in which youngsters learn to listen to others as well as to express their own views.
4. To create a new role for the teacher in which he/she becomes a resource rather than an authority.

Clearly these pedagogical goals centre around the process of learning rather than the product.

(ii) *Taba, H. (1972) The Taba Program in Social Science.* Addison-Wesley
This course aims to help pupils 'gain knowledge, skills and sensitivities that can give them an understanding of their own feelings, values and behaviour in a world of continuing change'. The whole course is based on concepts, main ideas and facts. The eleven concepts are: causality, conflict, co-operation, cultural change, differences, interdependence, modification, power, societal control, tradition and values. Each grade level has a different focus.

   Kindergarten: *Anuk's family of Bali* – readiness material, eighteen photographs.

Grade 1: *People in Families* – in Kenya, New York, France, Minnesota, Canada, Massachusetts, Mexico and California.

Grade 2: *People in Neighbourhoods* – examines inner-city, suburban and small town US neighbourhoods.

Grade 3: *People in Communities* – 'the student is helped to recognise dignity in cultures different from his own, and to grow in his respect for those differences'.
Examines the Bedouin of the Negev, the Yoruba of Ife, the Thai of Bangkok and the Norwegians of Hemnesberget.

Grade 4: *People in States* – examines agriculture in Mysore, industrialisation in Osaka, government decisions in Serbia, resources and culture in Nova Scotia.

Grade 5: *People in America* – pluralist society of today, early cultures, revolt, Civil War and migration.

Grade 6: *People in Change* – case studies of people interacting with their environment, representing different historical periods, different geographical regions and contrasting patterns of culture. Examines people in Canada, Australia, New Zealand, Brazil, Peru, Mexico, ancient Greece, Tudor England, French Revolution, Nazi Germany, ancient Mesopotamia, Arab tribes, Syria and Israel.

(iii) *Gross, R. and Mitchells, J. (1976) The People Program: Culture, Times, Places.* Addison-Wesley
This programme's four main goals are concerned to develop (a) concepts

and generalisations, (b) enquiry processes, (c) skills and (d) awareness of one's own attitudes and values as well as those of others. Amongst the concepts employed are roles, values, institutions, culture, environment, needs, wants, interdependence and change. The units include 'Working, Playing and Learning', 'Towns and Cities', 'People, Places, Products', 'Regions Round the World' and 'The Human Adventure'. 'The Human Adventure' is a world history which traces the development of man from earliest times to the present day with a brief conclusion on the Third World through figures such as Mao, Castro and Nyerere. There are comparisons of concurrent periods in Africa, Asia and the Americas.

(iv) *Fielder, W.R. (ed.) (1972) Holt Databank System.* Holt, Rinehart and Winston

This is intended to be a completely self-contained and self-sufficient teacher support system. There is a pupil book and a teacher book for each unit but, in addition, there is a databank containing filmstrips, sound filmstrips, records, games, data packs (booklets), data cards, simulations, data spirit masters and data foldouts (charts). These amount to a sophisticated and expensive information storage–retrieval system to be used by pupils pursuing their enquiry-based learning. There are also film loops available. The units cover the whole primary school age range and cover the following topics: 'Inquiring about Myself'; 'Inquiring about People'; 'Inquiring about Communities'; 'Inquiring about Cities'; 'Inquiring about Cultures'; 'Inquiring about Technology'.

## British primary school materials

Primary school teachers are not entirely without British materials, however. There is a wide range of short, well-illustrated print material available from the Centre for World Development Education, the Council for Education in World Citizenship, Oxfam, and the UK Committee for UNICEF.

*The World Studies 8–13 Project*, funded by the Schools Council and the Rowntree Charitable Trust, is based in Bristol and Lancaster. It is scheduled to run from 1980 to 1983 when it is planned to produce a teacher's resource book and handbook. *Planning and Teaching World Studies: An Interim Guide* is available from the Centre for Peace Studies or the World Studies Project. The Project has selected four themes which illustrate some of the main concepts and issues in World Studies. They are:

1. *Getting on with others.* This explores relationships in the classroom, home and community and extends to consider relationships between other groups. It will focus on the importance of communication, cooperation and the peaceful resolution of conflicts.
2. *Learning about other people.* This explores ways of teaching about other countries, especially the so-called developing countries and/or particular minority groups around the world. In particular it will be concerned with avoiding oversimplified stereotypes of other peoples.

Emphasis will be given to the various links between Britain and the societies to be studied.

3. *Understanding the news*. Children are very aware, via the media, of events in the wider world. Only occasionally however, as in *John Craven's Newsround*, are attempts made to explain such events at a child's level. The work on this theme will aim to develop ways of making world news more easily understood.

4. *The world tomorrow*. This explores the kinds of future children would like to see, for themselves as well as for the world. It encourages creative thinking about how choices and decisions are made and how events and trends in the local area are reflected in the wider world. This theme could involve consideration of issues to do with the environment and the use of the earth's resources.

The Schools Council Project *History, Geography and Social Science 8–13* produced a number of packs as exemplars of its approach to social studies. The project team was influenced by the work of Hilda Taba and based its rationale upon the need to develop in pupils critical thinking, empathy and autonomy. Thus it emphasised the development of intellectual, social and physical skills and the fostering of interests, attitudes and values that might be characterised by openness. The methodology is largely enquiry-based. The content, in the form of exemplar units, focuses upon substantive concepts – communication, power, values, beliefs, conflict and consensus, and upon methodological concepts – similarity/difference, continuity/change and cause/consequence.

The Inner London Education Authority (ILEA) has produced a booklet *Social Studies in the Primary School* which was the outcome of a project it undertook with its own teachers. The booklet is to be supplemented by a series of occasional papers, all obtainable from the ILEA Learning Materials Centre. It is intended to promote different ways of planning content and suggests approaches based on themes, topics and concepts. The concepts identified include the distribution of power and authority, division of labour, social control, conflict, interdependence, co-operation, tradition and social change. An enquiry-based approach would start with an issue and use a variety of methods ranging from interviewing to drama to develop understanding.

A project which raises moral dilemmas in a manner which is appropriate to this age range and which has encouraged many schools to develop class projects on global issues is the Schools Council's (1978) *Startline* published by Longman. The materials are varied and open-ended. Cards from the 'Making it Happen' section require pupils to act, paint, draw or write about situations which reflect concepts like interdependence, but at a personal level. Thus card 55 instructs the pupil to 'Write two different stories about the same people. In one story people care about others. In the other story they do not care. Talk about the two stories with someone else. Which story do you like best? Why is this?' Picture-cards of figures in the 'Setting the Scene' section are multicultural and can be used either as stimulus for creative writing or drama (reflects moral dilemmas) or for interpreting situations and discussing action. The whole project aims to 'Heighten perception and sensitivity to other people's needs, attitudes and feelings'. Further guidance is available in: McPhail. P. et al. (1978) *Moral Education in the Middle Years*. Longman

## Starting-points at the secondary level

Amongst the wealth of resource material which is now available at the secondary school level, certain items and projects suggest themselves as suitable starting-points, either because they are self-contained, or because they are sufficiently extensive to include a variety of activities, or because they offer suitable opportunities to obtain further resources.

Teachers are strongly recommended to begin by referring to the publications of the World Studies Project (see p. 205), the *Development Puzzle* published by the Centre for World Development Education (CWDE) and the *World Studies Resource Guide,* published by the Council for Education in World Citizenship (CEWC). For an introduction to the general philosophy of the field the best range of theoretical and background papers are to be found in *New Era* and the *World Studies Journal* (see p. 203).

## Existing disciplines in the secondary school curriculum

Apart from the resources which have been developed specifically for work in this field, there is a wealth of material available in existing school subjects: in literature, history, geography, and RE. These materials may be emphasised by those teachers already teaching the subject or they may be exploited by others working under different labels. It is important to remember, however, that these categories are not mutually exclusive and many items could well fit into more than one. The range of these materials is now so extensive that they are presented here as lists within accessible and existing categories.

(* Texts for pupils)

## English

There is a sense in which all literature can be said to concern itself with the human condition and dilemmas within it. But there are some works which may be used by teachers (without necessarily compromising the author's intention of treating his work as an art form which has to be considered as a whole) to highlight global issues, particularly war and man's inhumanity to man. Novelists like Steinbeck, Orwell and Huxley have highlighted political dilemmas associated with freedom, human rights, state control and ideology in works like *1984* and *Brave New World*. There are also useful collections and anthologies of shorter poems and prose, for example:

*Clements, S. *et al.* (ed) (1963) *Reflections*. Oxford UP
*Fowler, R. S. (ed) (1967) *Themes in Life and Literature*. Oxford UP

*Hewett, S. (1960) *This Day and Age*. Edward Arnold
*Jones, E. H. *et al.* (eds) (1972) *Themes: Aggression*. Routledge and Kegan Paul
*Jones, E. H. *et al.* (eds) (1972) *Themes: Rebels*. Routledge and Kegan Paul
*Smith, J. A. (1969) *The Living Stream*. Faber
*Thompson, A. (ed.) (1967) *Enquiries*. University Tutorial Press

## Geography

*Schools Council (1981) *Geography for the Young School Leaver*. Nelson. Has new material linking geography with development education. The original packs (1974) have items on world cities, migration, leisure in other countries.
Carnie, J. (1972) Children's Attitudes to Other Nationalities, in *New Movements in the Study and Teaching of Geography*. Temple Smith
*Church, D. and Ford, B. (1975) *Focus on World Problems*. Nelson
*Clare, R. (1974) *The Third World*. Macdonald
Cole, J. P. (1979) *The Geography of World Affairs*. Pelican
Cole, J. P. (1981) *The Development Gap*. Wiley
CWDE Geography Teachers Group *The Changing World of Geography*. Centre for World Development Education
*Dalgleish, N. (1975) *The Developing Nations*. Nelson.
*Dawson, J. and Thomas, D. (1975) *Man and His World*. Nelson
*Fyson, N. L. (1979) *Resources for World Geography*. Nelson. Titles include: Latin America and the Caribbean, Africa and Asia. Each includes sections on population, food, health, industry and trade.
Harrison, P. (1980) *The Third World Tomorrow*. Pelican
Hicks, D. W. (1980) *Bias in Geography Textbooks: Images of the Third World and multi-ethnic Britain*. Working paper No. 1, Centre for Multicultural Education, London University, Institute of Education
Hicks, D. W. (1980) *Images of the World: An Introduction to Bias in Teaching Materials*. Occasional Paper No. 2, Centre for Multicultural Education, London University Institute of Education
Hoyle, B. S. (1974) *Spatial Aspects of Development*. Wiley
Huckle, J. (ed.) (1981) *Geographical Education: Reflection and Action*. Oxford UP In-Focus Books
James, P. and Webb, K. (1980) *One World Divided*. Wiley
*Jones, D. and Kimplon, L. (1981) *Geography in a Changing World*. Hodder and Stoughton: (1) *Understanding Places;* (2) *Understanding Developing Places* – the developing world; (3) *Understanding Developed Places* – contrasts in developments; (4) *Understanding Man's World* – the world system; (5) *Understanding Man's Decisions* – local, national and international.
O'Dell, P. R. (1979) *Oil and World Power?* Pelican
O'Riordan, T. and d'Arge, R. (eds) *Progress in Resource Management and Environmental Planning*. Vol. 1, Wiley
O'Riorden, T. and Turner, R. D. (eds) *Progress in Resource Management and Environmental. Planning* Vol. 2, Wiley

Peet, R. (ed.) (1978) *Radical Geography: Alternative Viewpoints on Contemporary Social Issues*. Methuen

*Reed, A. (1979) *The Developing World*. Bell and Hyman

Shave, D. W. (1972) *One World*. John Murray

Smith, D. M. (1977) *Human Geography – A Welfare Approach*. Arnold

Smith, D. M. (1979) *Where the Grass is Greener: Living in an Unequal World*. Pelican

*Spicer, B. *et al*. (1975) The Global System series. John Murray: *Man and Space*; *Space and Change*; *Production and Space* (1977); *Space for Living* (1977)

*Stuart, J. (1977) *The Unequal Third*. Arnold

*Turner, J. (1978) *World Inequality*. Longman

UNESCO (1978) *Tropical Forest Ecosystems*. UNESCO

UNESCO (1978) *World Water Balance and the Water Resources of the Earth*. UNESCO

Waldichuk, M.(1978) *Global Marine Pollution*. UNESCO

*Wright, D. (1979) *West Indies*. Longman


# History

*Schools Council (1976) *History 13–16 Project*. Holmes McDougall
Introductory Unit: *What is History?*
World History Units: 'The Rise of Communist China'; 'Arab–Israeli Conflict'; 'The Move to European Unity'; 'The Irish Question'
Teachers' guide: *A New Look at History*
Evaluation book: *Explorations*

*ILEA (1976) *World History Themes: Africa; India; China* Heinemann

*ILEA World History Topics. ILEA Learning Materials Centre (1974) *Social Change: India, China, United States; (1974) Nationalist Movements*; (1975) *Communist Societies*; (1975) *Industrialisation*.

*Bareham, J. *et al*. (1971) *Towards Tomorrow: World History in the Twentieth Century*. Holmes McDougall

*Bareham, J. *et al*. (1976) *Changing World History* Book 3. Holmes McDougall

Bowle, J. (1977) *The Imperial Achievement*. Penguin

Bowle, J. (1979) *A History of Europe: A Cultural and Political Survey*. Secker and Warburg

Cornwell, R. D. (1969) *World History in the Twentieth Century*. Longman

Davidson, B. (1978) *Africa in Modern History*. Penguin

Fitzgerald, C. P. (1974) *A Concise History of East Asia*. Pelican

Galbraith, J. K. (1979) *The Age of Uncertainty*. André Deutsch.

Hagdoff, H. (1978) *Imperialism: From the Colonial Age to the Present*. Monthly Review Press

Heater, D. (1981) *Peace and War Since 1945*. Harrap

Langer, W. L. (1973) *An Encyclopaedia of World History*. Harrap

Lippman, J. (1978) A new framework for World History, *History Teacher*, **12** (1), Nov.

McEvedy, C. and Jones, R. (1978) *Atlas of World Population History*. Penguin
Mansfield, P. (1978) *The Arabs*. Pelican
Martell J. (1980) *The Twentieth Century World*. Harrap
Oliver, R. and Fage, R.D. (1975) *A Short History of Africa*. Penguin
Rayner, E. (1980) *International Affairs Since 1919*. Oxford UP
Roberts, J. M. (1980) *The Pelican History of the World*. Pelican
Sturdy, D. (1981) *Europe and the World: 1763–1960*. Harrap
Taylor, D. (1976) *A Short History of the Post War World 1945– 1970*. Dennis Dobson
Thomas, H. (1979) *An Unfinished History of the World*. Hamish Hamilton
Watson, J. (1981) *Success in Twentieth Century World Affairs*. John Murray
Wright, M. (1979) *Power Politics*. Penguin

## Moral and Religious Education

*Barford, G. *et al.* (1980) *Survival*. Archway Development Education Centre
Cole, W. O. (1978) *World Faiths in Education*. Allen and Unwin
Cole, W. O. (1978) *World Problems in the Classroom*. UNESCO
Cole, W. O. (ed.) (1978) *World Religions*. Commission for Racial Equality
CWDE (1979) *The Changing World and RE*. Centre for World Development Education
*Dalgleish, N. (1973) *Living in a Changing World* Book 1. Nelson
*Dalgleish, N. (1974) *Living in a Changing World* Book 2. Nelson
Downey, M. and Kelly, A. V. (1978) *Moral Education: Theory and Practice*. Harper and Row
Fraenkel, J. R. (1977) *How to Teach about Values*. Prentice-Hall
Judson, S. (1977) *A Manual on Non-violence and Children*. Religious Society of Friends, Philadelphia
Hersh, R. H. *et al.* (1980) *Models of Moral Education*. Longman
*Mabey, R. (ed) (1972) *Connexions: Food*. Penguin
McPhail, P. et al (1978) *Moral Education in the Middle Years*. Longman
Prutzman, P. et al. (1978) *The Friendly Classroom for a Small Planet*. Avery Publishing Group
*Richardson, R. (1977) *World in Conflict*. Nelson
*Rogers, J. (1975) *Connexions: Foreign Places, Foreign Faces*. Penguin
*Schools Council (1972) *Lifeline*: Project Packs, Longman
*School Council (1978) *Startline*: Project Packs. Longman
Sherratt, B.W. and Hawkin, D.J. *Gods and Men: A Survey of World Religions*. Blackie
Schools Council (1972) *World Affairs*. Longman
Snellgrove, D. L. (1978) *The Image of Buddha*. UNESCO
Sugarman, B. (1973) *The School and Moral Development*. Croom Helm
Taylor, N. and Richardson, R. *Change and Choice: Britain in an Interdependent World*. Centre for World Development Education
Ungoed-Thomas, R. (1972) *Our School*. Longman

Woodhouse, S. (1980) *Your Life, My Life*. Writers and Scholars Education Trust

## Economics

Baran, P. A. (1973) *The Political Economy of Growth*. Pelican
Dalton, G. (1974) *Economic Systems and Society: Capitalism, Communism and the Third World*. Penguin
Elkan, W. (1973) *An Introduction to Development Economics*. Penguin
Freeman, A. *et al.* (1973) *The Economics of Environmental Policy*. Wiley
Hopkins, T. K. and Wallerstein, I. (1980) *Processes of the World System*. Sage
Pickles, T. (1961) *The World at Work*. John Murray
Todaro, M. P. (1977) *Economic Development in the Third World*. Longman
Tudge, C. (1979) *The Famine Business*. Penguin
Walter, I. (ed.) (1976) *Studies in International Environmental Economics*. Wiley
Ward, B. (1979) *Progress for a Small Planet*. Pelican

## 'Integrated' Studies

There are several 'packages' of integrated curriculum materials which have been developed by various agencies, but mainly by the Schools Council, over the past decade. A feature of many of them is that they are intended to be used as the basis of enquiry work. Thus they contain evidence or data, stimulus material on a number of controversial issues, many of which are relevant to teachers developing global perspectives.

*Schools Council *Geography for the Young School Leaver*, Nelson
*Schools Council (1976) *History 13–16*, Holmes McDougall
*Schools Council (1975) *History, Geography and Social Science 8–13*, Collins/ESL
*Schools Council *Environmental Studies 5–13*, Longman. Focuses on ecology in order to make pupils aware of man's dependence on the natural environment. Publications include: *Education for the Environmental; Ethics and Environment*
*Schools Council *Project Environment 8–16*. Emphasises enquiry into local environment. Hart Davis
*Schools Council *General Studies Project* (16+), Longman. Includes packs of approximately ten booklets of stimulus/discussion material on: *World Studies; Science and Society; Population and Environment; European Studies; Politics*
*Schools Council *Humanities Curriculum Project* (14–16). Heinemann. Based on non-directive classroom discussion of controversial issues. Packs containing 200 items of evidence were produced on: *War; Poverty; Law and Order; Relations between the Sexes; Education; Cities; Work; Family*
*Schools Council *Integrated Studies Project* (11–16) Aims to develop pupils' imaginative understanding of the human situation. The materials are organised in four units:
Unit 1. *Exploration Man* – works on the pupils' own experiences and

includes packs on: *Language and Gesture; Myth and Meaning; Belonging to Groups*.

Unit 2. *Communicating with Others* has three packs.

Unit 3. *Living Together* – is useful to teachers in this field. It examines a simple, a complex and a changing society in packs on 'Dayaks of Borneo'; 'Imperial China'; the 'Manding of West Africa'.

Unit 4. *Groups in Society* – examines conflict faced by minorities.

★Schools Council *Startline*. Moral education 8–13. Longman. See p. 184

★Schools Council *Lifeline*. Moral education 14–16. Longman. Packs include: 'In Other People's Shoes' (Points of view, Sensitivity, Consequences); 'What Would You Have Done'?; 'Proving the Rule'

Teachers' books: McPhail, P. *et al.* (1972) *Moral Education in the Secondary School*; McPhail, P. (1972) *In Other People's Shoes: Teachers' Guide*; Ungoed-Thomas, R. (1972) *Our School*.

★*One World Trust World Studies Project*. Established in 1973, this project is the one most directly concerned with the production of resources on a significant scale. Directed by Robin Richardson, it has produced books for both teachers and pupils. *Learning for Change in World Society* and *Debate and Decision* are both full of ideas for teachers to use in the classroom, whilst *Ideas into Action* offers thirteen case studies of the way global perspectives have been implemented. Pupils' books are: Richardson, R. (1977) *World in Conflict*; Richardson, R. (1977) *Caring for the Planet*; Richardson, R. (1977) *Progress and Poverty*; Richardson, R. (1978) *Fighting for Freedom*; all published by Nelson

UNESCO *ASPRO*: UNESCO *Associated Schools Project* is concerned to get children actively involved in visits, exhibitions, correspondence and exchange of materials.

## NEW SUBJECTS IN THE SECONDARY SCHOOL CURRICULUM

(★Recommended texts for pupils)

Although global perspectives in the curriculum have been advocated since the 1930s it is the last decade in particular which has witnessed the appearance of new subjects such as World Studies, international relations and peace studies. They appeared first in higher education but are now making their presence felt at secondary level. Because they all share an interest in certain issues and because they all depend heavily on concepts like interdependence, conflict and co-operation, there is inevitably a large degree of overlap between them. The lists which follow, therefore, make no claim to be mutually exclusive and readers will find it helpful to refer to more than one section.

### World Studies

CEWC (1980) *World Studies Resource Guide*. Council for Education in World Citizenship

*ELY *Materials on World Studies Project.* Card sets: The Rich and the Poor;
  Energy and People. Ely Resource and Technology Centre
Fisher, S., Magee, F. and Wetz, J. (1980) *Ideas into Action.* One World Trust
Heater, D. (1980) *World Studies: Education for International Understanding.*
  Harrap
*Matthews, B. and Matthews, P. (1973) *Happily Ever After? People and
  World Problems.* Edward Arnold
O'Conner, E. (1980) *World Studies in the European Classroom.* Council of
  Europe
Richardson, R. (ed.) (1979) *Debate and Decision.* One World Trust
Richardson, R. (1976) *Learning for Change in World Society.* One World
  Trust
*Richardson, R. A. (1977) *World Studies series.* Nelson. Titles in the series
  include: *World in Conflict; Progress and Poverty; Caring for the Planet; Fight-
  ing for Freedom.*
Switzer, K. and Mulloy, P. (1979) *Global Issues: Activities and Resources for
  the High School Teacher.* Social Science Education Consortium
Taylor, N, and Richardson, R. (1980) *Change and Choice: Britain in an
  Interdependent World.* Centre for World Development Education
UNESCO (1978) *Suicide or Survival? The Challenge of the Year 2000.*
  UNESCO.
UNESCO (1978) *Some Suggestions on Teaching about Human Rights.*
  UNESCO
UNESCO (1978) *What Kind of World Are We Leaving Our Children?*
  UNESCO
United Nations (1980) *U. N. Demographic Yearbook.* United Nations
United Nations (1980) *U. N. Statistical Yearbook.* United Nations
World Bank (1980) *World Development Report 1979.* World Bank
World Bank (1981) *World Bank Atlas.* World Bank

## Development Education and Third World studies

CWDE, which is continuing the work previously carried out by the
Education Unit of the now defunct Voluntary Committee for Overseas Aid
and Development, provides an excellent range of materials designed to be
used in schools. Outstanding among the Centre's products is *The Devel-
opment Puzzle,* a 150-page sourcebook for teaching about 'Rich World/Poor
World' divisions, which contains many pages of suggestions for additional
resources in several media. *Learning about Africa* from the Development
Education Centre, Birmingham, is a helpful multi-media pack and the
School of Oriental and African Studies (SOAS) (1977) handbook has many
excellent suggestions for the classroom.
Allen, R. (1980) *How to Save the World.* Kogan Page
Bernstein, H. (ed.) (1974) *Underdevelopment and Development.* Penguin
Braun, D. and Pearson, J. (1981) *Priorities for Development.* Development
  Education Centre, Birmingham

Brookfield, H. (1975) *Interdependent Development*. Methuen

*CEWC/Oxfam. *Facts about Development*. Series. Population, World Food, World Trade, etc. Council for Education in World Citizenship

Clark, B. (1979) *The Changing World and the Primary School*. Centre for World Development Education

Donaldson, P. (1973) *Worlds Apart*. Penguin

Dwyer, D. J. (1975) *People and Housing in Third World Cities*. Penguin

Fyson, N. L. (1979) *The Development Puzzle*. Centre for World Development Education

George, S. (1976) *How the Other Half Dies*. Penguin

Harrison, P. (1979) *Inside the Third World*. Penguin.

Harrison, P. (1980) *The Third World Tomorrow*. Penguin

Hummel, C. (1977) *Education Today for the World of Tomorrow*. UNESCO

Lipton, M. (1977) *Why Poor People Stay Poor – Urban Bias in World Development*. Temple Smith

Mabogunje, A. L. (1980) *The Development Process*. Hutchinson

Mountjoy, A. (ed.) (1978) *The Third World: Problems and Perspectives*. Macmillan

*Overseas Development Administration (ODA) (1980) *ABC of Aid and Development*. Free ODA

Smith, D. M. (1979), *Where the Grass is Greener: Living in an Unequal World*. Penguin

SOAS (1977) *Development Studies: A Handbook for Teachers*. SOAS

*Stuart, J. (1977) *The Unequal Third*. Edward Arnold

Thomas, O. and McKenzie, A. (eds) (1976) *Involved in Mankind*. Centre for World Development Education

*Turner, J. (1978) *World Inequality*. Longman

*TWP (1977) *Third World Study Pack*. Third World Publications

UNESCO (1978) *Population Education: A Contemporary Concern*. UNESCO

## Minorities and Race

Banton, M. (1972) *Racial Minorities*. Jonathan Cape

Berger, J. and Mohr, J. (1975) *A Seventh Man: The Story of a Migrant Worker in Europe*. Penguin

Brody, H. (1975) *The People's Land: Eskimos and Whites in the Eastern Arctic*. Pelican

Brown, D. (1971) *Bury My Heart at Wounded Knee: An Indian History of the American West*. Picador

CARE (1975) *Problems and Effects of Teaching about Race Relations*. (1976) Centre for Applied Research in Education, Norwich

Commission for Racial Equality *Education for a Multi-cultural Society: Information Pack* 1. *Bibliography for Teachers*. 2. *Audiovisual aids for Teachers*. Commission for Racial Equality

Hall, S. (1978) *Policing the Crisis*. Macmillan

Herbstein, D. (1978) *White Man, We Want to Talk to You*. Pelican

Hicks, D. (1980) *Minorities: A Teacher's Resource Book*. Heinemann

Hodge, J. L. *et al.* (1975) *Cultural Bases of Racism and Group Oppression: An Examination of Traditional 'Western' Concepts, Values and Institutional Structures which support Racism, Sexism and Elitism.* Two Riders Press, PO Box 4129, Berkeley, California 94704

*Hurman, A. (1977) *As Others See Us.* Edward Arnold

*IDAF (1978) *This is Apartheid: A Pictorial Introduction.* International Defence and Aid Fund

Jeffcoate, R. (1979) *Positive Image: Towards a Multi-racial Curriculum.* Writers and Readers Publishing Co-operative

Marnham, P. (1977) *Nomads of the Sahel,* Report No. 33. Minority Rights Group

Miles, R. and Phizacklea, A. (1979) *Racism and Political Action in Britain.* Routledge

Milner, D. (1977) *Children and Race.* Penguin

*New Internationalist* (1979) Australia's shame: the undermining of the Aborigines, No. 77. Special issue

NUT (1978) *Race, Education, Intelligence: A Teacher's Guide to the Facts and the Issues.* National Union of Teachers

Padrun, R. and Guyot, J. (1978) *Migrant Women Speak.* Search Press/World Council of Churches

Political and Economic Planning (1967) *Racial Discrimination in Britain.* HMSO

Power, J. and Hardman, A. (1978) *Western Europe's Migrant Workers,* Report No. 28. Minority Rights Group

Rex, J. and Moore, R. (1967) *Race, Community and Conflict.* Institute of Race Relations

Roberts, J. (1978) *From Massacres to Mining: The Colonisation of Aboriginal Australia.* War on Want, Colonialism and Indigenous Minorities Research Association (CIMRA)

*Searle, C. (1977) *The World in a Classroom.* Writers and Readers Publishing Co-operative

Smith, D. J. (1977) *Racial Disadvantage in Britain.* Penguin

Tinker, H. (1977) *Race, Conflict and the International Order: From Empire to United Nations.* Macmillan

Watson, J. L. (ed.) (1977) *Between Two Cultures: Migrants and Minorities in Britain.* Blackwell

Wilson, A. (1978) *Finding a Voice: Asian Women in Britain.* Virago

## Human rights

Council of Europe (1981) *Human Rights Education Handbook.* Council of Europe

Cox, B. (1976) *Civil Liberties in Britain.* Penguin

Hicks, D. (1980) *Minorities.* Heinemann

*IDAF (1978) *This is Apartheid: A Pictorial Introduction.* International Defence and Aid Fund.

NCCL (1979) *Civil Liberty: the NCCL Guide.* Penguin

O'Mahoney, P. J. (1978) *The Fantasy of Human Rights*. Mayhew-McGrimmon

Searle, C. (1977) *The World in a Classroom*. Writers and Readers Publishing Co-operative

Street, H. (1977) *Freedom, the Individual and the Law*. Penguin

UNESCO (1968) *Suggestions on Teaching Rights*. UNESCO

★Woodhouse, S. (1980) *Your Life, My Life*. Writers and Scholars Educational Trust

Wren, B. (1977) *Education for Justice*. SCM

## International relations and peace studies

Abraham, H. (1973) *World Problems in the Classroom*. UNESCO/HMSO

Aluko, O. (ed.) (1977) *The Foreign Policies of African States*. Hodder & Stoughton

Blaisdell, D. C. (1977) *International Organisation*. Wiley

Clarke, M. (1978) *Resources for Teaching International Relations*. G. & A. Hesketh

Clarke, M. (1978) *Simulations in the Study of International Relations*. G. & A. Hesketh

★Committee on Poverty and the Arms Trade (1978) *Bombs for Breakfast*. Campaign Against the Arms Trade

DES (1979) *International Understanding*: Sources of Information on Organisations HMSO

Enloe, C. H. (1980) *Ethnic Soldiers: State Security in a Divided World*. Penguin.

Fotheringham, P. (1975) *International Relations*. Blackie.

Fraenkel, J. R. et al. (1973) *Peacekeeping: Perspectives in World Order*. Institute for World Order

Fraenkel, J. R. et al. (1975) *The Struggle for Human Rights*: A Question of values (Perspectives in World Order), Institute for World Order

Jones, R. B. (1980) *The Making of Contemporary Europe*. Hodder & Stoughton

★Noble, D. (1977) *The War and Peace Book*. Writers and Readers Publishing Co-operative

Quester, G. H. (1977) *Offence and Defence in the International System*. Wiley

Rundle, R. N. (1979) *International Affairs 1890–1939*. Hodder & Stoughton

Stevens, C. (ed.) (1981) *EEC and the Third World: A Survey*. Hodder & Stoughton

UNESCO (1976) *Moving Towards Change: Thoughts on the New International Economic Order*. UNESCO

UNESCO (1977) *Human Rights Aspects of Population Programmes*. UNESCO

UNESCO (1978) *Review of Research Trends*, UNESCO

UNICEF (1980) *An Approach to Peace Education*. UNICEF

## Filmstrips and slides for developing global perspectives

New Worldwide Filmstrips with teachers' notes. Student Recordings Ltd. A series of filmstrips 'introducing' countries with follow-up strips 'exploring' cities in each country. Includes, amongst many, Russia, United States, South Africa, China, Brazil, Malaysia, India, Israel, Kenya.

New Worldwide Colour Slides, with teachers' notes. Student Recordings Ltd. Several series: *People of the World* – Europe, Africa, Asia, North America. *Man and His World* – Man the builder, industrialist, farmer, physician, machine, fisherman, etc. *World Environment* – houses, towns and cities, ports, churches. *The World About Us* – physical geography. *World Agriculture. World Industries. World Transport. The World We Live In* – The Third World; The Hungry World; World Faiths and Religions, etc. *V.R. Series* – Life in Algeria, Bali, Saudi Arabia, an Indian Village, The Republic of China. *Getting to Know* – primary level: The Family of Man; How other People Live.

Colour slides folios from the Slide Centre, including notes.

*Great Political Thinkers* Series: Marx; Engels; Lenin; Mao; Castro. *The Modern World* Series, includes, amongst many: The Two World Wars; History of Russia; China.

*Geography of the World* Series – over 60 sets, includes: Life on a Kibbutz; Life in China's Communes; Co-operative Farming in China; Calcutta; Life Among the Arabs; South Africa – The People.

*Life-style slides* – suitable for primary and lower secondary: French farmer; New Guinea gatherer: Mexican mine-worker: Tanzanian co-operative farmer.

*The Third World* series: 14 sets including: What is the Third World?; Health in the Third World; Farming in the Third World; Industry in the Third World; Towns and Cities in the Third World; African Development. *Divided world.*

*Survival*: problems and change affecting Aboriginals; Dayaks; Brazil; Indonesia.

*Resources of the World; Energy; Population and Resources. World Religions*: Buddhism; Islam; Hinduism.

Sound filmstrips from Educational Audio Visual, Mary Glasgow Publications: Black Protest; China in the Modern World; Ecological Systems; The Ideas of Karl Marx; Imperialism; The Right to Pollute; Terrorism; Wealth and Poverty; Prejudice; Aggression; Man and Space.

Slide Sets from CWDE illustrate Third World cultures and economics. In addition several raise current issues directly, e.g.: Our Cup of Tea; Caribbean in Change; Shanty Towns.

Taylor, N. and Richardson, R. *Seeing and Perceiving – Films in a World of Change*. Concord Films Council. A very helpful book for considering the way in which films may be used.

195

## Films

*Africa: Historical Heritage*. (Naval Films) Examines aspects of African culture and myth of the 'dark continent'.

*Between Two Worlds*. (Concord) Contrast of cultures for a young African sampling 'western' life-style.

*Casimoro – Andean Journey*. (Concord) Contrast of rural and urban life in Bolivia.

*Children of Africa*. (Guild Sound and Vision) UNICEF's work in improving the quality of life of African children.

*Children in China*. (Gateway Films) Children in different types of school and as an important part of the economic structure.

*Due to Lack of Interest Tomorrow has been Cancelled*. (BBC) Explores global ecological issues and predictions.

*The Day Before Tomorrow*. (Concord) Examines the consequences of the population explosion. (International Planned Parenthood Federation)

*Energy: The Dilemma*. (Concord) Examines consequences for the environment of growth in demand for energy from fossil fuels.

*Energy: New Sources*. (Concord) Explores 'alternative' souces of energy and indicates potential.

*Energy in Perspective*. (BP) Examines growth in use of energy, the limits of conventional fuel sources and the availability of alternatives.

*Eye of the Storm*. (Concord) An experiment in teaching about racial prejudice.

*The Faces of India*. (Gateway Films) Four separate films illustrating cultural and religious differences: *Jhaoo Chowdhari* – a Muslim tradesman; *Raju* – a boy guide; *Swami Chidananda* – a Yogi; *Sampuran Singh* – a Sikh farmer.

*Family of Man*. (BBC) Series of six programmes comparing aspects of family life in five different cultures (two British). *Married Life* is good introduction to different bases of marriage.

*Five Minutes to Midnight*. (Concord) Many examples of poverty and problems of underdevelopment in several countries.

*Food for 6,000 million People*. (Guild Sound and Vision) Suggests strategies for coping with the world's food problem in the year 2,000.

*For Us to Choose*. (Concord) Contrasts nineteenth-century poverty with twentieth-century affluence – in the West! Contrast with Third World.

*Legacy of Empire*. (Concord) Early slavery, current immigration and the relationship between migration and underdevelopment.

*Living in a Developing Country*. (BBC) Examines life in Ghana.

*Not Enough*. (Concord) Examines problems faced by those requiring and those providing development aid.

*One Planet, Two Worlds*. (Concord) (i) Rural and urban proverty. The seeds of catastrophe; (ii) Malnutrition. The hidden killer; (iii) Rich and Poor. What can we do?

*The Other Way*. (BBC) Explores problems of 'Western' pursuit of growth, underdevelopment and the rich/poor divide.

*Population Explosion*. (Guild Sound and Vision) Animated film linking population and economic growth.

*Rural and Urban Poverty*. (Concord) Examines poverty in the Third World – in villages and in shanty towns (part of *Five Minutes to Midnight*).

*The Shadow of Progress*. (BP) Highlights the environmental consequences of economic progress – pollution, population explosion, limited resources.

*Spare a Thought*. (Christian Aid) Three-part film about interdependence, and the problems faced by Third World countries dependent upon a single commodity for economic survival.

*The Survival Game*. (Central Film Library) The gap between rich and poor nations and the way world trade currently perpetuates the inequality.

*Tanzania*. (Concord) Illustrates Nyerere's socialist philosophy. Rural development, co-operative villages and the place of education.

*Tea – The Deadly Cost* (Granada) Highlights the poverty-line conditions of workers on the Sri Lanka tea plantations owned by British and multinational companies.

*That All May Learn*. (Concord) Battle to eliminate illiteracy in Third World countries.

*Viracocha*. (Concord) Economic exploitation leads to conflict and contempt.

*The Vital Earth*. (Central Film Library) The importance of agriculture in the Third World, India.

*Water Supply*. (Naval) Descriptive/illustrative film showing problems to be overcome in providing hygienic water supply.

*What is it We're Looking at, Miss*? (Concord) A classroom project on Africa in an English school.

*Women in a Changing World*. (Concord) The changing role of women faced with social, economic, technological and political change.

*A World Away*. (Concord) Social change following technological innovation in an Indian village.

*The World Without*. (Film Forum) The villagers and the newcomers.

## Games and simulations

(Full details of authors referred to are given at the end of this list)

*Aid Committee Game*. Oxfam. Case studies requiring determination of priorities.

*The Arms Control Game* – see Clarke, M. (1978).

*BaFa BaFa* – see RaFa RaFa.

*The Bosnian Crisis Game* – see Clarke, M.(1978).

*Choices*. Campaign Against the Arms Trade. Arms Trade simulation.

*Confrontation*. Philmar Ltd, 47 Dace Road, London N3. Board game of international nuclear crisis.

*Congress of Vienna*. Longman Resources Kit. Conference diplomacy.

*Crisis*. Simile II, Scarce resources in six countries.

*Development Game* in Walford, R. (1969). Development problem for new state and old colonial power.

*Dignity*. Third World Publications. Considers power and oppression.

*Disunia*. Interact. Thirteen states on a new planet in 2087, face problems similar to US in 1780s.

*The EEC Wine Lake Game* – see Clarke, M. (1978).

*Extinction: The Game of Ecology*. Sinauer Associates. Decision-making to ensure survival of competing species.

*Game of Nations*. Waddingtons. Board game of Middle East politics and crisis.

*Genex Crisis Games* – see Clarke, M. (1978).

*Geography Games*. Longman. Various, including Urbanisation, Caribbean Fisherman and Breadline.

*The Grain Drain*. Centre for World Development Education. Board game illustrating problems faced by Third World countries on world markets.

*Guns or Butter*. Simile II. Choice between arms–dealing or international co-operation.

*History Games*. Longman. Various including The Scramble for Africa, Congress of Vienna and Frontier.

*Inter-Nation Simulation*. Science Research Associates. Pressures of international relations.

*Island*. Third World Publications. Problems of economic development.

*The Lebanon Crisis Game* – see Clarke, M. (1978).

*Living Together – survival*. Centre for World Development Education. Importance of trade and exchange.

*The Mali Cattle Game*. Centre for World Development Education. Problems of survival via cattle-breeding.

*The Poultry Game*. Centre for World Development Education. Economic survival through investment in poultry.

*The Poverty Game*. Centre for World Development Education. Problems of African subsistence farmers where fate is controlled by chance.

*Powderhorn*. Simile II. Frontier men establish hierarchy through trade.

*RaFa RaFa*. Simile II, Centre for World Development Education. Cross-cultural simulation.

*The Rich and the Poor*. Centre for World Development Education. Card games – ranking, comparing, contrasting.

*Starpower*. Simile II. Illustrates stratification and power.

*Sierra Leone Development Project*. Center for Educational Services and Research. Decisions in the economic development of a newly emerging nation.

*A Trade Game*. Centre for World Development Education. Consumers, retailers and dealers in market for foodstuffs.

*The Trading Game*. Christian Aid. Relationship of trade and national prosperity.

*World Energy Game*. Ely Resource and Technology Centre.

*World Politics* in Walcott, C. and Walcott, A. (1976). Economic interdependence.

Useful books on simulation and gaming:

Adams, D. M. (1973) *Simulation Games: An Approach*. C. A.Jones Publishing Co., Ohio

Clarke, M. (1978) *Simulations in the Study of International Relations*. G. & A. Hesketh

Tansey, P. J. (1971) *Educational Aspects of Simulation*. McGraw

Taylor, J. and Walford, R. (1972) *Simulation in the classroom*. Penguin

Walcott, C. and Walcott, A. (1976) *Simple Simulations*. American Political Science Association

Walford, R. (1969) *Games in Geography*. Longman

## Do it yourself resources

### Sources

Although there are now excellent 'purpose-built' resources available from the sources indicated above, it is advantageous to collect and to produce one's own, in addition. Features and photographs from newspapers, periodicals and colour supplements provide a convenient means of keeping teaching materials up to date. In addition, one can provide variety by recording music as records are released, and by taping radio and television broadcasts (subject to copyright restrictions).

The print sources of topical material do not need to be listed here. The daily newspapers speak for themselves and the appropriate journals are listed on pp. 202–3. It is worth bearing in mind, however, that, whilst newspapers like the *Guardian* incorporate a regular feature like the 'Third World Review' and the other 'heavies' include foreign news sections, the low reading age and the short time-span of concentration required by the tabloids means that they may be the most suitable for a large range of secondary pupils.

With such pupils music is particularly important because it provides a means of starting with their own interests and so it minimises the problem of initial motivation and relevance. Apart from the overtly political songs of 'protest' music and singers like Joan Baez, folk music provides a rich source. But it is popular music which probably has most potential, and the pupils themselves will often identify and contribute the appropriate records or albums. Many of John Lennon's songs like 'Revolution', 'Power to the People', 'Nowhere Man', 'Give Peace a Chance', and the Beatles' music after 1966, focus upon issues like peace, conflict and injustice. More recently groups like the Sex Pistols with their record 'Anarchy', Poison Girls with 'Alienation' and 'Hero' and, above all, the music of Crass, fall into this category. Rush, for example, have produced an album called 'Hemispheres' which is an allegorical tale containing verses such as the following:

Some fought themselves, some fought each other
Most just followed one another
Lost and aimless like their brothers.

For their hearts were so unclear
And the Truth could not appear.
Their spirits were divided
Into blinded hemispheres.

We can walk our road together
If our goals are all the same.
We can run alone and free
If we pursue a different aim.

## Retrieval

There is nothing more frustrating, having collected together many such resources, than to finish up unable to find the right one when it's required! Yet there are very simple storage and retrieval systems which are easy to organise, inexpensive to maintain and very effective in practice. These can incorporate resources in different media, for different age-groups, commercially produced or 'home-made'. At the simplest level each item is given a number, starting at 1 and progressing in sequence. It is then listed on an index card. The item itself is stored in that sequence, usually in an ordinary filing cabinet. If the index cards are made out in duplicate it becomes possible to store the second set by subject or some other categorical heading.

The major weakness of this system lies in the necessity to classify each item under one subject or category when many items do not fit neatly into a single category and some will cover more than one. This problem is easily overcome by using 'edge notch' or 'edge punch' cards, available in various sizes, with numbered holes punched along each edge. Each hole can stand for a characteristic that we may wish to use as the basis for retrieval. These characteristics may be features of the material such as concepts or topics or countries, or the age-group for which it is suitable, or the medium in which it is available. Each item is allocated a number which is then written on a card together with the title. The hole for each characteristic of the item is then 'notched' or slotted and the card can be filed in any order.

When we want to find items on a particular topic, or concept, or issue or country, they can be retrieved by pushing a needle through the appropriate hole in the stack of cards. The relevant cards are left behind, because they are slotted, when all the others are lifted out on the needle. The operation may be repeated several times until one has, say audio-visual items, on poverty, in the Third World, suitable for lower secondary pupils. When the user has the necessary information the cards are returned to the stack in any order. There is no tedious and time-consuming filing.

The important part of the whole process is the establishment of a thesaurus, the list of characteristics which will be used to classify the resource items. Ideally it should not be too long, when the classifying becomes tedious, nor should it be so short that it fails to include characteristics which are important to the course. The simplest procedure for teachers is to establish a trial list for a pilot run on, say, half a dozen items before compiling the final list. Once established, the list should not be altered without altering all the cards already indexed.

One of the greatest advantages of this system is that it can be operated by the pupils themselves. Teachers need only classify the items. The rest of the process actually provides pupils with the opportunity to develop logical library indexing and research skills as well as the opportunity to play a responsible part in their own learning.

There are more sophisticated systems such as optical co-ordinate coincidence indexes (OCCI) but these tend to be more appropriate for larger numbers of items than are usually held in a single faculty or department.

## Bibliography for organising resources

Aitchison, J. and Gilchrist, A. (1972) *Thesaurus Construction : A Practical Manual.*

Beswick, N. (1972) *School Resource Centres*, Schools Council Working Paper 43. Evans/Methuen

Beswick, N. (1975) *Organising Resources.* Heinemann

Beswick, N. (1977) *Resource Based Learning.* Heinemann

Foskett, A. C. (1971) *Guide to Personal Indexes.* Bingley

Jolley, J. L. (1974) Retrieval systems theory and resource centres, *Ideas*, 29 154–161

Jolley, J. L. (1977) *Punched Feature Cards for Co-ordinate Indexing in Schools.* Information Systems and Services Ltd, High Wycombe, Bucks.

Malcolm, A. H. (1973) *A Resource Centre...is a State of Mind.* Scottish Educational Films Association

Tucker, R. N. (1976) *The Setting Up of a Resources Centre.* Scottish Educational Films Association

## Sources of retrieval and indexing materials

Copeland-Chatterson Company Ltd, Seymour House, 17 Waterloo Place, London SW1Y 4AR

Information Systems and Services Ltd, Westbourne House, Westbourne Street, High Wycombe, Bucks HP11 2PZ

## Developing Education Centres

National Association of Development Education Centres, Development Education Project, 9a Didsbury Park, Manchester M20 8RR

Birmingham Development Education Centre, Gillett Centre, Selly Oak Colleges, Birmingham 29

Bridgend Overseas Development Education Centre, Bridgend College of Technology, Cowbridge Road, Bridgend, Mid-Glamorgan

Bristol Development Education Centre, c/o The Breadline, Old Market, Bristol 1

Cambridge Third World Centre, Brunswick Teachers' Centre, Newmarket Road, Cambridge CB5 8EG

Cardiff Welsh Centre for International Affairs, Temple of Peace, Cathays Park, Cardiff CF1 3AP

Edinburgh SEAD (Scottish Education and Action for Development), 9 Union Street, Edinburgh EH1 3LT

Exmouth Development Education Centre Project, Rolle College, Exmouth, Devon EX8 2AT

Hove TWIC (Third World Information Centre), 31 Western Road, Hove, East Sussex BN3 1AF

Leamington TWIC (Third World Information Centre), 32a Bath Street, Leamington Spa, Warwickshire CV31 3AE

Leeds Development Education Centre, 29 Blenheim Terrace, Leeds 2

London Archway Development Education Centre, 173 Archway Road, London N6

London One World Shop (Euston), 78 Eversholt Street, London NW1

London Ujamaa Centre, 14 Brixton Road, London SW9

Manchester Development Education Project, Didsbury School of Education, 9a Didsbury Park, Manchester M20 8RR

Manchester Shanti Third World Centre, 178 Oxford Road, Manchester M13 9QX

Northern Ireland World Development Education Projects, 45 Clarendon Street, Londonderry

Norwich Third World Centre. 17–19 St John Maddermarket, Norwich NR2 1DN

Ormskirk Development Education Project, Edge Hill College of Higher Education, St Helen's Road, Ormskirk, Lancs. L39 4QP

Oxford 'The Rest of the World' Development Education Centre, 72 Cowley Road, Oxford

Sheffield India Alive Project, 23 Steade Road, Sheffield S7 1DS

Sheffield Third World Resources Centre, Sheffield Caribbean Workshop, Sharrow Lane, Sheffield S11 8AE

Southampton World Studies Centre, St John's School, Castleway, Southampton S01 0AS

Workington Development Education Centre, Cumbria Schools World Development Project, 28 Finkle Street, Workington, Cumbria

**Journals and periodicals** – useful to teachers

| | |
|---|---|
| *Action for Development* | Centre for World Development Education |
| *Broadsheets* | Council for Education in World Citizenship |
| *Bulletin of Environmental Education* | Town and Country Planning Association |
| *Children's Book Bulletin* | Children's Rights Workshop |
| *Cultures* | UNESCO |
| *Development Forum* (free) | Centre for Economic and Social Information |
| *Ecologist* | Edward Goldsmith (ed.) 73 Molesworth St, Wadebridge, Cornwall PL27 7ES |

| | |
|---|---|
| *IDS Bulletin* | Institute of Development Studies |
| *Impact* | UNESCO/HMSO |
| *Intercom* | Centre for Global Perspectives |
| *Journal of Development Studies* | Frank Cass |
| *MOST* | Modern Studies Association, Scotland |
| *New Era* | World Education Fellowship/World Studies Project |
| *New Internationalist* | Oxfam/Christian Aid |
| *Newsletter* | World Studies Teacher Education Network |
| *Orbit* | Voluntary Service Overseas |
| *Outlook* | War on Want |
| *Sanity* | Campaign for Nuclear Disarmament |
| *Social Education* | National Council of Social Studies, USA |
| *Social Science Teacher* | Association for Teaching the Social Sciences |
| *South* | South Publications Ltd, London |
| *Spur* | World Development Movement |
| *Social Studies* | Helen Dwight Reid Educational Foundation |
| *State of Affairs* | Jordanhill College |
| *Teaching Politics* | Politics Association |
| *Third World Quarterly* | Third World Foundation |
| *UNESCO Courier* | UNESCO |
| *World Development Reports* | World Bank |
| *World Studies Journal* | Groby Community College, Leics. |

## Addresses of useful organisations

Africa Bureau, Montague House, High Street, Huntingdon, Cambs. PE18 6EP

Amnesty International, Tower House, 8–14 Southampton Street, London WC2E 7HF

Association for Teaching the Social Sciences, Didsbury Faculty, Manchester Polytechnic, Wilmslow Road, Manchester M20 8RR

Bradford School of Peace Studies, Bradford University, W. Yorks BD7 1DP

British Film Institute, 127 Charing Cross Road, London WC2H OEA

Campaign Against the Arms Trade, 5 Caledonian Road, London N1 9DX

Campaign for Nuclear Disarmament, 11, Goodwin Street, London N4

Catholic Fund for Overseas Development, 21a Soho Square, London W1Y 6NR

Catholic Institute for International Relations, 1 Cambridge Terrace, London NW1 4JL

Centre for Applied Research in Education, University of East Anglia, Norwich NR4 7TJ

Centre for Peace Studies, St. Martin's College, Lancaster LA1 3JD

Center for Teaching about Peace and War, 754 University Center Building, Wayne State University, Detroit, MI. 48202, USA

Centre for Teaching International Relations, University of Denver, Denver, Colorado 80208, USA

Centre for World Development Education, 128 Buckingham Palace Road, London SWlW 9SH

Central Film Library, Government Building, Bromyard Avenue, Acton, London W3 7JB

Central Office of Information, Publications Sections, Hercules Road, London SE1 7DU

Children's Rights Workshop, 4 Aldebert Terrace, London SW8

Christian Aid, PO Box No.1, London SW9 8BH

Commission of the European Community, 20 Kensington Palace Gardens, London W8 4QQ

Commission for Racial Equality, 10–12 Allington Street, London SW1E 5EH

Commonwealth Institute, Kensington High Street, London W8 6NQ

Concord Films Council, Nacton, Ipswich, Suffolk IP3 9BJ

Conservation Trust, 246 London Road, Earley, Reading RG6 1AJ

Contemporary Films Ltd, 55 Greek Street, London W1V 6DB

Council for Education in World Citizenship, 26 Blackfriars Lane, London EC4V 6EB

Council for Environmental Education, School of Education, University of Reading, London Road, Reading RG1 5AQ

Educational and Television Films Ltd, 247 Upper Street, London N1 1RU

EMI Special Films Unit, 135 Wardour Street, London W1

Fergus Davidson Associates Ltd, 376 London Road, West Croydon, Surrey CRO 2SU

Friends of the Earth, 9 Poland Street, London W1V 3DG

Future Studies Centre, 15 Kelso Road, Leeds LS2 9PR

Global Development Studies Institute, PO Box 522, Madison, New Jersey 07946, USA

Global Perspectives in Education, 218E 18th Street, New York, NY 10003, USA

Guild Sound and Vision, Oundle Road, Peterborough PE2 9PZ

ILEA Learning Resources Centre, Highbury Station Road, London N1 1SB

Institute of Development Studies, University of Sussex, Brighton BN1 9RE

Institute for World Order, 1140 Avenue of the Americas, New York, NY 10036, USA

International Defence and Aid Fund, 2 Amen Court, London EC4M 7BX

Jordanhill Project in International Understanding, Jordanhill College of Education, Glasgow G13 1PP

Mid-America Program for Global Perspectives, 513 North Park Avenue, Bloomington, Indiana 47401, USA

Minority Rights Group, 36 Craven Street, London WC2N 5NG

National Association of Development Education Centres, Development Education Project, 9A Didsbury Park, Manchester M20 8RR

National Association for Multi-racial Education, 86, Station Road, Mickleover, Derby DE3 5FP

National Association for Race Relations Teaching and Action Research, 22 Laneham Close, Bessacarr, Doncaster

National Centre for Alternative Technology, Llwyngwern Quarry, Machynlleth, Powys, Wales

National Council for Civil Liberties, 186 Kings Cross Road, London WC1X 9DE

One World Trust, 24 Palace Chambers, Bridge Street, London SW1

Overseas Development Institute, 10 Percy Street, London W1P OJB

Oxfam, 274 Banbury Road, Oxford OX2 7DE

Pax Christi, St. Francis of Assisi Centre, Pottery Lane, London W11 4NQ

Politics Association, 16 Gower Street, London WC1E 6DP

Richardson Institute for Peace and Conflict Research, Fylde College, University of Lancaster, Lancaster LA1 4YF

Runnymede Trust, 62 Chandos Place, London WC2N 4HG

School of Oriental and African Studies, University of London, Malet Street, London WC1E 7HP

Scottish Central Film Library, 74 Victoria Crescent Road, Glasgow G12 9JN

Slide Centre Ltd, 143 Chatham Road, London SW11 6SR

Social Science Education Consortium, 855 Broadway, Boulder, Colorado 80302, USA

Student Recordings Ltd, 88 Queen Street, Newton Abbot, Devon

Third World First, 232 Cowley Road, Oxford OX4 1UH

Third World Foundation, New Zealand House, 80 Haymarket, London SW1Y 4TS

UNICEF, 46 Osnaburgh Street, London NW1 3PU

United Nations Association, 3 Whitehall Court, London SW1A 2EL

United Nations Information Centre, 14 Stratford Place, London W1N 9AF

Voluntary Service Overseas, 9 Belgrave Square, London SW1X 8PW

War on Want, 467 Caledonian Road, London N7 9BE

World Bank, 1818H Street NW, Washington, DC 20433, USA

World Development Movement, Bedford Chambers, Covent Garden, London WC2E 8HA

World Education Center, 1730 Grove Street, Berkeley, California 94707, USA

World Education Fellowship, 33 Kinnaird Avenue, London W4 3SH

World Future Society, PO Box 30369, Bethesda Branch, Washington, DC 20014, USA

World Studies Project (see One World Trust, above)

World Studies Teacher Education Network, Westminster College, North Hinksey, Oxford

Worldwatch Institute, 1776 Massachusetts Avenue. NW Washington DC20036, USA

World Without War Publications, 67 East Madison, Chicago, Illinois 60603, USA

# References

Action for Development/Food and Agricultural Organisation (1975). *Joint UN Plan of Support and Action for Development Education Activities, 1975–80,* Rome

Alger C. (1977) 'Foreign Policies of US Publics', *International Studies Quarterly,* **21,** 277–318

Anderson, L. (1979) *Schooling and Citizenship in a Global Age: An Exploration of the Meaning and Significance of Global Education.* Social Studies Development Center, Mid-America Program for Global Perspectives in Education, Indiana University, Bloomington, Indiana, USA

Anderson, L. and Becker, J. (1968) An examination of the structure and objectives of International Education. *Social Education.* **Vol 22,** November 1968 639-647

Anderson, L. and Becker, J. (1977) Education for involvement. *The New Era,* **58** (2), 40–3.

Aucott, J., Cox, H., Dodds, A. and Selby, D. (1979) World Studies on the runway: One year's progress towards a core curriculum, *The New Era,* **60** (60), 212–29

Bailey, C. H. (1975) Neutrality and rationality in teaching, in Bridges, D. and Scrimshaw, P. (eds) *Values and Authority in School.* Hodder & Stoughton. London

Bailey, P. (1979) One day in Africa, *Teaching Geography,* **4** (4). (Patrick Bailey edits this journal.) A more detailed report can be found in *West Africa '77: Kasewe Hills Report,* University of Leicester School of Education library

Baldwin, J. and Wells, H. (eds) (1979) *Active Tutorial Work,* Books 1–5. Blackwell, Oxford

Ballard, M. (1970) Change and the curriculum, Ch. 11 in Ballard, M. (ed.) *New Movements in the Study and Teaching of History.* Temple Smith, London

Banks, J. A. (1974) Curricular model for an open society, Ch. 4. pp 43–63 in Della–Dora, D. and House, J.E. (eds) *Education for an Open Society.* Association for Supervision and Curriculum Development, Washington

Bloom, B. S. *et al.* (1956) *A Taxonomy of Educational Objectives:* the Classification of Educational Goals: Cognitive and Affective Domains (2 handbooks). Longman, London

Bobbitt, F. (1924) *How to Make a Curriculum.* Houghton Mifflin, Boston.

Booker, C. (1980) *The Seventies.* Penguin, London

Bourdieu, P. (1960) The school as a conservative force: scholastic and cultural inequalities, reprinted in Dale, R., Esland, G. and Macdonald, M.(eds) (1976) *Schooling and Capitalism.* Routledge & Kegan Paul, London

Bowker, J. (1973) *Sense of God.* Oxford UP, London, New York, 1977

Bowles, T. S. (1978) *Survey of Attitudes Towards Overseas Development.* HMSO, London

Brandt, W. (ed.) (1980) *North-South: A Programme for Survival.* Pan, London and Sydney

Braun, D. and Pearson, J. (1981) *Priorities for Development: A Teacher's Handbook for Development Education.* Development Education Centre, Birmingham

Bridges, D. (1975) *Only One Earth–Perspectives on a Consultation.* World Studies Project, London

Bridges, D (1978) *Materials on World Studies: interim report for the Overseas Development Ministry,* Ely Resource and Technology Centre, Black Hill, Ely, Cambs. Cyclostyled

Bridges, D. (1979) *Education Democracy and Discussion.* National Foundation for Educational Research, Windsor, UK (distributed in USA by Humanities Press Inc., New Jersey).

Brown, G. N. (1978) International understanding and national inertia: a curriculum reform which hasn't happened, *The New Era*, **59** (4), 128–33

Bruner, J. S. (1960) *Process of Education*. Harvard University Press

Bruner, J. S. (1966) *Toward a Theory of Instruction*. Harvard University Press

Buchanan, K. (1974) Reflections on a 'dirty word', reprinted in Peet, R. (ed.) (1978) *Radical Geography*. Methuen, London

Burns, R. (1975) *Higher Education and Third World Development Issues: An International Comparative Study*, Action for Development/Food and Agricultural Organisation, Rome

Burton, J. (1972) *World Society*, Cambridge UP

Buttimer, A. (1976) Grasping the dynamism of lifeworld, *Annals of the Association of American Geographers*, **66**, 277–92

Caldwell, M. (1977) *The Wealth of Some Nations*. Zed Press, London

Calthrop, K. and Owens, G. (eds) (1974) *Teachers for Tomorrow: Diverse and Radical Views About Teacher Education*. Heinemann, London

Camus, A. (1961) *Resistance, Rebellion and Death*. Hamish Hamilton, London

Carby H. (1980) *Multicultural Fictions*, Centre for Contemporary Cultural Studies, University of Birmingham (mimeo).

City of Birmingham (1975a) *Agreed Syllabus of Religious Instruction*. City of Birmingham Education Department

City of Birmingham (1975b) *Living Together: a Teacher's Handbook of Suggestions*. City of Birmingham Education Department

Clarke, R. (1975) *Notes for the Future: An Alternative History of the Past Decade*. Thames & Hudson, London

Coggin, P. (1980) *Education for the Future: The Case for Radical Change*. Pergamon Press, Oxford

Cripwell, K. R. (1979) *Man and Language*. Harrap, London

Cullinan, T. (1975) *If the Eye Be Sound*. Catholic Institute for International Relations, London

DES (1972) *Education: A Framework for Expansion*. OMND 5174, HMSO, London

DES (1976) Circular 9/76, *Unesco Recommendation: Education for International Understanding*. DES, London

DES (1977) *Education in Schools: A Consultative Document*. HMSO, London

DES (1980) *Framework for the School Curriculum*. HMSO London

Dhondy, F. (1978) Teaching young blacks, *Race Today*, May/June, 80–6

Dunlop, O. J. (ed.) (1977) *Modern Studies: Origins, Aims and Development*. Macmillan Education, London

Eliade, M. (1959) *Sacred and Profane*. Harcourt, Brace & Co., New York

Elliott, J. (1973) Neutrality, rationality and the role of the teacher, *Proceedings of the Philosophy of Education Society of Great Britain*, **7** (1), 39–65, Basil Blackwell, Oxford

Elliott, J. (1975) The values of the neutral teacher, in Bridges, D. and Scrimshaw, P. (eds) *Values and Authority in Schools*. Hodder & Stoughton, London

Fisher, S., Magee, F. and Wetz, J. (1980) *Ideas into Action: Curriculum for a changing world*. One World Trust, London

Galtung, J. (1973) *The European Community: A Superpower in the Making*. Universitetsforlaget, Oslo, and George Allen & Unwin, London

Galtung, J. (1976) Peace Education: problems and conflicts, in Haavelsrud, M. (ed.) *Education for Peace: Reflection and Action*. IPC Science and Technology Press, Guildford

Gates, B. E. (1980) *Afro–Caribbean Religions*. Ward Lock, London

# References

Gribbin, J. (1979) Climatic change and world food, *Times Educational Supplement*, Environmental Studies Extra, 10 June

GRIHE (1975) *Interdisciplinarity*. Group for Research and Development in Higher Education, Nuffield Foundation

Grimmitt, M. (1973) *What Can I Do In RE*? Mayhew–McCrimmon Ltd

Guest, I. (1978) *Shishir of Bangladesh*. UNICEF Development Education School Series No. 1, Geneva

Hall, S. (1980) Teaching Race, *Multiracial Education*, **9** (1) Autumn, 3–13

Halstead, F. (1978) *Out Now! A Participant's Account of the American Movement Against the Vietnam War*. Monad Press, New York

Hampden–Turner, C. (1970) *Radical Man*. Schenkman Publishing Company, United States, and George Duckworth, London

Hannam, C. (1970) Prejudice and the teaching of history, pp. 26–36 in Ballard, M. (ed.) *New Movements in the Study and Teaching of History*. Temple Smith, London

Hampshire Education Authority (1978) *Agreed Syllabus for R.E.* Hampshire Education Authority

Hanvey, R. (1976) *An Attainable Global Perspective*. Box 1064, Bloomington, Indiana, IN 47402. Centre for War Peace Studies, 218 East 18th Street, New York 10003, USA

Hanvey, R. (1979) Strategies of change in global education: recommendations for the United States, *The New Era*, **60** (4), London

Hardy, T. (1981) *Tess of the d'Urbervilles*. (1957) Macmillan, London and Basingstoke

Harper, R. (1972) Environmental education as an arena of creative conflict, *International Understanding at School*, No. 23, UNESCO

Heater, D. (1980) *World Studies: Education for International Understanding in Britain*. Harrap, London

Henderson, J. (1975) A note on World Studies: the key concepts, background paper for a meeting of the Education Advisory Committee of the One World Trust at the House of Commons, 29, April

Hepworth, T. (1979) What ought we to do? Values and action in the classroom, *The New Era*, **60** (2), World Education Fellowship, London

Hicks, D. W. (1977a) The role of contemporary global issues in teacher training courses, M.Sc., University of Lancaster

Hicks, D. (1977b) The Third World: what should we be teaching? *Teaching Geography*, **3** (1),

Hicks, D. W. (1979) Two sides of the same coin: an exploration of the links between multicultural education and development education, *New Approaches in Multiracial Education*, **7** (2) 1–5

Hicks, D. W. (1981) *Minorities: A Teacher's Resource Book for the Multi-ethnic Curriculum*. Heinemann Educational, London

Higgins, R. (1978) *The Seventh Enemy*. Hodder & Stoughton, London

Higgins, R. (1979) Countering the 'Seventh Enemy', *World Studies Journal*, **1** (1), 4

Hirst, P. H. (1973) Toward a Logic of Curriculum Development, *The Curriculum: Research Innovation and Change*. Eds. Taylor, P. and Walton, J., Ward Lock Educational, London

Hodge, J., Struckmann, D. and Trost, L. (1975) *Cultural Bases of Racism and Oppression*. Two Riders Press, California

Huckle, J. (1978) Geography and values in higher education, *Journal of Geography in Higher Education*, **2** (1), 57–67

208

Hull, J. M. (1975) Agreed syllabuses, past, present and future, in Smart, N. and Horder, D. (eds) *New Movements in R. E.* Temple Smith, London

Hutchinson, A. (1980) Development education and the voluntary agencies: Constraints v. needs, *World Studies Journal*, **1** (3), 23–7

ILEA (1980) *Assemblies in County Schools*. GLC Supplies Dept., London

Institute of Race Relations (1980) Anti-racist not multicultural education, *Race and Class*, **22** (1), 81–3

James, A. (1980) The 'multicultural' curriculum, *New Approaches to Multiracial Education*, **8** (1), 1–5

Jeffcoate, R. (1976) Curriculum planning in multiracial education, *Educational Research*, **18** (3), 192–200

Johnston, R.A. (1979) *Geography and Geographers: Anglo-American Human Geography since 1945*. Arnold, London

Katz, J. (1978) *White Awareness: A Handbook for Anti-racist Training*, University of Oklahama Press, Norman, Oklahoma

Keddie, N. (Ed.) (1973) *Tinker, Tailor.. the Myth of Cultural Deprivation*. Penguin Education, Harmondsworth

King, E. (1971) *The World: A Context for Teaching in the Elementary School*. Wm C. Brown

King, E. (1973) *Educating Young Children: Sociological Interpretations*. Wm. C. Brown

Krathwohl, D.R. et al. (1964) *A Taxonomy of Educational Objectives: the Classification of Educational Goals: Handbook 2, Affective Domain*. Longman, London

Lawrence, J. (1975) *Take Hold of Change: Alternatives for Society at the End of the Second Millennium*. SPCK Press Ltd, London

Laxton, W. (ed.) (1980) *Paths to Understanding: A Handbook of RE in Hampshire Schools*, Globe Education/Hampshire Education Authority

Leech, K. (1973) *Youthquake: The Growth of a Counter-Culture Through Two Decades*. Sheldon Press, London

Lewy. G. (1974) *Religion and Revolution*. Oxford, London and New York

Lindholm, S. (1975) *Seeing for Oneself*. Swedish International Development Authority, Stockholm

Lyall, A. (1967) *History Syllabuses and a World Perspective*. Longman, London

Lodge, B. (1976) Training cuts will put 1500 out of work, union warns. *Times Educational Supplement*. 12 November.

Marcuse, H. (1976 edn) Repressive tolerance, in Connerton, P. (ed) *Critical Sociology*. Penguin, Harmondsworth

Marratt, H. (1979) *RE and the Training of Primary Teachers*. RE Council, Farnham

Martin, D. (1978) *A General Theory of Secularisation*. Blackwell, Oxford, and Harper, New York

Mazrui, A. (1975) The new interdependence, Ch. 3, pp. 38–54 in Erb, G.F. and Kallab, V. (eds) *Beyond Dependency: The Developing World Speaks Out*. Overseas Development Council, Washington

McNeill, W. (1970) World history in the schools, pp. 16–25 in Ballard, M. (ed.) *New Movements in the Study and Teaching of History*. Temple Smith, London

McPhail, P., Ungoed-Thomas, J. R. and Chapmen, H. (1972) *Moral Education in the Secondary School*. Longman, London

Meadows, D. H., Meadows, D. L., Randers, J. and Behrens, W. W. (1972) *The Limits to Growth*. Universe Books, New York and Earth Island Ltd, London

Medllin, R. (1976) Research partners, quoted p. 33 in Richardson, R., *Learning for Change in World Society*. One World Trust, London

# References

Mesarovic, M. and Pestel, E. (1975) *Mankind At The Turning Point*. Hutchinson, London

Mill, J. S. (1971 edn) On Liberty, in *Three Essays by John Stuart Mill*. Oxford UP, London

Morrish, I. (1971) *Background of Immigrant Children*. Allen & Unwin, London

Mullard, C. (1981) *Racism in Society and Schools: History, Policy and Practice*. University of London Institute of Education

Musgrove, F. (1973) The curriculum for a world of change, pp. 27–37 in Taylor, P. and Walston, J. (eds) *The Curriculum: Research Innovation and Change*. Ward Lock, London

Musgrove, F. (1974) *Ecstasy and Holiness: Counter Culture and the Open Society*, Methuen, London

NATFHE (1976) World teachers' meeting, *National Association of Teachers in Further and Higher Education Journal*, Issue 7

National Society (1980) *The Durham Report: The Fourth R*. Society for Promoting Christian Knowledge, London

Needleman, J. and Baker, G. (1978) *Understanding the New Religions*. Seabury, New York.

Niblett, W.R. (1966) 'The RE clauses of the 1944 Act', in Wedderspoon, A. (ed.) *RE 1944–84*, Allen & Unwin, London

Nicklas, H. and Ostermann, A. (1979) The psychology of deterrence and the chances of peace, *Bulletin of Peace Proposals*, 4, 368–73

Ngugi wa Thiong'o (1977) *Petals of Blood*. Heinemann, London

Owen, J., Baker, J. and Flux, A. (1976) 'A Third World Study Visit: West Africa '74', *Teaching Geography*, 1 (5), 206–10

Paton, K. (1979) Talking with (other) racists, in Clark, H. *et al.* (eds) *Taking Racism Personally*. Peace News Collective, Nottingham

Peet, R. (1978) *Radical Geography: Alternative Viewpoints on Contemporary Social Issues*, Methuen, London

Pollard, H. M. (1957) *Pioneers of Popular Education 1760–1850*. Greenwood, London and New York

Price, R. F. (1977) *Marx and Education in Russia and China*. Croom-Helm. London; Rowman & Littlefield, New Jersey

*Primary Education in England: A Survey by HM Inspectors of Schools*, HMSO, London

Pryce, K. (1979) *Endless Pressure*. Penguin Books, Harmondsworth

Reich, C.A. (1970) *The Greening of America*. Random House, New York and (1971) Penguin

Richardson, R. (1974a) Tensions in world and school: an outline of certain current controversies, *Bulletin of Peace Proposals*, 5, 263–273, International Peace Research Institute, Oslo

Richardson, R. (1974b) World Studies, Ch. 12 in Collier, G., Wilson J. and Tomlinson, P. (eds) *Values and Moral Development in Higher Education*. Croom Helm, London

Richardson, R. (ed.) (1976) *Learning for Change in World Society: Reflections, Activities, Resources*, World Studies Project, London (2nd edn 1979)

Richardson, R. (1977) Studying world society: some approaches to the design of courses, *The New Era*, **58**, (6), 175–84

Richardson, R. (1978) *Caring for the Planet; World in Conflict; Fighting for Freedom; Progress and Poverty*. Nelson, London

Richardson, R., Flood, M and Fisher, S. (1979) *Debate and Decision: Schools in a World of Change*. One World Trust, London

Richardson, R. and Poxon, J. (1979) *The Third World in Initial Teacher Training*, Oxfam.

Richmond, J. (1970) *Theology and Metaphysics*. SCM Press, London; Schocken, New York

Robinson, J. A. T. (1968) *In the End, God*. Collins, London; Harper & Row, New York

Rolle College (1976) *Proposed Diploma in Higher Education/BA African Studies: Outline Syllabus*. Rolle College of Education, Exmouth

Roszak, T. (1970) *The Making of a Counter Culture*. Faber, London

Sartre, J. P. (1946) Portrait of the anti-Semite, pp. 270–86 in Kaufmann, W. (ed.) (1956) *Existentialism from Dostoevsky to Sartre*, Meridian Books, New York; Thames & Hudson, London

Sathyamurthy, T. V. (1975) The course on political change in the Department of Politics, University of York, *Case Studies in Interdisciplinarity 3: Integrated Social Sciences*, Nuffield Foundation, London

The Schools Council/Nuffield Humanities Project (1970) *The Humanities Project: An Introduction*. Heinemann, London

Schumacher, F. (1974) *Small is Beautiful*. Abacus, London

Schutz, A. (1964) The stranger, reprinted in Cosin, B. et al. (eds) *School and Society: A Sociological Reader*. Routledge & Kegan Paul, London

Scotttish Education Dept; (1979) *The Future of In-Service Training in Scotland*. HMSO, Edinburgh

Searle, C. (1973) *This New Season: Our Class, Our Schools, Our World*. Calder and Boyars, London

Searle, C. (1975) *Classrooms of Resistance*. Writers and Readers Publishing Co-operative, London

Searle, C. (1977) *The World in a Classroom*. Writers and Readers Publishing Cooperative, London

Selby, D. E. (1980) Globalizing sixth-form general studies, *Good Practice in Sixth-Form General Studies*, General Studies Association, Occasional Publications No. 4

Shirman, D. & Conrad, D. (1977) Awareness, understanding and action: a global conscience in the classroom, *The New Era*, **58** (6), 163–67

Sivanandan, A. (1976) *Race, Class and the State : The Black Experience in Britain*. Institute of Race Relations, London

Skilbeck, M. (1975) The school and cultural development, Ch. 3 in Golby, M., Greenwald, J. and West, R. (eds) *Curriculum Design*. Croom Helm, London

Smalley, K. (1975) Freetown town trail, *Teaching Geography*, **1** (5), 210–2

Smart, N. (Forthcoming) *Varieties of Religious Identity*. Collins, London

Smith, D. M. (1977) *Human Geography: A Welfare Approach*. Arnold, London

Smith, M. (1977) *The Underground and Education*. Methuen, London

Smoker, P. (1976) *Critical mass and social technology*, Peace and Conflict Programme, Lancaster University

Social Morality Council (1970) *Moral and Religious Education in Primary Schools*. London; (1973) *Future of broadcasting* (mimeo), London; (1975) *Education and drug dependence* (mimeo), London; (1977) *A plan for moral education in schools* (mimeo), London.

Starkey, H. (1978a) 'Not problems but politics' – Some comments on approaches to the development of new resources for World Studies, *Cambridge Journal of Education*, **8** (2 & 3), 161–4

Starkey, H. (1978b) *The Rich and the Poor*. Ely Resource and Technology Centre

# References

Starkey, H. (1979a) The World Energy Game – Developing new materials for teaching about energy, *Environmental Education*. **11**, 42–4

Starkey, H. (1979b) Looking to our future: an evening class for school and community, *The New Era*, **60** (4), 141–4

Starkey, H. and Panayides, A. (1978) 'Things we never knew existed' – perceptions of a course in World Studies, *The New Era*, **59** (4), 140–5

Stavrianos, L.S. (1976) *The Promise of the Coming Dark Age*. W.H. Freeman & Co., San Francisco

Stenhouse, L. (1970) Some limitations of the use of objectives in curriculum research and planning. *Paedagogica Europeaea*, **6**. 73–83

Stenhouse, L. (1975) *An Introduction to Curriculum Research and Development*. Heinemann, London

Stone, M. (1981) *Education of the Black Child in Britain*. Fontana, London

Street-Porter, R. (1978) *Race, Children and Cities*. E361 Block V, Open University, Milton Keynes

Stuart, J. S. (1977) *The Unequal Third*. Arnold, London

Sumner, H. Once Upon a Time – Fairy Tales as a social studies resource. Briefings No. 6, ATSS *The Social Science Teacher*, **Vol. 6**, No. 2

Taba, H. (1971) *Curriculum Development: Theory and Practice*. Harcourt Brace Jovanovitch, London

Taba, H. (1971) *A Teacher's Handbook for Elementary Social Studies*. Addison-Wesley, London

Taylor, N. and Richardson, R. (1979) *Seeing and Perceiving: Films in a World of Change*. Concord Films Council, Ipswich

Taylor, N. and Richardson, R. (1980) *Change and Choice: Britain in an Interdependent World*. Centre for World Development Education, London

Taylor, P. H. (1970) *How Teachers Plan their Courses: Studies in Curriculum Planning*, Fernhill

Taylor, T. (1977) *A New Partnership for our Schools*. HMSO

Taylor, W. (1969) *Society and the Education of Teachers*. Faber, London

Thompson, E. P., and Smith, D. (eds) (1980) *Protest and Survive*. Penguin, Harmondsworth

Toffler, A. (1970) *Future Shock*. Bodley Head, and (1971) Pan Books, London

Turner, J. (1978) *World Inequality*. Longman, London

Tweedie, J. (1979) What about poor Arabs, sexy Chinese, and timid Iranians? *The Guardian*, 13 Dec.

Tyler, W. *Basic Principles of Curriculum and Instruction*. University of Chicago Press.

ULIE (1980) Introducing development education in schools, *Development Education: Education for Life in a Changing World*, 3.1–3.12, University of London Institute of Education.

UNESCO (1974) *The Recommendation Concerning Education for International Understanding, Cooperation and Peace and Education Relating to Human Rights and Fundamental Freedoms*. UNESCO, Paris

UNESCO (1976a) *International Meeting of Experts on the Role of Social Studies in Peace and Respect for Human Rights* at Michigan State University; EP-76/Conf. 631/5, UNESCO, Paris

UNESCO (1976b) *The Report of a Meeting of Experts on the Implementation of the 1974 UNESCO Recommendation*. UNESCO, Paris

UNESCO (1979) *The Final Report of the European Regional Seminar on the Implementation of the 1974 UNESCO Recommendation, Sofia, Bulgaria*. UNESCO, Paris

UNESCO (1980a) *An Evaluation of the UNESCO Associated Schools Project (1953–80) Arising from an International Meeting of Experts.* UNESCO, Paris

UNESCO (1980b) *Report on Education for International Understanding in the Context of Teacher Education, Helsinki.* UNESCO, Paris

Verma, G. and Bagley, C. (1978) Teaching styles and race relations: some effects on white teenagers, *The New Era,* **59** (2) 53–7 World Education Fellowship, London

Verma, G. and MacDonald, B. (1971) Teaching race in schools: some effects on the attitudinal and sociometric patterns of adolescents, *Race,* **13** (2), 187–202

Vickers, G. (1973) Educational criteria for time of change, *Journal of Curriculum Studies,* **5,** 13–24

Voltaire (1971) *Philosophical Dictionary.* Translated by Bestermann, J., Penguin, Harmondsworth

Walford, R. (1979) Listening to the learner, *Journal of Geography in Higher Education,* **3** (1), 54–9.

Warnock, M. (1975) The neutral teacher, in Brown, S.C. (ed.) *Philosophers Discuss Education.* Macmillan, London

Watson, J. W. (1977) On the teaching of value geography, *Geography,* **62,** 198–204

Wheeler, D. K. (1967) *Curriculum Process.* University of London Press

Whitaker, P. (1980) Education, World Studies and films, *World Studies Journal,* **1** (3), 28–34

White, J. P. (1973) *Towards a Compulsory Core Curriculum.* Routledge & Kegan Paul, London

Wilson, J. (1972) *Practical Methods of Moral Education.* Heinemann, London

Wolsk, D. (1975) *An Experience-Centred Curriculum.* UNESCO, Paris

Wren, B. (1977) *Education for Justice,* SCM Press, London

Wright, D. (1972) Wrestling with concepts, *Times Higher Education Supplement,* 15 Dec.

Wright, D. (1979) Not world enough, *Times Educational Supplement,* 28 Dec.

Yergin, D. (1977) *Shattered Peace : the Origins of the Cold War and the National Security State.* Harvard UP and André Deutsch, London

213

# Index

# Index